FLORIDA

SCIENCE

FUSION

fusion [FYOO • zhuhn] a mixture or blend formed by fusing two or more things

This Interactive Student Edition belongs to

_____

Teacher/Room

_____

HOUGHTON MIFFLIN HARCOURT

Consulting Authors

Michael A. DiSpezio
Global Educator
North Falmouth, Massachusetts

Marjorie Frank
Science Writer and Content-Area Reading Specialist
Brooklyn, New York

Michael Heithaus
Director, School of Environment and Society
Associate Professor, Department of Biological Sciences
Florida International University
North Miami, Florida

Donna Ogle
Professor of Reading and Language
National-Louis University
Chicago, Illinois

 HOUGHTON MIFFLIN HARCOURT

Copyright © 2012 by Houghton Mifflin Harcourt Publishing Company

Printed in the U.S.A.

ISBN-13 978-0-547-36591-6

1 2 3 4 5 6 7 8 9 10 1421 19 18 17 16 15 14 13 12 11 10
4500000000   ABCDE

Program Advisors

Paul D. Asimow
Associate Professor of Geology and
Geochemistry
California Institute of Technology
Pasadena, California

Bobby Jeanpierre
Associate Professor of Science
Education
University of Central Florida
Orlando, Florida

Gerald H. Krockover
Professor of Earth and Atmospheric
Science Education
Purdue University
West Lafayette, Indiana

Rose Pringle
Associate Professor
School of Teaching and Learning
College of Education
University of Florida
Gainesville, Florida

Carolyn Staudt
Curriculum Designer for Technology
KidSolve, Inc.
The Concord Consortium
Concord, Massachusetts

Larry Stookey
Science Department
Antigo High School
Antigo, Wisconsin

Carol J. Valenta
Senior Vice President and Associate
Director of the Museum
Saint Louis Science Center
St. Louis, Missouri

Barry A. Van Deman
President and CEO
Museum of Life and Science
Durham, North Carolina

Florida Reviewers

Janet M. Acerra
Forest Lakes Elementary
Oldsmar, Florida

Shannan Combee
Inwood Elementary
Winter Haven, Florida

Amber J. Cooley
Jacksonville Heights Elementary
Jacksonville, Florida

Donna de la Paz
Trinity Oaks Elementary
New Port Richey, Florida

Nancy Carrier Duncan
Eustis Heights Elementary
Eustis, Florida

Marsha Dwyer
Kenwood K-8 Center
Miami, Florida

Jessica S. Fowler
Susie E. Tolbert Elementary
Jacksonville, Florida

Pat Houston
Northwood Elementary
Crestview, Florida

Timothy W. Peterson
Romeo Elementary
Dunnellon, Florida

Rosanne Phillips
Kenwood K-8 Center
Miami, Florida

Rose M. Sedely
Eustis Heights Elementary
Eustis, Florida

Gerilyn Stark-Jerry
Chain of Lakes Elementary
Winter Haven, Florida

Deborah S. Street
Southport Elementary
Southport, Florida

Janine Townsley
Norwood Elementary
Miami, Florida

Jessica Weiss
Westchase Elementary
Tampa, Florida

Power Up with Science Fusion!

Your program fuses . . .

Online Virtual Experiences

Hands-on Explorations

Active Reading

. . . to generate new science energy for today's science learner—*you*.

Active Reading

Be an active reader and make this book your own!

You can write your ideas, answer questions, draw graphs, make notes, and record your activity results right on these pages.

By the end of the school year, this book becomes a record of everything you learn in science.

uses objects
object to stop moving

Active R As you read these t ges, draw circles around
two words tha e types of forces.

hat have you pus or pulled
ay? Maybe you p ed open a
d on your shoes ush or a
ce. Suppose you w change
mething is moving.
n object's speed or dire

Many ces act on you. Gravity is a for
that pulls o ects down to Earth. Gr
keeps you on the ground
Friction is a
against the dire
slow things dow

Hands-on Explorations

Science is all about doing.

Ask questions and test your ideas.

Draw conclusions and share what you learn.

How Does Drought Affect Plants?

A drought happens when a place gets much less rainfall than normal. What happens to plants when their environment changes and they do not get the usual amount of water?

Materials
5 plastic cups
black marker
125 seeds
potting soil
water
measuring cup

1. Label the cups A through E.

2. Fill each cup with moist potting soil. Plant 25 seeds in each cup.

3. Water the cups according to the following schedule:
   • Cup A—50 mL of water each day
   • Cup B—25 mL of water each day
   • Cup C—50 mL of water every other day
   • Cup D—50 mL of water once a week
   • Cup E—no water

4. Make a hypothesis how the seeds different cups

5. Place the cups on windowsill. Obser cups for two week

There are lots of exciting investigations on the Inquiry Flipchart.

Online Virtual Experiences

Explore cool labs and activities in the virtual world—where science comes alive and you make it happen.

See your science lessons from a completely different point of view—a digital point of view.

Science Fusion
is new energy... just for YOU!

Contents

© Houghton Mifflin Harcourt Publishing Company

ix

PHYSICAL SCIENCE

The lesson I'm most interested in learning about is

_____

_____ .

LIFE SCIENCE

© Houghton Mifflin Harcourt Publishing Company   (t) ©Dan Suzio/Photo Researchers, Inc.

Scientists at Work

Big Idea 1

The Practice of Science

Big Idea 2

The Characteristics of Scientific Knowledge

Kissimmee Prairie, FL

I Wonder Why

Why do some scientists work outdoors and other work inside a laboratory? *Turn the page to find out.*

Here's Why Scientists work to answer questions. Some questions can be answered with outdoor investigations. Others require tools in a lab.

Track Your Progress

Essential Questions and Florida Benchmarks

Big Idea 1   *The Practice of Science*

Big Idea 2   *The Characteristics of Scientific Knowledge*

Now I Get the Big Idea!

SC.5.N.1.6 Recognize and explain the difference between personal opinion/interpretation and verified observation. SC.5.N.2.1 …science is grounded in empirical observations that are testable; explanation must always be linked with evidence. SC.5.N.2.2 …when scientific investigations are carried out, the evidence produced by those investigations should be replicable by others.

Essential Question

What Is Science?

Engage Your Brain!

Find one answer to the following question in this lesson and write it here.

What are some science skills you could use when studying fish in an aquarium?

_____

_____

_____

Active Reading

Lesson Vocabulary

List the terms. As you learn about each one, make notes in the Interactive Glossary.

_____

_____

_____

_____

Use Headings

Active readers preview headings and use them to pose questions that set purposes for reading. Reading with a purpose helps active readers focus on understanding what they read in order to fulfill the purpose.

© Houghton Mifflin Harcourt Publishing Company (bkg) ©Frans Lemmens/Getty Images

What All Scientists Do

Digging up fossils. Peering through telescopes. Mixing chemicals in a lab. Using computers to make weather predictions. These are only a few of the things scientists do.

As you read these two pages, turn the heading into a question in your mind, and underline sentences that answer the question.

Does solving puzzles and searching for buried treasures sound like fun? If so, you might like being a paleontologist. Paleontologists are scientists who study the history of life on Earth. Like all scientists, they try to explain how and why things in the natural world happen. They answer questions by doing investigations. An **investigation** is a procedure carried out to carefully observe, study, or test something in order to learn more about it.

In addition to knowing a lot about living things of the past, paleontologists have to use many skills. In fact, all scientists use these skills. All scientists **observe**, or use their five senses to collect information. And all scientists **compare**, finding ways objects and events are the similar and different.

Observe

Write one observation you could make about the fossil.

_____

_____

Paleontologists use fossils to answer questions such as, "What was Earth's environment like in the past?"

Paleontologists also work in labs, cleaning and studying fossils.

This paleontologist needs to observe the landscape to predict where fossils might be hidden. Once he finds the fossils, he compares them to fossils found in other parts of the world.

Paleontology is just one branch of science. **Science** is the study of the natural world and involves making observations and performing investigations. Scientists learn by thinking critically about the results of their investigations.

Compare

Observe these two skulls. List two ways they are similar and two ways they are different.

Similarities	Differences
_____	_____
_____	_____
_____	_____

Prove It!

In the 1600s, there were not many ways to keep meat fresh. Rotting meat quickly filled with squirming, worm-like maggots. Yuck! Where did the maggots come from?

Active Reading On these two pages, circle the examples of evidence.

Rotten Meat turns into Maggots!

▶ Draw a large *X* through the explanation that was shown *not* to be true.

Travel back in time to the 1660s. Most people think flies, worms, and mice come from nonliving objects and rotting food. As *evidence,* or proof, they show how a dead animal's body soon becomes loaded with squirming maggots.

To a scientist, **evidence** is information collected during a scientific investigation. Some evidence, such as seeing a fossil dinosaur skull, is direct evidence that the dinosaur existed. Evidence can be indirect, such as finding a fossil footprint of a dinosaur.

Meet Dr. Francesco Redi, a scientist in Italy. A book Dr. Redi reads leads him to think maggots come from the eggs of flies. Redi **plans and conducts investigations** to gather evidence. He traps some maggots

The meat in the open jar soon became "wormy," while the meat in the sealed jar did not.

Redi placed fresh meat in two jars. He covered one jar and left the other jar uncovered.

inside jars with pieces of meat. He watches the maggots turn into adult flies. He observes adult flies laying eggs and more maggots come out of these eggs.

Redi then sets up an experiment. He places meat in several jars. Some jars are sealed and others are left open to the air. Redi observes that only the meat in jars he left open have maggots.

Redi experiments many times over. He tries dead fish, frogs, and snakes. All the evidence supports his idea: Living insects can only come from other living insects.

▶ Fill in the blanks in this sequence graphic organizer.

Make observations and ask
_____.

↓

Plan and conduct
_____.

↓

Use _____ to explain observations.

Maggots Hatch from eggs that flies lay.

A Sticky Trap

Humans are too big to get stuck in a spider's web. But there are some sticky traps you need to avoid when thinking like a scientist.

Active Reading As you read these two pages, turn the main heading into a question in your mind. Then underline sentences that answer the question.

▶ Look at the words in the spider web below. Star the things you *should* use to draw conclusions properly. Cross out the others.

Opinions

Favorites

Observations

How to Draw Conclusions

Scientists draw conclusions from the results of their investigations. Any conclusion must be backed up with evidence. Other scientists judge the conclusion based on how much evidence is given. They also judge how well the evidence supports the conclusion.

Don't jump to conclusions too quickly. That's a sticky trap in science! As Dr. Redi did, repeat your investigations. Think about what you can infer from your observations. And then—only then—draw your conclusions.

Suppose you spend a week observing spiders. You might conclude that all spiders build webs to catch their food. This may be true of the spiders you observed, but it's not true of all spiders. Some spiders, such as wolf spiders, hunt for their prey instead.

Inferences

Evidence

Feelings

Observation Information collected by using the senses	The insect is stuck in the spider web.
Inference An idea or a conclusion based on an observation	A spider is going to use the bug for food later.
Opinion A personal belief that does not need proof	Spiders are really gross!

Opinion or Evidence?

An **opinion** is a belief or judgment. It doesn't have to be proved, or backed up with evidence. It might be your opinion that spiders are gross and disgusting. Others may disagree, but you are welcome to stick with your opinion!

Personal feelings and opinions should not affect how you do investigations. Nor should they affect your conclusions. It's hard to do, but science is about keeping an open mind. For example, don't ignore evidence just because you don't like what it means.

▶ Write one observation, one inference, and one opinion about what you see in the photo.

Observation	
Inference	
Opinion	

Knowledge Grows

How is a man investigating electricity and wires more than 350 years ago connected to the latest video game release?

Stephen Gray, a scientist born in 1666, was working at home when he discovered that electrical energy could move along a short metal wire. Gray carried his materials to friend's homes. He showed them how the materials worked and, together, they made the wire longer and longer.

Today there are so many ways for scientists to **communicate**, or share, the results of investigations. When scientists communicate clearly, others can repeat their investigations. They can compare their results with those of others. They can expand on one another's ideas. In these ways, scientific knowledge grows.

energy by living organisms

DATA

Communicate

List several ways you can communicate.

_____

_____

_____

_____

1729 Stephen Gray shows that electrical energy can be carried through a wire.

1882 Thomas Edison opens the first electricity generating station.

Knowledge grows when it is communicated. Each science discovery leads to new questions. More is learned and new things invented.

The first video game was invented in 1958. The inventor was a scientist named William Higinbotham. The reason? To make Visitor's Day at his lab more interesting for the public! Hundreds of people lined up to play the game.

Take a look at the timeline. The science behind Higinbotham's game goes back hundreds of years or more.

1947 The transistor, needed to make radios and computers, is invented.

1953 The first computer is sold.

1958 William Higinbotham invents the first video game.

1967 First hand-held calculator invented.

1971 First coin-operated arcade video games in use.

The first arcade games were not very complex.

1972 The first home video game systems are sold.

1977 The first handheld video games sold.

2009 Scientists use super-fast video game cards inside computers to investigate the structure of molecules.

The video games of today are fast, complex, and interactive.

Meet Scientists

There are more people working as scientists today than ever before in history. Yet, there are plenty of unanswered questions left for you to answer!

Active Reading As you read these two pages, underline what each type of scientist studies.

Astronomer

Astronomers ask questions about how the universe works. Because novas, black holes, and galaxies are so far away, they use time/space relationships to investigate them. For example, astronomers measure space distances in units called light-years. That's how far light can travel in one Earth year.

Do the Math!
Use Fractions

Earth and Jupiter travel around the sun. Each time Earth makes one complete trip, Mars makes about $\frac{1}{2}$ of its trip.

1. How many trips does Earth make around the sun in the time it takes Mars to make one trip?

_____

2. In the drawing below, put an X where Mars will be after Earth completes five trips around the sun.

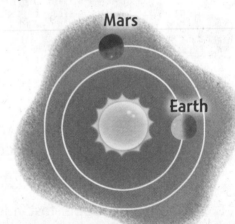

You don't have to be a pro to do astronomy. People have discovered many comets and exploding stars using telescopes in their back yards!

Order

When you **order**, you place objects or events one after another in the correct sequence. Write the numbers *1, 2, 3,* and *4* to show the order of the images below.

_____   _____

_____   _____

Botanist

Botanists investigate questions about plants. For example, some botanists study how environmental conditions affect a plant's life cycle.

Taxonomist

Taxonomists are scientists who identify types of living things and classify them by how they are related. When you classify, you organize objects or events into categories based on specific characteristics.

Classify

Look at the butterflies on this page. What are some ways you could classify them?

_____

_____

_____

Lexias damalis
Asia

Yon

Amyruta smolfildia
Africa

Agric

Doxopoca agathina
America

Marpesta petrous
America

Prepona dexamenes
America

ona *emophon*
America

When you're done, use the answer key to check and revise your work.

Read the summary, and fill in the missing words.

The goal of a scientist is to understand the natural world. To do this, a scientist plans and conducts 1. _____ .

Scientists use the 2. _____ they gather to draw

3. _____ .

A good scientist does not let his or her personal beliefs, or

4. _____ , influence their study.

There are many important skills that scientists use. For example, when scientists 5. _____ , they use their observations and prior knowledge to determine what is happening.

Read each of the statements below. Write the science skill that each student used.

6. Angela made a list of how the two planets were alike.

_____

7. Krystal sorted the rocks into five groups based on their color.

_____

8. Robbie explained the results of his investigation to his classmates.

_____

9. Dmitri noted how the feathers looked and felt.

_____

10. Juan organized the steps of the process from first to last.

_____

Name _____

Word Play

1 Complete the crossword puzzle. If you need help, use the terms in the yellow box.

Across

1. The study of the natural world through investigation
5. Collecting information by using the senses
6. An idea or a conclusion based on an observation
7. Facts and information collected over time
8. To put things into groups
9. A belief or a judgment

Down

2. The sharing of information
3. The observations and information that support a conclusion
4. The process of studying or testing something to learn more about it
5. To arrange things by when they happened or by their size

---

classify   communication   evidence*   inference   investigation*

knowledge   observing   opinion*   order   science*

* Key Lesson Vocabulary

Apply Concepts

2 Compare these two birds. List how they look similar and different.

Similarities:

_____

_____

Differences:

_____

_____

3 Suppose someone tells you they saw a bird never before seen in your state. What kinds of evidence would you ask for?

_____

_____

_____

4 What, in your opinion, is the scariest animal on Earth? How should this affect your investigations?

_____

_____

_____

5 One morning you see an outdoor garbage can tipped over. Plastic bags are torn open. What could you infer?

_____

_____

_____

Take It Home! How can you communicate with people around the world, collect real data, and help answer a question? Research citizen science projects online. Choose an interesting project. Participate with your family.

Name _____

SC.5.N.2.1 Recognize and explain that science is grounded in empirical observations that are testable; explanation must always be linked with evidence.

Essential Question

How Do Scientists Learn About the Natural World?

Set a Purpose
What will you learn from this investigation?

_____

_____

_____

_____

Think About the Procedure
How did you choose what predictions to write on your origami predictor?

_____

_____

_____

_____

Record Your Data
In the table below, record your results.

Date	Origami Prediction	Weather Service Prediction	Actual Weather

Draw Conclusions

Of the two kinds of weather predictions, which one was more likely to be correct? Explain.

_____

_____

_____

_____

Analyze and Extend

1. What results do you think you would get if you continued your investigation for a whole month?

_____

_____

_____

2. How do you think the weather service makes its predictions?

_____

_____

3. Why is it important that scientists make good weather predictions?

_____

_____

_____

_____

4. The line graph shows average October air temperatures in Houston, TX. Can you predict the air temperature in Houston next October? If so, how?

_____

_____

_____

Average Temperature in Houston in October

5. What else would you like to find out about how scientists make predictions? Write each idea as a question.

_____

_____

_____

_____

_____

_____

_____

Directions

1. Carefully tear this page out of your book.

2. Cut out the square below. You will use it to make your origami weather predictor.

3. On each set of lines, write a weather prediction.

4. Follow the instructions on the back of this page to fold and use your origami weather predictor.

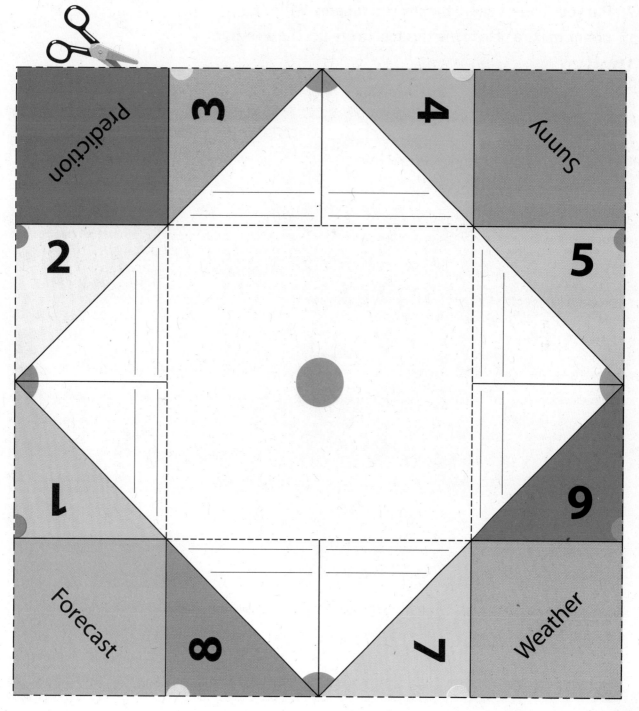

Directions (continued)

5. Fold the blue dots into the blue circle. Turn the paper over, and fold the green dots into the green circle.

6. Fold the paper in half so that the yellow dots touch each other. Make a crease, and unfold the paper. Fold it in half again so that the pink dots touch each other.

7. Put your fingers under the colorful squares. With your group, make a plan to use this tool to predict the weather.

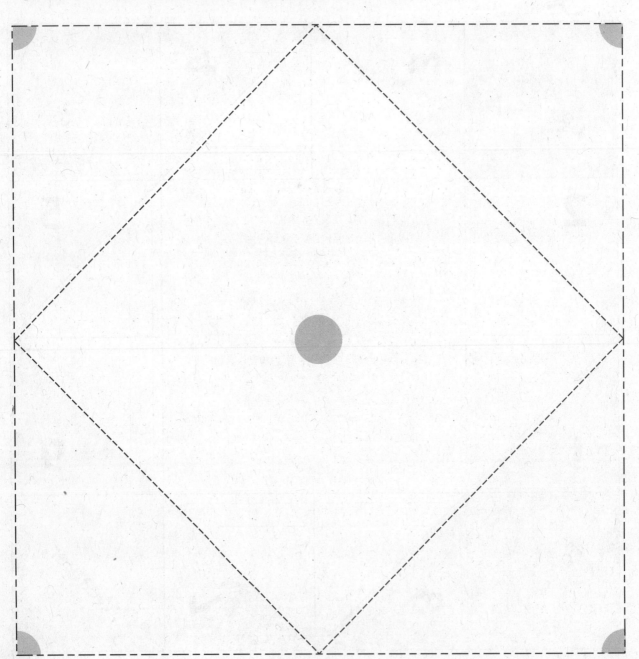

SC.5.N.1.1 ...plan and carry out scientific investigations.... SC.5.N.1.2 Explain the difference between an experiment and other types of scientific investigation. SC.5.N.1.3 Recognize and explain the need for repeated experimental trials. SC.5.N.1.4 Identify a control group and explain its importance.... SC.5.N.1.5 ... scientific investigation frequently does not parallel the steps of "the scientific method."

Essential Question

What Are Some Types of Investigations?

Engage Your Brain!

Find one answer to the following question in this lesson and write it here.

What did this scientist do prior to starting her experiment with plants?

_____

_____

_____

_____

Active Reading

Lesson Vocabulary

List the terms. As you learn about each one, make notes in the Interactive Glossary.

_____

_____

_____

_____

Main Ideas

The main idea of a paragraph is the most important idea. The main idea may be stated in the first sentence, or it may be stated elsewhere. Active readers look for main ideas by asking themselves, What is this paragraph mostly about?

A Process for Science

Testing bridge models, mapping a storm's path, searching the sky for distant planets—each of these investigations uses scientific methods.

How does the shape of the room affect the sound of a voice?

How does having a cold affect a person's singing?

Can a human voice shatter glass?

How high a note can a singer sing?

Start with a Question

Scientists observe the world and then ask questions that are based on their observations. But not all questions are the same. A good scientific question is one that can be answered by investigation. A scientific investigation always begins with a question.

Plan an Investigation

Once a scientist has a testable question, it is time to plan an investigation. **Scientific methods** are ways that scientists perform investigations. There are many ways that scientists investigate the world. But all scientific methods use logic and reasoning.

▶ Suppose you've just heard an opera singer warm up her voice. Write your own science question about the sounds a singer makes.

_____

_____

_____

Experiments

In an experiment, scientists control all the conditions of the investigation. Scientists study what happens to a group of samples that are all the same except for one difference.

Repeated Observations

Scientists use repeated observation to study processes in nature that they can observe but can't control.

Using Models

Scientists use models when they cannot experiment on the real thing. Models help scientists investigate things that are large (like a planet), expensive (like a bridge), or uncontrollable (like the weather.)

Investigations Differ

The method a scientist uses depends on the question he or she is investigating. An **experiment** is an investigation in which all of the conditions are controlled. Models are used to represent real objects or processes. Scientists make repeated observations to study processes in nature without disturbing them.

Drawing Conclusions

Whatever scientific methods are used, scientists will have results they can use to draw conclusions. The conclusions may answer the question they asked before they began. They may point to other questions and many more ideas for investigations.

▶ Write the type of investigation you should use to answer the following questions.

How do different bridge designs react to strong winds?

_____

How fast does the wind blow where a bridge will be built?

_____

Which type of paint works best to keep a bridge from rusting?

_____

Explosive Observations

How does a hurricane affect animals? Are coral reefs dying? How do whales raise their young? These are some science questions that can be answered with repeated observation.

Active Reading As you read these two pages, place a star next to three examples of repeated observation.

Old Faithful

Some science questions can only be answered by making observations. This is because some things are just too big, too far away, or too uncontrollable for experiments. However, much can be learned from repeated observation.

In Yellowstone National Park, heated water and steam shoots out of holes in the ground. This is called a geyser. Old Faithful is a famous geyser that erupts about every hour. Observations of the geyser collected over many years can be used to predict when the next eruption will occur. A prediction is a statement, based on information, about a future event.

The time until Old Faithful's next eruption is affected by how long the previous eruption lasted. Suppose the last eruption was at 3:05 p.m. and lasted 3 minutes 15 seconds. Predict when it will erupt next.

_____

How long an eruption lasts	1 min 30 sec	2 min	2 min 30 sec	3 min	3 min 30 sec	4 min	4 min 30 sec	5 min
Time until next eruption	50 min	57 min	65 min	71 min	76 min	82 min	89 min	95 min

The first observation of a whale is often its spout.

Scientists have many questions about whales—the largest mammals on Earth. How long do whales live? How do they communicate? How do they care for their young? How far can they travel in a year? These questions can be answered with repeated observation.

For example, the tail flukes of whales are different from one whale to another. Scientists take photos of the flukes and use them to identify individual whales. Once they know which whale is which, they can recognize them each time they are seen in the ocean.

▲ = volcanic eruption

Predict

Scientists have observed and recorded volcanic eruptions for hundreds of years. The map to the left shows that data. Which location—A, B, or C— is most likely to have a volcanic eruption? _____

Why do you think scientists call this region the "Ring of Fire."

_____

_____

Super Models

How does a bat fly? How might Saturn's rings look close up? How does a heart work? These are some science questions that can be answered with models.

Active Reading Circle different types of models that are described on these two pages.

Complex models can be made on a computer. This model shows where the most damage would occur if an earthquake were to strike.

When Modeling Is Needed

When scientists cannot experiment with the real thing, they can use models. Scientific models are needed to understand systems that have many hidden parts, such as an ant colony or the Internet. Scientists draw conclusions and make predictions by studying their models.

The closer the model represents the real thing, the more useful it is. So scientists change their models as they learn more.

Earthquakes are difficult to predict, and they can cause damage. New structures are designed to prevent damage.

Types of Models

Models are made in different ways. One way is to build a physical model. An earthquake shake table with model buildings on it is a physical model. Another way is to program computer simulation models. Scientists can speed up time in computer models so that they can see what might happen long in the future. Drawing diagrams and flow charts is a third way to make models. These two-dimensional models can be used to show how ideas are related.

Scientists build "shake tables" that model the motion of real earthquakes. This photo shows two types of houses being tested. Which house seems to be safer in an earthquake?

Use Models

How is an earthquake model made of gelatin like a real earthquake? How is it unlike a real earthquake?

Alike: _____

_____

Different: _____

_____

You can model the effects of an earthquake, using gelatin for the ground and buildings made of blocks.

How to Excel in Experimentation

You're enjoying a frozen juice pop. The heat of your tongue melts the pop. As you slurp the liquid, you think about how different substances freeze.

I know that water freezes at 0 degrees Celsius. How does adding other substances to water affect the temperature at which it freezes?

Active Reading As you read the next four pages, circle lesson vocabulary each time it is used.

Ask Questions

You know a freezer is cold enough to freeze water. You also know that juice is mostly water. You ask "Does adding substances to water affect its freezing point?"

Many science questions, including this one, can be answered by doing experiments. An **experiment** is a procedure used to test a *hypothesis*. It's a good idea to make some observations before stating a hypothesis. For example, you might put a small amount of orange juice in a freezer. Then you'd check it every few minutes to look for changes.

Hypothesize

A hypothesis is a statement that can be tested and will explain what can happen in an investigation. In the case of the freezing question, you think about what you already know. You can also talk to other people. And you can do research such as asking an expert.

You find out that the freezing point and melting point of a material should be the same temperature. An expert suggests that it is better to measure the melting point than the freezing point.

Design an Experiment

A well-designed experiment has two or more setups. This allows you to compare results among them. For the freezing/melting experiment, each setup will be a cup of liquid.

A **variable** is any condition in an experiment that can be changed. In most experiments, there are many, many variables to consider. The trick is to keep all variables the same in each setup, except one. That one variable is the one you will test.

Among the setups should be one called the control. The **control** is the setup to which you will compare all the others.

You've decided to dissolve different substances in water and freeze them. Then you plan to take them out of the freezer and use a thermometer to check their temperatures as they melt.

© Houghton Mifflin Harcourt Publishing Company

Hypothesize

Fill in the blank in the hypothesis. Any substance dissolved in water will _____ the temperature at which the mixture freezes and melts.

Identify and Control Variables

When you identify and control variables, you determine which conditions should stay the same and which one should be changed. Circle the variable that will be tested. Underline the variables that will remain the same.

- the kinds of cups

- the amount of water

- the material that is dissolved in the water

- the temperature of the freezer

- the types of thermometers

- the amount of time you leave the cups in the freezer

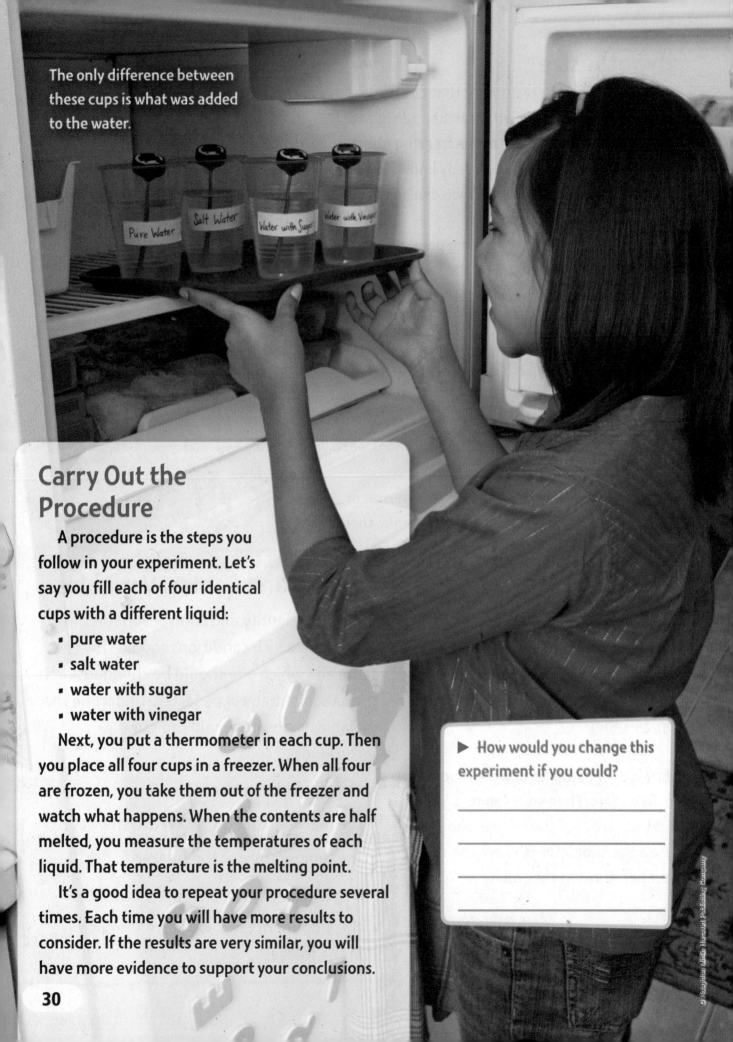

The only difference between these cups is what was added to the water.

Pure Water
Salt Water
Water with Sugar
Water with Vinegar

Carry Out the Procedure

A procedure is the steps you follow in your experiment. Let's say you fill each of four identical cups with a different liquid:

- pure water
- salt water
- water with sugar
- water with vinegar

Next, you put a thermometer in each cup. Then you place all four cups in a freezer. When all four are frozen, you take them out of the freezer and watch what happens. When the contents are half melted, you measure the temperatures of each liquid. That temperature is the melting point.

It's a good idea to repeat your procedure several times. Each time you will have more results to consider. If the results are very similar, you will have more evidence to support your conclusions.

▶ How would you change this experiment if you could?

_____

_____

_____

_____

Record and Analyze Data

You could write down your observations as sentences. Or you could make a table to fill in. No matter how you do it, make sure you record correctly. Check twice or have a team member check.

Once the experiment is completed and the data recorded, you can analyze your results. If your data is in the form of numbers, math skills will come in handy. For example, in the data table below, you'll need to know how to write, read, and compare decimals.

Melting Point Experiment	
Substance	Melting Point
Pure Water	0.0 °C
Salt Water	−3.7 °C
Sugar Water	−1.8 °C
Vinegar Water	−1.1 °C

Draw Conclusions and Evaluate the Hypothesis

You draw conclusions based on your results. Remember that all conclusions must be supported with evidence. The more evidence you have, the stronger your conclusion.

Once you've reached a conclusion, look at your hypothesis. Decide if the hypothesis is supported or not. If not, try rethinking your hypothesis. Then design a new experiment to test it. That's what scientists do—build on what they learn.

Draw Conclusions

What conclusion can you draw based on this experiment?

_____

_____

_____

_____

_____

_____

Special Delivery: Data Displays

Once you've completed a science investigation, you'll want to share it. What's the best way to communicate the data you collected?

As part of their investigations, scientists collect, record, and interpret data. There is more than one way to display, or communicate, your data. Some kinds of displays are more suited to certain kinds of data than others.

Food Eaten by Orangutans

Other 5%
Flowers 5%
Insects 10%
Leaves 15%
Fruits 65%

Line graphs are suited to show change over time, especially small changes. If you want to show how much you grow each year, use a line graph.

Estimated Number of Orangutans in Sumatra

Number of Individuals

14,000
12,000
10,000
8000
6000
0

1990 1994 1998 2002 2006 2010

Year

Circle graphs are suited to comparing parts to the whole. If you want to show fractions or percents, use a circle graph.

Orangutan Using Tool to Feed

Diagrams are suited to show data that do not include numbers. This diagram shows how an orangutan uses a tool to eat seeds in fruit.

Orangutans at the Zoo

Number of Individuals

Adult Males | Adult Females | Young

Bar graphs are suited to compare things or groups of things. When your data are in categories, use a bar graph.

Do the Math!
Draw a Bar Graph

Draw a bar graph on this page. Use the data in the table below. Decide whether you want the bars to be vertical or horizontal. Carefully label the intervals on each axis. Draw the bars. Then title and label all the parts of your graph.

Number of Orangutans Counted	
Day	Number
Monday	7
Tuesday	13
Wednesday	10
Thursday	2
Friday	6

Sum It Up!

When you're done, use the answer key to check and revise your work.

The outline below is a summary of the lesson. Complete the outline. When you are done, use the answer key to check and revise your work.

Summarize

I. Scientific Methods

  A. All start with a question

  B. Investigations differ

    1. experiments

    2. **1** _____

    3. **2** _____

  C. All have results from which to

    3 _____

II. Repeated Observations

  A. Some things are just too big, too far away, or too uncontrollable for experiments

  B. Examples

    1. solar eclipses

    2. **4** _____

III. Using Models

  A. Needed to understand systems that have many hidden parts

  B. Types of models

    1. diagrams and flow charts

    2. **5** _____

    3. **6** _____

IV. Controlled Experiments

  A. Ask questions

  B. Hypothesize

  C. **7** _____

  D. Carry out the procedure

  E. **8** _____

  F. Draw conclusions

V. Organizing and Displaying Data

  A. Data displays help communicate

  B. Kinds of data displays

    1. circle graphs

    2. **9** _____

    3. **10** _____

    4. **11** _____

Name _____

Word Play

① **Read each clue. Then find and circle the term in the word search puzzle.**
Clues

1. All the ways scientists do investigations:
   _ _ _ _ _ _ _ _ _ _
   _ _ _ _ _ _ _

2. These should be as similar as possible to the real thing: _ _ _ _ _ _ _

3. The part of an experiment used to compare all the other groups:
   _ _ _ _ _ _ _

4. What scientists do that is the basis for their investigations:
   _ _ _ _ _ _ _ _ _ _ _ _ _ _ _

5. Any condition in an experiment that can be changed: _ _ _ _ _ _ _ _ _

6. A type of graph suited to show change over time: _ _ _ _ _ _ _ _ _ _

7. A statement that can be tested and that explains what you think will happen in an experiment:
   _ _ _ _ _ _ _ _ _ _

8. The steps you follow in your experiment:
   _ _ _ _ _ _ _ _ _

9. To use patterns in observations to say what may happen next:
   _ _ _ _ _ _ _ _

10. An investigation that is controlled:
    _ _ _ _ _ _ _ _ _ _ _ _

```
R T A S N O I T S E U Q K S A R S
C O L L E C T D A T A R S A T S I
S C I E N T I F I C M E T H O D S
B B N Z X E J E O E S T S A U Y E
A Z E Y N P I D D V U L O T Q S H
R F G L A C E A A U F Q E A T V T
G W R A M D N R E P L P T D V L O
R C A N C I I R I W N C I D O D P
A E P A C A D G R M I U N R A M Y
P I H A B G K N I D E P T O B Z H
H N K L Y R H L E A H N Y C C U A
R Y E W D A X R V M O A T E N R A
A N G L B M P R O C E D U R E Y D
```

CHALLENGE: How many other important words from this lesson can you find in the word search? Write them below.

_____
_____
_____
_____
_____
_____

Apply Concepts

2 For each question, state which kind of investigation works best: repeated observations, using models, or controlled experiments. Then explain how you would do the investigation.

What kinds of birds visit a feeder at different times of the year?

_____

_____

_____

Does hot water or cold water boil faster?

_____

_____

_____

What are the parts of an elevator and how does it work?

_____

_____

_____

How does the length of a kite's tail affect the way it flies?

_____

_____

_____

3 Ryan hypothesizes that darker colors heat up faster. He places a thermometer inside a red wool sock, a green cotton glove, and a black nylon hat. What's wrong with his procedure?

_____

_____

_____

Take It Home!

Use scientific methods to help your family enjoy a healthy snack. Design an experiment to find out whether coating apple slices in lemon juice can stop them from turning brown. Perform your experiment.

36

SC.5.N.1.2 Explain the difference between an experiment and other types of scientific investigation. **SC.5.N.1.5** Recognize and explain that scientific investigation frequently does not parallel the steps of "the scientific method."

Name _____

Essential Question

How Do You Perform a Controlled Experiment?

Set a Purpose
What will you learn from this experiment?

_____

_____

_____

_____

_____

_____

Think About the Procedure
What is the tested variable in this experiment?

_____

_____

Each time you try the same test, it is called a trial. Why is it important to do repeated trials of this experiment?

_____

_____

_____

Record Your Data
In the table below, record your results.

Surface Material	Height Ball Bounced					
	Trial 1	Trial 2	Trial 3	Trial 4	Trial 5	Average

Draw Conclusions

What can you conclude based on your experiment?

_____

_____

_____

_____

Analyze and Extend

1. Think about the materials the ball bounced on. What was it about them that affected the height of the bounce?

_____

_____

_____

_____

2. What other floor materials could you test? Predict the results.

_____

_____

_____

_____

3. Tennis is played on three types of surfaces: grass, packed clay, and hard courts. Hard courts are often made from asphalt, the black road surface material, with paint on top. Predict how these surfaces would affect ball bounces. Then do some research. Find out the pros and cons of each type.

_____

_____

_____

_____

4. What else would you like to find out how balls bounce?

_____

_____

_____

_____

_____

_____

SC.5.N.1.1 ... plan and carry out scientific investigations of various types....

Lesson 5

Essential Question

What Are Some Science Tools?

Engage Your Brain!

Find the answer to the following question in this lesson and write it here.

This scientific equipment is filled with liquids. What tools can scientists use to measure the volume of a liquid?

_____

_____

_____

Active Reading

Lesson Vocabulary

List the terms. As you learn about each one, make notes in the Interactive Glossary.

_____

_____

_____

_____

Compare and Contrast

Many ideas in this lesson are connected because they explain comparisons and contrasts—how things are alike and different. Active readers stay focused on comparisons and contrasts when they ask themselves, How are these things alike? How are they different?

Field Trips

If you like school field trips, you might want to become a field scientist. Field scientists travel around the world studying science in the wild. They pack their tools and take them along.

Active Reading As you read these two pages, box the names of all the science tools.

Field scientists go "on location" to investigate the natural world. Their investigations are often in the form of repeated observations. They use tools to increase the power of their senses. Their choices of tools depend on the questions they ask.

Collecting Net

What kinds of animals swim near the shore of a pond? A scientist might use a collecting net and an observation pan to answer this question. By carefully pulling the net through the water, they can catch small animals without harming them.

Hand Lens

How does an ant move? How does it use its mouthparts? A hand lens might help answer these questions. Hold the hand lens near your eye. Then move your other hand to bring the object into view. Move the object back and forth until it is in sharp focus.

Do the Math!
Estimate by Sampling

Scientists photograph ducks from a plane and then draw a grid over the photo. How many ducks do you estimate are on the whole lake?

_____

Why might your estimate differ from the actual number of ducks?

_____

_____

_____

Cameras

What do lion fish eat? How do they catch their food? To investigate, a scientist might use an underwater video camera. Cameras help scientists record events.

Into the Lab

What's living in a drop of pond water? Lots of tiny critters! Some behave like animals. Others are like plants. All are too small to be seen with only a hand lens.

Active Reading As you read these two pages, draw lines connecting the pairs of tools being compared to each other.

Science tools can be heavy and expensive. If you want to observe the tiniest pond life, you'll need science tools that are too big or too delicate to be carried into the field. For example, scientists use computers to record and analyze data, construct models, and communicate with other scientists.

Use Numbers

Some tools help scientists count things. Some scientists estimate, while others perform complex mathematical calculations. All scientists must be comfortable **using numbers**.

▶ To find the magnification of a light microscope, multiply the power of the eyepiece lens by the power of the objective lens. The letter X stands for how many times bigger objects appear.

Eyepiece Magnification	Objective Magnification	Total Magnification
10X	40X	
15X	60X	
8X	100X	

Light Microscope

The tiny living things in pond water are **microscopic**, or too small to see with just your eyes. A light microscope magnifies things, or makes them look bigger. The object to be viewed is placed on a clear slide. Light passes through the object and two lenses. You look through the eyepiece and turn knobs to focus an image.

Dropper

A dropper is a tube with a rubber bulb on one end. Squeeze the bulb and then dip the tip into a liquid. Release the bulb, and the liquid will be sucked up the tube. When you slowly squeeze the bulb, the liquid drops out.

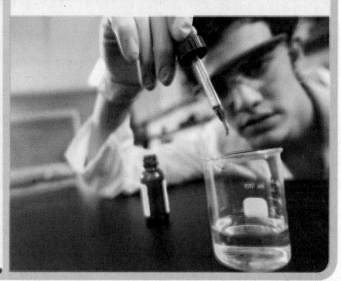

Electron Microscope

Light microscopes have been around for 500 years. But technology, or people's use of tools, has improved. Today a scanning electron microscope (SEM) can magnify an object up to one million times. The SEM shoots a beam of electrons at the object. An image of the surface of the object appears on a computer screen.

Pipette

A pipette is a tool like a dropper, but it's more exact. It is used to add or remove very small amounts of liquids. Pipettes often have marks on the side to measure volume. One kind of pipette makes drops so tiny that they can only be see with a scanning electron microscope!

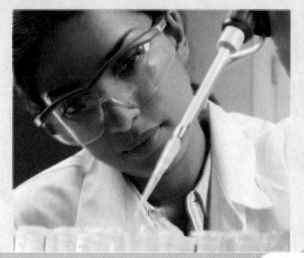

Measuring Up

What do a digit, a palm, a hand, a dram, a peck, a rod, and a stone have in common? They all are, or were at one time, units of measurement!

Active Reading As you read the next four pages, circle all the units of measurement.

When you **measure**, you make observations involving numbers and units. Today most countries use the International System (SI) units in daily life. If you were to visit these countries, you'd purchase fruit or cheese by the *kilogram*. In the United States, most everyday measurements use units from the time when English colonists lived in America.

However, scientists around the world—including those in the United States—use the SI, or metric system.

The metric system is based on multiples of 10. In the metric system, base units are divided into smaller units using prefixes such as *milli-, centi-,* and *deci-*. Base units are changed to bigger units using prefixes such as *deca-* and *kilo-*.

Measuring Length

Length is the distance between two points. The base metric unit of length is the *meter*. Rulers, metersticks, and tape measures are tools used to measure length.

A caliper can be used to measure the distance between the two sides of an object.

Measuring Time

Time describes how long events take. The base unit of time is the second. Larger units are the minute, the hour, and the day. Smaller units include the millisecond and microsecond. Clocks, stopwatches, timers, and calendars are some of the tools used to measure time.

Measure Your Science Book

Use a metric tool and units to measure the length, width, and thickness of your science book.

Length: _____

Width: _____

Thickness: _____

Measuring Temperature

Temperature describes how hot or cold something is. Thermometers are used to measure temperature. Scientists measure temperature in degrees Celsius. So do most other people around the world. In the United States, degrees Fahrenheit are used to report the weather, to measure body temperatures, and in cooking.

Pan Balance

A **balance** is a tool used to measure mass. *Mass* is the amount of matter in an object. The base unit of mass is the kilogram. One kilogram equals 1,000 grams.

With this balance, you can directly compare the masses of two objects. Put one object in each pan. The pan that sinks lower contains the greater mass.

To measure in grams, place an object in one pan.

Always carry a balance by holding its base.

Add gram masses to the other pan until the two pans are balanced. Then add the values of the gram masses to find the total mass.

This pan balance has drawers where the masses are stored.

Three Beams

A triple-beam balance measures mass more exactly than the pan balance. It has one pan and three beams. To find the number of grams, move the sliders until the beam balances.

Digital Mass

An electronic balance calculates the mass of an object for you. It displays an object's mass on a screen.

How Strong?

A **spring scale** is a tool used to measure force. Force is a push or a pull. When an object hangs down from the scale, the force of gravity, or weight, is measured. When the spring scale is used to pull an object, it measures the force needed to move the object. Either way, the base unit is called a newton.

▶ Draw lines to match the tools to what they measure and the units.

Tool	What It Measures	Units
	▪ force ▪	▪ seconds, minutes, hours, days, years, etc.
	▪ temperature ▪	▪ grams, milligrams, kilograms, etc.
	▪ length ▪	▪ newtons
	▪ mass ▪	▪ degrees Celsius, degrees Fahrenheit
	▪ time ▪	▪ meters, kilometers, millimeters, etc.

More Measuring

It's a hot day and you're thirsty. How much lemonade would you like? 1,000 milliliters or 1,000 cubic centimeters? Not sure? Read on!

Units of Volume

Volume is the amount of space a solid, liquid, or gas takes up. There are two base metric units for measuring volume. A *cubic meter* is one meter long, one meter high, and one meter wide. The *liter* is the base unit often used for measuring the volume of liquids. You're probably familiar with liters because many drinks are sold in 1-liter or 2-liter bottles. These two metric units of volume are closely related. There are 1,000 liters (L) in one cubic meter (m^3).

▶ One cubic centimeter (cm^3) is equal to 1 milliliter (mL). Both are equal to about 20 drops from a dropper.
Which is greater—1,000 mL or 1,000 cm^3?

_____

1 cm
1 cm
1 cm

Finding Volume

You can find the volume of a rectangular prism by multiplying length times width times height. To find the volume of a liquid, use a measuring cup, beaker, or graduated cylinder. Use water to find the volume of an irregular solid. Put water in a graduated cylinder. Note the volume. Then drop the object in and note the new volume. Subtract the two numbers to find the volume of the object.

> The surface of a liquid in a graduated cylinder is curved. This curve is called a *meniscus*. Always measure volume from the center of the meniscus.

Accurate Measurements

When a measurement is close to the true size, it is **accurate**. Try to measure as accurately as you can with the tools you have. Make sure a tool is not broken and that you know how to use it properly. Also pay attention to the units on the tools you use. Accurate measurements are important when doing science investigations, when baking, and when taking medicines.

Follow these tips to improve your accuracy:

☑ Handle each tool properly.

☑ Use each tool the same way every time. For example, read the measurement at eye level.

☑ Measure to the smallest place value the tool allows.

☑ Measure twice.

☑ Record your measurements carefully, including the units.

▶ Write the math sentence for finding the volume of the toy.

_____

Sum It Up!

When you're done, use the answer key to check and revise your work.

There are many kinds of tools that scientists use. Tools help scientists observe, measure, and study things in the natural world. Fill in the blank boxes with examples of tools that scientists use.

1 _____

dropper

2 _____

camera

Other Tools

3 _____

Science Tools

5 _____

4 _____

6 _____

Tools for Observing

Tools for Measuring

binoculars

7 _____

telescope

8 _____

beaker and graduated cylinder

stopwatch

Answer Key: 1 and 2—computer or collecting net; 3 and 4—microscope or hand lens; 5, 6, 7, and 8—thermometer, balance, spring scale, and ruler or meterstick.

Name _____

Word Play

1 Put the scrambled letters in order to spell a science term.

1. treem   ◯ _ _ ◯ _   A metric unit of length

2. amrg   _ _ ◯ _   A metric unit of mass

3. rdsgeee seCisul   _ _ _ _ _ _ ◯ _ _ _ _ _ ◯   A metric unit for temperature

4. taceurca   _ _ _ ◯ _ _ _ ◯   A measurement close to the true size

5. townne   _ _ _ ◯ _ _   A unit used to measure force

6. trile   _ _ _ _ ◯   A metric unit of volume

7. acnsrl spgei   _ _ _ _ _ ◯ _   A tool used to measure force

8. nap cablane   _ ◯ _ _ _ _ _   A tool used to measure mass

9. dceson   ◯ _ _ _ _ _   A metric unit of time

10. veumol   _ _ _ ◯ _ _   The amount of space a solid, liquid, or gas takes up

11. tagurdade lycnidre   ◯ _ _ _ _ _ _ _ _ _ _ ◯ _ _   A tool used to measure volume

Riddle: Place the circled letters in order to solve the riddle below.

Why did the captain ask for a balance?

He wanted to _ _ _ _ _ _ _ _ _

the mass of the _ _ _ _ _ _ _ _ _ _ _ _ .

Apply Concepts

2 Tell how you use one or more of these tools to investigate each question.

How are two fossil teeth similar and different?

_____

_____

_____

Which kinds of butterflies are found in a field?

_____

_____

_____

What do scientists already know about the bottom of the ocean?

_____

_____

_____

Does the mass of a ball affect how far it rolls?

_____

_____

_____

3 Identify what each tool measures and the metric units it uses.

_____   _____   _____

_____   _____   _____

Take It Home!

At your school or public library, find a book about how scientists work or the tools they use. Read and discuss the book with your family. Prepare a brief summary to present to your classmates.

SC.5.N.1.1 ... plan and carry out scientific investigations of various types such as: systematic observations....
SC.5.N.1.2 Explain the difference between an experiment and other types of scientific investigation.

Name _____

Essential Question

How Can Scientists Learn from Observations?

Set a Purpose
What will you learn from this investigation?

_____
_____
_____
_____

Think About the Procedure
What planning must I do before this investigation?

_____
_____
_____
_____
_____

What tools are used in this investigation. What measurements, if any, are taken with them?

_____
_____
_____
_____
_____

Record Your Data
In the space below, record your results.

Soil Sample: _____

My Observations:

Amount of water held by
100 mL of soil: _____

Mass Before Drying: _____

Mass After Drying: _____

Draw Conclusions

Compare your data with the data from other groups. What can you conclude?

_____

_____

_____

_____

Analyze and Extend

1. Why is it important that soils be able to hold some water?

_____

_____

_____

_____

2. Why would a farmer want to know about the soil on his or her farm?

_____

_____

_____

_____

3. How was this investigation different from a controlled experiment?

_____

_____

_____

_____

4. Why was it important to know the mass of the soil before it was dried for one week?

_____

_____

_____

_____

5. What else would you like to find out about different types of soils?

_____

_____

_____

_____

Ask a Zoologist

wombat

Q. Do zoologists work in a zoo?

A. Some, but not all, zoologists work in zoos. Zoologists are scientists who study animals. The word "zoo" comes from the Latin word for animal.

Q. Do zoologists get to play with animals?

A. No. Most zoologists study wild animals in their habitats. They try to observe animals without disturbing them.

Q. Do zoologists get to have wild animals as pets?

A. Wild animals do not make good pets. Zoologists do not take wild animals home. Pets such as cats and dogs have grown used to living with people. Wild animals have not.

Now It's Your Turn!

What question would you ask a zoologist?

_____

_____

_____

Wombats live in Tasmania and southeastern Australia.

Careers in Science *continued*

Animals That Start with "K"

Some zoologists study animal behavior, or how animals act. A zoologist spotted some interesting behaviors in Australia and wrote these journal entries. Match the sentences with the pictures by entering the day of the journal entry near the picture it describes.

Day 1 This afternoon we saw an adult koala carrying a young koala on its back.

Day 2 Today our team saw a kangaroo. It had a joey (a young kangaroo) in its pouch.

Day 3 Our team saw a kangaroo hopping quickly. We measured its speed—nearly 15 miles per hour!

Day 4 This morning we saw a koala. It was eating leaves from a eucalyptus tree.

Day 5 We saw two kangaroos boxing with each other.

Day _____

Day _____

Day _____

Day _____

Day _____

Name _____

Multiple Choice

Identify the choice that best answers the question.

SC.5.N.1.1

1 Gabrielle counts the number of people who visit the community pool each day for 1 week. She displays her data using a bar graph.

Number of Pool Visitors

How many more people did Gabrielle observe at the pool on Sunday than on Thursday?

(A) 20   (C) 75
(B) 30   (D) 100

SC.5.N.1.1

2 Observations are made using our five senses. We can then use those observations to draw conclusions. Which of the following is an example of a conclusion?

(F) "The object is flat."
(G) "The flower smells like mint."
(H) "Crickets chirp to attract mates."
(I) "The food is both sweet and salty."

SC.5.N.2.1

3 Scientists are not the only ones who gather information. For example, historians gather information to describe what has happened in the past. However, scientists gather information differently than others. Which way of gathering information do **only** scientists use?

(A) reading
(B) observing
(C) recording
(D) experimenting

SC.5.N.2.1

4 Leon likes doing science experiments. However, he could not understand why the directions said to repeat the experiment three times. Why do scientists repeat their experiments?

(F) to avoid making observations
(G) to throw out the information they collected earlier
(H) to develop a new procedure that they can use later
(I) to make sure that the information they collect is reliable

SC.5.N.1.1

5 Asa watches his mom rub soap on her finger to help her get a ring unstuck. He thinks that soap must reduce friction. He designs an investigation to test his theory. He pulls a weight across a board and records the force with a spring scale. He then puts soap on the board and pulls the weight again. Which of the following variables is Asa measuring?

(A) the speed with which the weight is pulled
(B) the amount of weight being pulled
(C) the force needed to pull the weight
(D) the type of surface the weight is being pulled across

SC.5.N.1.1

6 Gabriella is learning how to accurately read a thermometer. She places the following thermometer in the sun for 1 hour.

What temperature does Gabriella read on the thermometer?

(F) 38° Celsius   (H) 38° Fahrenheit
(G) 100° Celsius   (I) 105° Fahrenheit

SC.5.N.1.1

7 Lia measured the volume of a liquid using a graduated cylinder. The following illustration shows three positions from which she could take a reading.

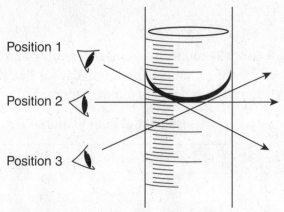

From which position should Lia observe the cylinder to get an accurate reading?

(A) Position 1
(B) Position 2
(C) Position 3
(D) All of the positions give accurate readings.

SC.5.N.1.1

8 Four students threw darts at the center of a dart board. Which target shows the **most** accurate results?

© Houghton Mifflin Harcourt Publishing Company (border) ©NDisc/Age Fotostock

SC.5.N.1.1

9 Different systems for making measurements use different units. Which system of measurement is generally used by scientists?

(A) customary

(B) English

(C) Imperial

(D) metric

SC.5.N.1.4

10 Joshua has been growing plants that receive $\frac{1}{2}$ cup of water two times per week. Now he wants to see what happens to the plants when the amount of water is reduced, as shown in the chart.

Plant	Amount of water
1	no water
2	$\frac{1}{2}$ cup once every two weeks
3	$\frac{1}{2}$ cup once per week
4	$\frac{1}{2}$ cup two times per week

Which plant is the control?

(F) 1   (H) 2

(G) 3   (I) 4

SC.5.N.1.2

11 Scientists want to determine if walls that are painted a certain color will raise a person's blood pressure. They plan to set up four rooms. Which variable should change in each room?

(A) the color used

(B) the type of room used

(C) the instruments used to test the blood pressure

(D) the amount of time the person spends in the room

SC.5.N.1.2

12 Sandy observes the phases of the moon during a two-week period. She sketches and labels the phases and shares her drawings with the class. Which statement best describes Sandy's investigation?

(F) It involves modeling.

(G) It involves experimentation.

(H) It involves repeated observations.

(I) It involves both experimentation and repeated observations.

SC.5.N.1.4

13 Scientists include controls in their experiments. Why is a control important?

(A) It helps scientists share results.

(B) It helps scientists form their first hypothesis.

(C) It helps scientists record their repeated observations.

(D) It helps scientists compare their results to a standard.

SC.5.N.1.4

14 A teacher writes the following note on a student's experimental design: "You did not identify and control variables." Why is it important to identify and control variables?

(F) because a scientist must observe data

(G) because a scientist must form a hypothesis

(H) because a scientist must know which variable causes change

(I) because a scientist must know which variable to use for making a model

SC.5.N.1.6, SC.5.N.2.1

15 Michael rides a bike made by Company A. Luis rides a bike made by Company B. How can Michael and Luis determine in a scientific way whose bike has tires that last longer?

Ⓐ Read information about the tires from each manufacturer.

Ⓑ Ask ten classmates who ride each bike which tires last longer.

Ⓒ Each student should ride their own bike for 25 days, then compare the tires.

Ⓓ Use a machine to test the bikes in the same way for 25 days, then compare the tires.

SC.5.N.1.6, SC.5.N.2.1

16 A doctor says that drinking two glasses of milk in the morning will give students more energy. Which of the following would be good scientific evidence for or against the doctor's claim?

Ⓕ a brochure from the doctor stating the benefits of milk

Ⓖ data from scientific investigations about drinking milk in the morning

Ⓗ a TV advertisement that drinking milk in the morning gives people plenty of energy

Ⓘ statements from five people about how drinking milk in the morning gives them energy

SC.5.N.1.3

17 When Andrew conducts an investigation, he repeats the investigation several times. Why does Andrew do this?

Ⓐ to create inventions

Ⓑ to get consistent results

Ⓒ to do the work very safely

Ⓓ to be sure the work is correct

SC.5.N.1.6

18 Sameh's friends wanted to see a different movie than he did. To get his friends to see the movie he wanted, Sameh told them about the exciting preview he saw. In scientific terms, which of the following **best** describes what Sameh was doing?

Ⓕ predicting

Ⓖ giving his opinion

Ⓗ stating a conclusion

Ⓘ surveying his friends

SC.5.N.2.1

19 Study the following pictures of common classroom objects.

| 1 | 2 | 3 | 4 |
| Pencil | Ruler | Pen | Chalk |

Which objects would be classified together?

Ⓐ 1, 2, 4   Ⓒ 2, 3, 4

Ⓑ 1, 3, 4   Ⓓ 1, 2, 3

SC.5.N.2.1

20 Sometimes, the results of an investigation are not what was expected. When this happens, what should a scientist do?

Ⓕ Change the results.

Ⓖ Defend the results as correct.

Ⓗ Plan another investigation to test the results of the first one.

Ⓘ Ignore the first set of results and plan a different investigation.

The Solar System and the Universe

Big Idea 5

Earth in Space and Time

Kennedy Space Center

I Wonder Why

This rocket carried the *Cassini* space probe into space. Why do scientists launch space probes? *Turn the page to find out.*

Here's Why Space probes can take images and collect and analyze samples from objects in the solar system. They provide data that would not be possible to get from Earth.

Track Your Progress

Essential Questions and Florida Benchmarks

Big Idea 5 *Earth in Space and Time*

Now I Get the Big Idea!

SC.5.E.5.2 Recognize the major common characteristics of all planets and compare/contrast the properties of inner and outer planets. **SC.5.E.5.3** Distinguish among the following objects of the Solar System—Sun, planets, moons, asteroids, comets—and identify Earth's position in it.

Essential Question

What Objects Are Part of the Solar System?

Engage Your Brain!

Find the answer to the following question in this lesson and record it here.

Which planets have rings, and what are the rings made of?

_____

_____

_____

Active Reading

Lesson Vocabulary
List the terms. As you learn about each one, make notes in the Interactive Glossary.

_____   _____

_____   _____

_____

Compare and Contrast
Many ideas in this lesson are connected because they explain comparisons and contrasts—how things are alike and different. Active readers stay focused on comparisons and contrasts when they ask themselves, How are these things alike? How are they different?

The Solar System

The sun, Earth, and its moon form a system in space. Earth revolves around the sun. That means Earth travels around the sun in a path called an orbit. The moon revolves around Earth. Read on to learn about other objects in space.

Active Reading As you read this page, underline two details that tell how all planets are alike.

Earth and its moon are part of a larger system in space called a solar system. A **solar system** is made up of a star and the planets and other space objects that revolve around it. A **planet** is a large, round body that revolves around a star. In our solar system, the planets and other objects revolve around a star we call the sun.

There are eight planets in our solar system. All of them rotate, or spin, about an axis. This is an imaginary line that goes through the center of a planet. Earth rotates on its axis once every 24 hours. This is the length of one day on Earth.

Unlike planets, some objects don't revolve directly around the sun. *Moons* are small, natural objects that revolve around other objects. Many planets have moons. Earth has only one. It revolves once around Earth about every 27 days.

Earth is about 150 million kilometers from the sun!

Diagram not to scale.

The planets in our solar system are very far from each other.

The orbits of the planets in our solar system are not perfect circles. They are oval-shaped, or elliptical [eh•LIP•tuh•kuhl].

Some planets have many moons. Earth has only one. Venus and Mercury have none!

Around and Around

Draw an orbit for the planet. Then draw a moon and its orbit.

sun

planet

The Inner Planets

At times, the brightest object in the night sky is not the moon or a star. It is Venus, one of Earth's closest neighbors in space.

Active Reading As you read this page, underline ways in which the inner planets are alike.

Mercury

Mercury, the smallest planet in our solar system, is less than half the size of Earth. Its surface is filled with craters, much like Earth's moon. Mercury is the closest planet to the sun. On Mercury, the sun would look three times as large as it does on Earth.

Planets in our solar system can be classified based on their distance from the sun. The four inner planets are the closest to the sun. In order from closest to farthest, the inner planets are Mercury, Venus, Earth, and Mars.

The inner planets are very dense and rocky. They have thin atmospheres and small diameters. A planet's diameter is the distance from one side of the planet, through its center, to the other side. The inner planets have large solid cores at their centers. They have few moons, and their revolution times are short compared to the other planets in the solar system.

Venus

Venus is so hot that lead would melt at its surface! Thick clouds surround Venus, and its atmosphere is made up mostly of carbon dioxide. Lava flows from more than 1,000 volcanoes on Venus's surface.

Planets not to scale.

sun

Earth

Earth is the third planet from the sun. It has an atmosphere made of mostly nitrogen, oxygen, and carbon dioxide. Earth is the only planet known to have abundant liquid water, which helps to keep Earth at temperatures that allow life.

No Home for Me

List three reasons why people could not live on Venus.

1. _____
_____

2. _____
_____

3. _____
_____

Mars

Sometimes you can see Mars in the night sky. Mars is known as the "Red Planet" because of its red, rocky surface. Giant dust storms often cover the entire planet, forming huge sand dunes. Mars, like the other inner planets, has many volcanoes.

The Outer Planets

On a clear night, Jupiter might appear to be a large, bright star in the night sky. But in fact, Jupiter is one of the outer planets in our solar system.

Great Red Spot

Active Reading As you read this page, underline ways in which the outer planets are alike.

Jupiter

Jupiter is the largest planet in the solar system. In fact, all of the other planets would fit inside Jupiter! Its Great Red Spot is about as wide as three Earths. The red spots are massive, spinning storms. Jupiter's faint rings were discovered by the *Voyager 1* space probe in 1979.

Jupiter, Saturn, Uranus, and Neptune are the outer planets. In that order, they are the farthest planets from the sun. The outer planets are also called the gas giants, because they are huge and made up mostly of gases. They don't have a solid surface, and their cores are very small.

Because the gas giants are so far away from the sun, their surfaces are much colder than the inner planets. All of the outer planets have many moons and ring systems. Saturn's ring system is more visible than those of the other outer planets.

Planets not to scale.

Saturn

Saturn, the second largest planet, has thousands of rings around it. The rings are made up of ice and chunks of rock. Some of Saturn's moons are found inside these rings. Like Jupiter, Saturn has large storms.

What Makes Them Unique?

Write one thing that is unique about each of the outer planets.

Jupiter

_____

_____

Saturn

_____

_____

Uranus

_____

_____

Neptune

_____

_____

sun

Uranus

The axis of Uranus is tilted so far that, compared to other planets, it rotates on its side. This makes seasons on Uranus last more than 20 years! Deep inside Uranus, heated gases bubble and burst onto the surface, causing bright clouds to form. Uranus has a system of at least 13 faint rings.

Neptune

Neptune is the windiest planet in our solar system. Its winds move at speeds of about 2,000 km/hr (1,250 mi/hr). These winds blow Neptune's Great Dark Spot around the planet. This spot is a storm, about the size of Earth, known to vanish and reform! Neptune has nine rings around it.

Compare Inner and Outer Planets

Size, surface features, and distance from the sun are just some differences between the inner and outer planets. Look at this chart to learn about other differences.

Planet	Period of Revolution (in Earth days and years)	Period of Rotation (in Earth hours and days)	Surface Temperature Range (inner planets) Top of the Clouds Temperatures (outer planets)	Number of Moons	Density	Diameter
INNER PLANETS						
Mercury	88 days	59 days	–173/427 °C	0	5.43 g/cm^3	4,878 km (3,031 mi)
Venus	225 days	243 days	–45/462 °C	0	5.24 g/cm^3	12,104 km (7,521 mi)
Earth	365 days	1 Earth day	–88/58 °C	1	5.52 g/cm^3	12,756 km (7,926 mi)
Mars	687 days	about an Earth day	–87/–5 °C	2	3.94 g/cm^3	6,794 km (4,221 mi)
OUTER PLANETS						
Jupiter	12 years	about 10 hours	–148 °C	63	1.33 g/cm^3	142,984 km (88,850 mi)
Saturn	29 years	about 10 hours	–178 °C	61	0.70 g/cm^3	120,536 (74,901 mi)
Uranus	84 years	about 17 hours	–216 °C	27	1.30 g/cm^3	51,118 km (31,764 mi)
Neptune	165 years	about 16 hours	–214 °C	13	1.76 g/cm^3	49,528 km (30,776 mi)

Do the Math!

Find an Average

In the space below, find the average density of the four inner planets. Repeat for the four outer planets.

Inner planets:

Outer planets:

How do the average densities compare?

_____

_____

_____

The density of water is 1 gram per cubic centimeter (g/cm³). Saturn would float because its density is less than the density of water. Earth would sink.

Patterns in Data

Look at the data table on the previous page. Describe two trends in the data between the inner and outer planets.

_____

_____

_____

_____

The Flying Objects

Besides planets, there are many other bodies that orbit the sun. Let's find out more about some of them.

As you read these two pages, find and underline two facts about asteroids.

Moons

Other moons are very different from Earth's moon. Europa, one of Jupiter's moons, may have a liquid ocean under a layer of ice. Another of Jupiter's moons, Io [EYE•oh], has the most active volcanoes of any body in the solar system.

Io

Dwarf Planets

Pluto was once called a planet. But in 2006, it was reclassified as a dwarf planet. **Dwarf planets** are nearly round bodies whose orbits cross the orbits of other bodies. Most are found in a region of the solar system beyond Neptune's orbit called the Kuiper belt. These objects are far away and hard to study. Quaoar, shown above, was discovered in 2002.

Asteroids

Asteroids are rock and iron objects that orbit the sun. Millions of them are found in the wide region between Mars and Jupiter known as the *asteroid belt*. Some asteroids are as small as a city block. Others could fill up an ocean. Some asteroids even have their own moons!

Meteoroids, Meteors, and Meteorites

Each day, tons of meteoroids hit Earth's atmosphere. *Meteoroids* are pieces of rock that break off of asteroids and travel through space. Most meteoroids burn up in Earth's atmosphere, causing a streak of light called a *meteor*. Meteoroids that reach Earth's surface are called *meteorites*.

Where's the Sun?

In the drawing of a comet, put an *S* to indicate the direction toward the sun. Put a *T* over each tail.

Comets

A **comet** is a chunk of frozen gases, rock, ice, and dust. Comets have long orbits around the sun. As comets pass close to the sun, part of their frozen surface begins to break away and turn into gases and dust. These particles reflect the sun's light and become visible as long tails. A comet's tails always point away from the sun.

Space Watch

Some objects in space cross each others' orbits. Often, nothing happpens. But sometimes the objects hit each other. Scientists look out for objects that may cross Earth's orbit.

Pictures of the surface of the moon tell a story. Over millions of years, space objects such as comets, meteoroids, and asteroids have impacted, or hit, the moon. Impact craters of all sizes can be found on the moon's surface.

Space objects have also hit other bodies in the solar system. A comet named Shoemaker-Levy 9 impacted Jupiter in 1994. Pictures of the impact were taken by the *Galileo* space probe.

Scientists know that large objects have also hit Earth. In fact, a huge one impacted Earth about 65 million years ago. Many scientists think it caused changes in the environment that killed all the dinosaurs. Luckily, impacts like that one do not happen often.

Scientists use telescopes to scan space for near-Earth asteroids. These are objects that may cross Earth's orbit. Scientists keep track of their size, position, and motion. They analyze this data to determine if the objects could impact Earth.

The impact of Shoemaker-Levy 9 caused bubbles of hot gas to rise into Jupiter's atmosphere, as well as dark spots to form on its surface.

The Barringer Meteor Crater, in Arizona, was formed by a meteorite that struck Earth about 50,000 years ago.

Impacts can happen anywhere on Earth! This map shows some impact crater sites from around the world.

Impact Crater Diameter

- 10–25 km
- 25–50 km
- greater than 50 km

▶ On these pages, underline effects of impacts. Then circle a picture that shows evidence of an impact on Earth.

Observatories have powerful telescopes that enable scientists to track the movement of objects in space.

Sum It Up!

When you're done, use the answer key to check and revise your work.

Read the summary, and then place the information in the list into the correct box below.

The sun is at the center of the solar system. Planets, dwarf planets, moons, and other smaller objects make up the solar system. The eight planets in the solar system can be divided into inner planets and outer planets. Each group has different characteristics.

small and dense	longer revolutions	many moons	few moons
giant size	closest to sun	gaseous surface	low density
rings	rocky surface		

1   **Inner Planets**

2   **Outer Planets**

Fill in the missing information to describe the object shown below.

3

Io

a. Object Type: _____

b. Space Neighbors: _____

c. Key Feature: _____

d. How It's Different from Earth: _____

_____

_____

Answer Key: 1. Inner Planets: small and dense, rocky surface, few moons, closest to sun 2. Outer Planets: gaseous surface, giant size, rings, many moons, low density, longer revolutions 3a. moon 3b. Jupiter and its other moons 3c. active volcanoes 3d. Io orbits a planet. Earth is a planet, so it orbits the sun. Io is farther from the sun than Earth.

76

© Houghton Mifflin Harcourt Publishing Company

Name _____

Word Play

1 Use each of the terms in the box to label the objects in the diagram below.

planet	comet	asteroid	solar system	dwarf planet
moon	orbit	gas giant	sun	

* Key Lesson Vocabulary

(x 1) • **Pluto**

9. _____

Neptune

(x 27) **Uranus**

1. _____

8. _____

(x 13)

7. _____

Jupiter

Saturn

(x 63)

(x 61)

5. _____

6. _____

← 4. _____

Mercury

Earth

Mars

2. _____

3. _____

Venus

Apply Concepts

2 In the space below, draw pictures to show the key physical characteristics of an inner planet and an outer planet. Then describe your drawings.

_____   _____

_____   _____

_____   _____

_____   _____

3 Describe the features of a comet.

_____

_____

_____

_____

4 What is a meteoroid, and how does it become a meteorite?

_____

_____

_____

_____

5 Identify each of the following large objects in the solar system.
Write how you are able to identify each one.

_____
_____

_____
_____

_____
_____

_____
_____

6 A scientist discovers an object in the solar system. She describes it as bigger than an asteroid, smaller than Mercury, and farther from the sun than Neptune. What kind of object could it be? Explain.

_____

_____

7 Complete the Venn diagram in order to compare and contrast an asteroid and a comet.

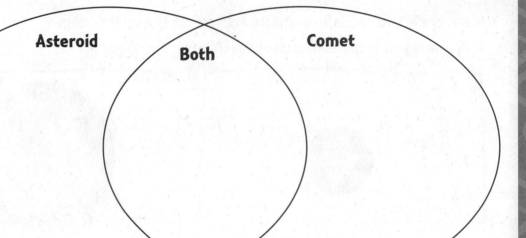

Asteroid   Both   Comet

8 Draw a picture of an object that might impact a planet. Label and describe the object. What evidence is there that these objects collide with planets and moons?

_____

_____

_____

Take It Home! Many newspapers give the location of Venus, Mars, and Jupiter in the sky. Find out where in the sky these planets may appear. See if you can find them. They are among the brightest objects in the night sky.

Name _____

SC.5.N.1.2 Explain the difference between an experiment and other types of scientific investigation.
SC.5.N.2.1 Recognize and explain that science is grounded in empirical observations that are testable; explanation must always be linked with evidence.
SC.5.E.5.2 Recognize the major common characteristics of all planets and compare/contrast the properties of inner and outer planets.

Essential Question

How Do We Observe Objects in the Solar System?

Set a Purpose

What do you think you will learn from this investigation?

_____

_____

Think About the Procedure

Why do you think you will observe the object in different ways?

_____

_____

_____

Why is it important that you work together as a team in this investigation?

_____

_____

Record Your Data

In the space below, record the observations you made using all three methods.

Draw Conclusions

Think about how scientists view objects in space. What did observing the object from far away represent?

_____

_____

_____

What did using binoculars represent?

_____

_____

_____

What did viewing the object up close represent?

_____

_____

_____

Analyze and Extend

1. How did your observations from far away differ from those made using binoculars? Give an example.

_____

_____

_____

2. How did your observations made using binoculars differ from the observations made when a student walked to the poster? Give an example.

_____

_____

_____

3. How do space probes help scientists learn about objects in space?

_____

_____

_____

4. Think about objects in the solar system. How do scientists use time and space relationships to observe them?

_____

_____

_____

5. Think of other questions you would like to ask about how scientists study objects in space. Write your questions.

_____

_____

_____

82

SC.5.E.5.1 Recognize that a galaxy consists of gas, dust, and many stars, including any objects orbiting the stars. Identify our home galaxy as the Milky Way.

Lesson 3

Essential Question

What Are Stars and Galaxies?

Engage Your Brain!

Find the answer to the following question in this lesson and record it here.

Space is not completely empty. There are small particles in space. What happens when these particles come together?

_____

_____

_____

A nebula, such as the Pelican Nebula shown here, is a giant cloud of gas and dust.

Active Reading

Lesson Vocabulary

List the terms. As you learn about each one, make notes in the Interactive Glossary.

_____

_____

_____

Signal Words: Details

Signal words show connections between ideas. *For example, for instance,* and *such as* signal examples of an idea. *Also* and *in fact* signal added facts. Active readers remember what they read because they are alert to signal words that identify examples and facts about a topic.

© Houghton Mifflin Harcourt Publishing Company (bkg) ©Stocktrek Images/Corbis

TWINKLING STARS

You see stars as tiny points of white light in the night sky. Stars are not tiny, and they are not all white. Find out how scientists study stars.

Active Reading As you read these two pages, draw boxes around words or phrases that signal a detail or an added fact.

People have always looked at objects in the sky. **Astronomy** is the study of objects in space and their characteristics. *Astronomers* are scientists who study space and everything in it. They use many types of telescopes to observe objects in space, such as stars and planets.

Stars are huge balls of hot, glowing gases that produce their own heat and light. The sun is the star you know the most about. It seems much larger than other stars only because it is much closer to Earth.

Do the Math!
Dividing by 3-digit Numbers

A small telescope magnifies objects 150 times. A large observatory telescope magnifies an object 3,300 times. How many times as great is the magnification of the observatory telescope than the small telescope?

_____

© Houghton Mifflin Harcourt Publishing Company · (t) ©Gregory MacNicol/Photo Researchers, Inc. (c) ©TONY GENTILE/Reuters/Corbis; (bkgd) ©Stephen Studd/Getty Images

► The sun is a medium-size yellow star. Many stars are larger or hotter than the sun. A supergiant, for example, can be more than 100 times the size of the sun.

A STAR IS BORN

Stars form when gravity causes gas and dust particles found in space to pull together. These particles are squeezed together under great pressure. Eventually, energy stored in the particles is released as heat and light. A star is born.

Stars are classified by their color, temperature, brightness, and size. The color of a star can tell us about its temperature.

For example, blue stars are the hottest. A blue star's average temperature is about 15,000 °C.

Stars have a wide range of sizes. White dwarf stars, for instance, can be as small as a planet. Giant and supergiant stars are many times bigger than the average-size star. The largest stars are also usually the brightest. A star's brightness is related to the amount of visible light it gives off.

Super Hot and Just Hot

Draw a rectangle around the hottest stars in the diagram. Draw a circle around the brightest stars.

Blue Giant   Super Giant

Red Giant

Brightest

sun

White Dwarf

Temperature

GOING GALACTIC

Our solar system is huge. Yet it is only a tiny part of a much larger system in space. Our sun is one star in a group of billions of stars found in the Milky Way galaxy.

Active Reading As you read the next four pages, circle details about the ages of stars in each type of galaxy.

Milky Way Galaxy

YOU ARE HERE

Once, people thought Earth was at the center of the universe. The universe is everything that exists. Now we know that we are not even at the center of our own galaxy!

► In the space below, describe the position of the solar system within the Milky Way.

_____

_____

_____

_____

FEATURES OF GALAXIES

A **galaxy** is a group of billions of stars, the objects that orbit the stars, gas, and dust. A galaxy is held together by gravity. There are billions of galaxies in the universe. Galaxies are separated by large distances. On a cloudless night, you might see what looks like a faint band of clouds among the stars. This is a part of our home galaxy, the Milky Way. Most other galaxies can be seen only by using powerful telescopes.

TYPES OF GALAXIES

In the 1920s, astronomer Edwin Hubble was the first to study galaxies. He classified them by shape. Through his telescope, Hubble observed pinwheel-like groups of stars that he called *spiral galaxies*.

Some spiral galaxies, called *barred spiral galaxies*, have a center shaped like a long bar. Recent evidence suggests that the Milky Way is a barred spiral galaxy.

SPIRAL GALAXIES

Spiral galaxies consist of a rotating disk of young stars, gas, and dust and a central bulge made of older stars.

BARRED SPIRAL GALAXIES

Barred spiral galaxies may have two or more spiral arms. Unlike regular spirals, there are young stars at the center of barred spiral galaxies.

MORE TYPES OF GALAXIES

Most of the brightest galaxies in the universe have spiral shapes. But spiral galaxies are not the only type of galaxy. In fact, they make up only about 20 percent of all galaxies. The dimmer *irregular galaxies* and *elliptical galaxies* make up about 80 percent of all galaxies in the universe.

IRREGULAR GALAXIES

Irregular galaxies do not have any particular shape. The stars are randomly scattered. There is lots of gas and dust to form new stars. About 20 percent of all galaxies are irregular. Some astronomers think that gravity from nearby galaxies causes irregular galaxies to form.

ELLIPTICAL GALAXIES

Elliptical galaxies are brightest at their center. About 60 percent of all galaxies in the universe are elliptical. They can be shaped like a perfect sphere or a flattened globe. Large ellipticals are made up of old stars and have too little dust or gas to form new ones.

COSMIC **CRASHES**

Sometimes galaxies collide, or crash together, in space! Why? Gravity pulls galaxies toward each other. Although galaxies may collide, single stars and planets almost never do.

Many things can happen when galaxies collide. Often, large amounts of dust and gas are pressed together. This causes a starburst, or rapid formation of many new stars. Sometimes, a smaller galaxy becomes part of a larger galaxy. A collision of galaxies can also form a large, irregular galaxy. Scientists believe that many irregular galaxies were once spiral or elliptical galaxies that were involved in a cosmic crash.

Galaxies do not stand still. They are always moving. Galaxies can move away from each other or toward each other.

Look at pictures 1–5. Draw a picture to show what you think will happen next to these two galaxies. Write a sentence to describe it.

_____

_____

Sum It Up!

When you're done, use the answer key to check and revise your work.

The universe is composed of billions of galaxies. Dust, gas, and billions of stars make up a galaxy. The idea web below summarizes information about stars and galaxies. Complete it using the words and phrases from the box.

Types of Galaxies	Elliptical	Temperature
Spiral	Characteristics of Stars	Size
Color	Irregular	

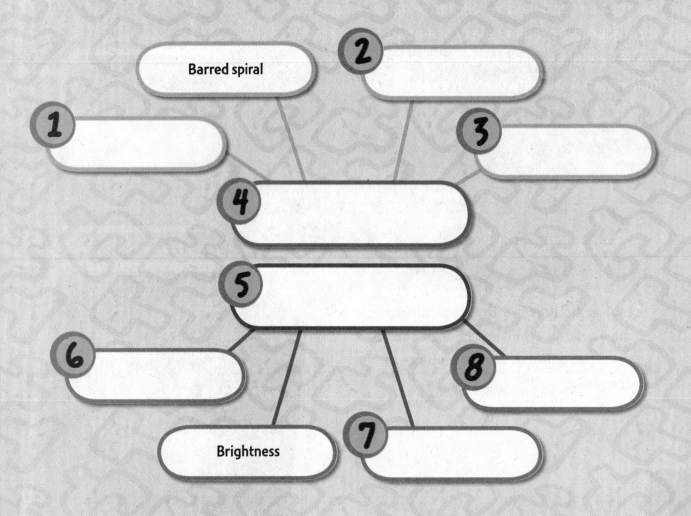

- Barred spiral
- 2
- 1
- 3
- 4
- 5
- 6
- 8
- Brightness
- 7

Name _____

Word Play

1 Complete the puzzle. If you need help, use the words in the box below the clues.

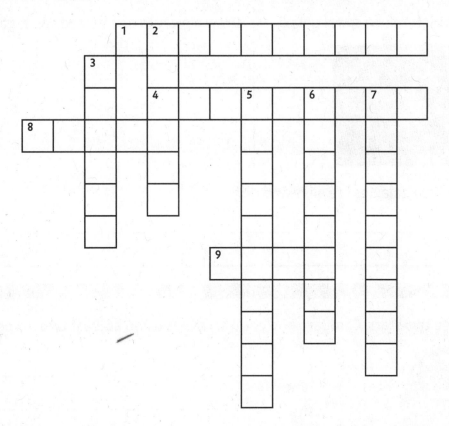

Across

1. A person who studies the universe
4. A galaxy with no particular shape
8. Characteristic that is related to a star's temperature
9. A ball of hot, glowing gases

Down

2. A pinwheel-like galaxy
3. A group of stars, dust, and gases
5. A galaxy shaped like a flattened globe
6. Everything that exists—planets, stars, dust, and gases
7. The study of the objects in space and their properties

| spiral | elliptical | astronomy* | irregular | galaxy* | star* |
| astronomer | color | universe* | * Key Lesson Vocabulary | | |

Apply Concepts

2 What are some ways in which galaxies differ?

_____

_____

3 Look at this picture of a spiral galaxy. | Draw a picture of a barred spiral galaxy.

Tell how the two galaxies are alike and different.

_____

_____

4 Look at these two stars. Compare and contrast them using at least two properties.

red giant   blue star

_____

_____

_____

5 How do these stars compare to the sun?

_____

_____

Take It Home! Find out which are the brightest stars that are visible this time of year in your area. With an adult, observe the stars. Make a diagram of the night sky showing where to find the brightest stars.

Meet Two Space Explorers

Kalpana Chawla

On her first mission, Kalpana Chawla traveled more than six million miles in 15 days!

As a little girl in India, Kalpana Chawla dreamed about flying airplanes. She came to the United States and studied hard. She soon earned her degree as an aerospace engineer. Kalpana Chawla could fly many kinds of airplanes. Her dreams had come true! But she kept dreaming. She wanted to fly in space. She went to work for NASA and became an astronaut. Soon, Kalpana Chawla became the first Indian-born woman in space!

Claudia Alexander

Claudia Alexander explores outer space, too. But she never leaves Earth! She studies the moons of the planet Jupiter. She was in charge of NASA's *Galileo* mission. The mission sent an unmanned spacecraft to Jupiter. The spacecraft left Earth in 1989. It took six long years to reach Jupiter. Claudia Alexander directed it over 385 million miles! Under her command, *Galileo* was the first spacecraft to take detailed photos of Jupiter and its moons.

Galileo space probe

Two Ways to Study Space

Kalpana Chawla and Claudia Alexander study space in different ways. Write the statements that apply to each scientist in the correct circle.

Kalpana Chawla

Claudia Alexander

The Hubble Space Telescope sends scientists pictures of space from its orbit high above Earth.

- I lead space missions without leaving Earth.
- I traveled on the space shuttle.
- I study the moons of Jupiter.
- I grew up in India and learned to fly many types of airplanes.
- I study objects in space.

Many scientists study space from Earth by using a telescope, such as this one, in an observatory.

Name _____

Multiple Choice

Identify the choice that best answers the question.

SC.5.E.5.2, SC.5.N.2.1

1 Scientists use models to represent or explain things in the natural world. Why are models useful for the study of the solar system?

(A) because models cannot be proven wrong

(B) because models are always accepted by all scientists

(C) because models describe the way things actually are

(D) because models can be used to describe how things work

SC.5.E.5.2

2 The illustration below shows several planets orbiting a star.

What type of group is the figure illustrating?

(F) constellation   (H) galaxy system

(G) solar system   (I) universe

SC.5.E.5.1

3 Galaxies are composed of many different objects. What kind of objects make up most of the visible matter in a galaxy?

(A) asteroids   (C) dust

(B) planets   (D) stars

SC.5.E.5.1

4 Astronomers use the term brightness to describe how much light a star produces, not how bright a star appears from Earth. The diagram below compares the size, temperature, and brightness of some stars that can be seen from Earth.

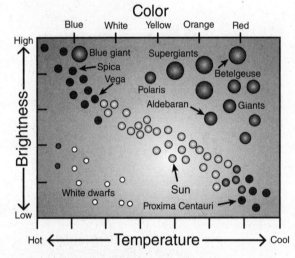

Which of these stars produces the most light?

(F) Betelgeuse

(G) sun

(H) Proxima Centauri

(I) Vega

SC.5.E.5.1

5 Some elliptical galaxies appear to be perfect spheres. How are the stars distributed within this kind of galaxy?

(A) The stars are evenly distributed through the galaxy.

(B) The center is very dense with many stars, and density decreases farther out.

(C) Most of the stars are near the outside of the sphere, with dust clouds in the center.

(D) The stars are spread throughout the sphere in bands that look like the arms of spiral galaxies.

SC.5.E.5.1

6 There are many different colors of stars. Each of the images below shows two stars of the same color. Which picture and statement is correct?

(F)

The larger star must be brighter.

(G)

The smaller star must be hotter.

(H)

The smaller star must be closer to Earth.

(I)

Stars that are the same color are usuallly the same size.

SC.5.E.5.2

7 All the planets in the solar system orbit the sun. What is the main difference between the orbits of the inner and outer planets?

(A) The inner planets travel a greater distance than the outer planets do.

(B) The inner planets have almost round orbits, and the outer planets do not.

(C) The outer planets rotate as they orbit the sun, and the inner planets do not.

(D) The outer planets take longer to orbit the sun than the inner planets do.

SC.5.E.5.3

8 The diagram below shows the orbit of Earth and the orbit of Borrelly.

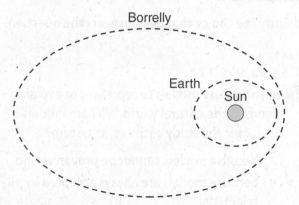

Borrelly

Earth

Sun

Which of these types of space objects is Borrelly most likely to be?

(F) an asteroid

(G) a moon

(H) a comet

(I) a planet

SC.5.E.5.2

9 Ming is doing a project on planets in other solar systems. She learns about a planet, called Planet Z. Planet Z is very large, has a thick atmosphere, and has a low density. Which of these planets in our solar system is Planet Z most similar to?

(A) Earth   (C) Saturn

(B) Mercury   (D) Mars

SC.5.E.5.1

10 Earth is part of the Milky Way galaxy. How does the Milky Way appear in the night sky from Earth?

(F) a small, very dim group of stars

(G) a bright, narrow band of stars

(H) a large number of stars in a broad, spiral shape

(I) a large cloudy band of stars spreading across the sky

96   Unit 2

Weather, Climate, and the Water Cycle

Big Idea 7

Earth Systems and Patterns

Fort Lauderdale, FL

I Wonder Why

Sometimes, the weather is stormy and cold. At other times, it is sunny and hot. Why does the weather change? *Turn the page to find out.*

Here's Why Weather changes because air moves constantly. Moving air changes local temperature and moisture—key factors affecting weather.

Track Your Progress

Essential Questions and Florida Benchmarks

Big Idea 7 *Earth Systems and Patterns*

Now I Get the Big Idea!

SC.5.E.7.1 Create a model to explain the parts of the water cycle. Water can be a gas, a liquid, or a solid and can go back and forth from one state to another. SC.5.E.7.2 Recognize that the ocean is an integral part of the water cycle and is connected to all of Earth's water reservoirs via evaporation and precipitation processes.

Lesson 1

Essential Question

What Is the Water Cycle?

Find the answer to the following question in this lesson and record it here.

Where is all this water going?

_____

_____

_____

_____

Active Reading

Lesson Vocabulary

List the terms. As you learn about each one, make notes in the Interactive Glossary.

_____ _____

_____ _____

_____ _____

Sequence

In this lesson, you'll read about a process of change called the water cycle. As you read about the *water cycle*, focus on the sequence, or order, of events in the process. Active readers stay focused on a sequence when they mark the transition from one step in a process to another.

Water
on the Move

The water that you drink may have once been underground or high in the sky. How does water get from Earth's surface to the air and back again?

Active Reading As you read the next page, circle the parts of the text that describe processes shown in the water cycle diagram.

▶ On the diagram, draw an X in three places where evaporation may be taking place.

Condensation   Transpiration

Evaporation

After it rains, this birdbath is filled with water. When the sun comes out, its energy heats the water. The birdbath becomes empty as water changes to water vapor and returns to the atmosphere.

100

About 75% of Earth's surface is covered by water. Most of Earth's water is salt water stored in oceans. Water moves between Earth's surface and the atmosphere through a process called the **water cycle**.

The sun provides the energy needed for water to move in the water cycle. When the sun shines on the ocean's surface, for example, some water particles heat up and evaporate. **Evaporation** is the change from a liquid to a gas. When water evaporates, it forms an invisible gas called *water vapor*.

Water vapor rises into the atmosphere. The **atmosphere** is the mixture of gases that surrounds Earth. In the atmosphere, water vapor cools to form clouds. Generally, clouds cover about 60% of Earth.

Water can evaporate from the leaves of plants. This process is called *transpiration*. Clouds can help transport water from one place to another.

Precipitation

Precipitation

Glacier

Lake

Surface Runoff

River

Groundwater

What goes up, comes down

What happens to water vapor after it rises into the air? How does it become puffy white clouds or raindrops that fall on your head?

Active Reading As you read these pages, write numbers next to the sentences that show the order of events from evaporation to precipitation.

Condensation

Think again of the ocean. Water from the ocean's surface evaporates. As this water vapor rises into the atmosphere, it cools. When it loses enough heat energy, it condenses to form liquid water. **Condensation** is the change of a gas into a liquid.

Even though the Earth's atmosphere is a mixture of gases, it contains some solids. It has tiny particles of salt from the ocean and dust from the land. Water vapor in the air condenses around these solid particles. A water droplet forms around a tiny solid particle. On their own, the water droplets are almost too small to see. When billions of droplets are close together, a cloud forms. Clouds can be made of water droplets, ice crystals, or both. They can form high in the sky or just above the ground.

Water droplets in the atmosphere form around tiny particles of dust and salt.

Dew is water vapor that condenses on cool surfaces near the ground. Droplets may form on a cold glass or a cool blade of grass. Water vapor may also condense in cool air near the ground to form fog.

102

In a cloud, water droplets collide and join together. It takes many droplets to form a single raindrop. Raindrops fall quickly to Earth.

Precipitation

Air currents keep clouds in the air. But as the cloud's droplets or snow crystals grow in size, they become too heavy to be held up by the air currents. They fall to the ground as precipitation. **Precipitation** is water that falls from clouds to Earth's surface. Forms of precipitation include rain, snow, and hail.

Precipitation often falls into the oceans, where it may quickly evaporate back into the atmosphere. Precipitation that falls on land may be temporarily stored. It may flow across the land, or it may be used by living things. Depending on where it falls, water from precipitation may move quickly or slowly through the water cycle.

Do the Math!
Compare Diameters

The diagram below compares the average diameter (d) of raindrops, a cloud's droplets, and of tiny particles of dust and salt in the air using metric units called *micrometers* (μm).

Large droplet
d = 100 μm

Average droplet
d = 20 μm

Dust particle
d = 0.2 μm

Raindrop
d = 2,000 μm

1. How much bigger is an average droplet than a dust particle?

_____

2. How much bigger is a large droplet than an average droplet?

_____

3. How much bigger is an average raindrop than an average droplet?

_____

Where Does Water Go?

Most precipitation falls into oceans and evaporates back into the air. But some water takes a more roundabout path on its way through the water cycle.

Active Reading As you read these pages, find and circle new key terms you need to know.

Picture a storm. Heavy rain falls on the ground. Some of this water will evaporate from shallow puddles as soon as the sun comes out. It goes from Earth's surface directly back into the atmosphere.

Much of the rainfall will not reenter the atmosphere right away. Some will seep into the ground. Water that is stored underground is called *groundwater*. Groundwater can be found near the surface or deep underground.

Rainwater fills up spaces between particles of soil or cracks in rock. Groundwater moves very slowly. Eventually, groundwater may reach a river, a lake, or an ocean. Then it moves on through the water cycle.

Not all of the water that falls on land evaporates right away or seeps into the ground. **Runoff** is water that cannot soak into the ground and instead flows across Earth's surface. It flows downhill into low-lying areas, rivers, or streams. Once runoff enters a river, it flows toward an ocean or a lake. Some of this water may evaporate before it reaches its destination.

Precipitation that falls in cold places may become part of a glacier. A *glacier* [GLAY•sher] is a large, slow-moving mass of ice. Water can be stored in glaciers for a very long time. But eventually, glaciers melt. Meltwater from glaciers can form lakes, flow into oceans, or become groundwater. Melting glaciers can increase the amount of runoff in an area.

In regions where lots of snow builds up in winter, spring runoff is common. The ground cannot soak up all the snowmelt, so water flows across the land.

Runaway Water

The picture shows runoff on a city street. In the space below, describe what might happen to this runoff.

_____

_____

_____

A Precious Resource

Can you name all the ways that you use water? Water is an important resource used by all living things. People often need to share and conserve their sources of clean, fresh water.

Active Reading As you read these two pages, find and underline at least three facts about aquifers.

SOUTH CAROLINA

MISSISSIPPI

ALABAMA

GEORGIA

LOUISIANA

ATLANTIC OCEAN

Gulf of Mexico

FLORIDA

LEGEND

Floridan aquifer system

When you turn on a faucet, water flows out. Where does it come from? People can get fresh water from rivers or lakes. They can also get fresh water from aquifers. An *aquifer* [AH•kwuh•fuhr] is a body of rock that stores groundwater. People can drill into an aquifer and pump the water to the surface.

Some aquifers are used by several states. The water in the aquifers can run low or be polluted by human activities. States that share aquifers work together to find solutions to these problems. They want to make sure that there is enough fresh, clean water for everyone.

The Floridan Aquifer covers about 60,000 square kilometers. Billions of gallons of water are pumped out of the Floridan Aquifer each day. Large cities such as Savannah and Orlando get their water from this aquifer.

Where Does Your Water Come From?

Find out the source of your water at school or at home.

_____

_____

People cannot live without water. We use water for many different purposes, including recreation.

Aquifers are huge underground water reservoirs [REZ•er•vwarz]. Precipitation adds water to aquifers in places called *recharge zones*. The water in some aquifers slowly makes its way to rivers, springs, lakes, and oceans. It may take groundwater in an aquifer up to a year to travel only 25 cm.

River

Recharge Area

Lake

Spring

Aquifer

Well   Shallow

Sand

Clay

Limestone

Deep Aquifer

Sum It Up!

When you're done, use the answer key to check and revise your work.

Write the term that matches each photo and caption.

1 Water can be stored for a long time in a large, slow-moving mass of ice.

_____

2 Water can also be stored underground between the spaces in particles of soil or cracks in rocks.

_____

3 During heavy rains, some water might not soak into the ground. Instead, it flows down slopes and across Earth's surface.

_____

Summarize

Fill in the missing words to describe the water cycle.

The water cycle shows how water moves from Earth's surface to the 4. _____ and back again. The 5. _____ provides the energy for the water cycle. Water on the surface of the ocean heats up. During 6. _____ , it changes from a liquid to a gas. As 7. _____ rises into the atmosphere, it cools. During 8. _____ , it changes from a gas to a liquid. Billions of water droplets form a 9. _____ . When the droplets get too large for air currents to keep them up, they fall to Earth's surface as 10. _____ .

Name _____

Word Play

1 Use the clues to fill in the missing letters of the words.

1. g __ __ __ __ __ w __ __ ◯ __   Water stored underground
   (10)

2. __ o __ d __ __ __ __ __ __ __ __   The changing of water from a gas to a liquid

3. __ a __ __ __ __ ◯ c __ __   The movement of water from Earth's surface to the
   (7)   atmosphere and back again

4. __ t __ __ __ p __ __ __ ◯   Mixture of gases that surround Earth
   (4)

5. __ r __ ◯ i __ __ __ __ __ t __ __ __   Water that falls from clouds to Earth's surface
   (8)

6. ◯ u __ __ __ __ __   Water that flows across Earth's surface
   (5)

7. g ◯ __ ◯ i __ __   A huge mass of frozen water that moves slowly
   (9) (6)

8. __ r __ n __ __ i __ __ ◯ __ __ __   The evaporation of water from the leaves of plants
   (3)

9. ◯ __ t __ __ __ a __ __ __   Water as a gas
   (1)

10. __ v __ __ o __ ◯ t __ o __   The changing of water from a liquid to a gas
    (2)

Bonus: Solve the Riddle!

Use the circled letters in the clues above to solve the riddle.

What is water's favorite way to travel?

On a __ __ __ __ __ __ __ __ __ __
      1 2 3 4 5 6 7 8 9 10

Apply Concepts

2 The sentences below show the steps that lead to the formation of a cloud. Number the steps to place them in the proper order.

_____ Water vapor cools and condenses around tiny particles.

_____ Water is heated by the sun.

_____ Water evaporates into the air.

_____ Billions of water droplets join together.

3 In the picture below, show how groundwater can return to the atmosphere. Use arrows to show how the water moves and use wavy lines to show evaporation.

4 What would happen if water could not condense in the atmosphere?

_____

_____

_____

_____

5 In the spaces below, draw and label examples of water in the atmosphere as a solid, a liquid, and a gas. Hint: Wavy lines may be used to represent water vapor.

_____ _____ _____

_____ _____ _____

6 Label each of the following scenes as an example of evaporation, precipitation, or condensation. Then briefly describe what happens during each process.

_____ _____ _____

_____ _____ _____

_____ _____ _____

7 The picture shows stored water being used to irrigate crops. Circle and label the source of the water. How may this stored water be renewed?

_____

_____

8 During an ice age, water is stored in glaciers. The picture below shows land area before and after an ice age. How are the land area and the oceans affected during an ice age?

Land Area
■ Current Day
■ Last Ice Age

_____

_____

_____

_____

_____

_____

Take It Home!

Share what you have learned about water with your family. Tell them why it is important to conserve water. Set up a barrel outside to catch rainwater. Use the rainwater to wash your car or water your garden.

Name _____

SC.5.N.1.1 … plan and carry out scientific investigations…. SC.5.N.1.5 … authentic scientific investigation frequently does not parallel the steps of "the scientific method." SC.5.E.7.1 Create a model to explain the parts of the water cycle…. SC.5.E.7.2 Recognize that the ocean is an integral part of the water cycle and is connected to all of Earth's water reservoirs via evaporation and precipitation processes.

Essential Question

What Happens During the Water Cycle?

Set a Purpose

How do models help you study processes such as the water cycle?

_____

_____

_____

_____

Think About the Procedure

Why did the mountain models take up only one-fourth of the containers?

_____

_____

_____

Why did you add salt to the water?

_____

_____

_____

_____

Why did you put the containers on a sunny windowsill?

_____

_____

_____

_____

Record Your Data

In the space below, write or draw your results.

Observations of Models	
Model without Ocean Water	Model with Ocean Water

Draw Conclusions

How did your models work?

_____

_____

_____

_____

Analyze and Extend

1. What role do oceans play in the water cycle?

_____

_____

_____

_____

2. Suppose you kept the models under a lamp overnight. What would happen to the models?

_____

_____

_____

_____

3. What is the role of the plastic wrap in the model? What does it represent?

_____

_____

_____

_____

4. What would happen if you left the models uncovered in the sunlight?

_____

_____

_____

_____

5. Draw what would happen if you left the models outdoors in a place with freezing temperatures. Describe your drawing on the lines below.

_____

_____

_____

6. Think of other questions you would like to ask about the water cycle.

_____

_____

_____

SC.5.E.7.3 Recognize how air temperature, barometric pressure, humidity, wind speed and direction, and precipitation determine the weather in a particular place and time.
SC.5.E.7.4 Distinguish among the various forms of precipitation (rain, snow, sleet, and hail), making connections to the weather in a particular place and time.

Essential Question

How Do We Measure Weather?

Engage Your Brain!

Find the answer to the following question in this lesson and record it here.

What is the weather like in this place and what tools could be used to measure it?

_____

_____

_____

_____

Active Reading

Lesson Vocabulary
List the terms. As you learn about each one, make notes in the Interactive Glossary.

_____

_____

_____

_____

Compare and Contrast
In this lesson, you will read about types of weather and the tools used to measure it. An author often compares and contrasts related things. Active readers ask themselves, How are these things alike? How are they different?

What's the Weather Like?

Crack! Boom! These are the sounds of a thunderstorm. Thunderstorms are one kind of weather. What other kinds of weather can you think of?

Active Reading As you read these pages, connect two images that show similar types of weather.

Look outside. What is the weather like? It might be sunny or rainy. It might be stormy or windy. It might be hot or cold. **Weather** is what the atmosphere is like at a given time and place. Weather can change from day to day, or even from hour to hour.

Meteorologists [mee•tee•uh•RAHL•uh•jists] are scientists who study weather. They measure factors such as air temperature, amount of cloud cover, and how much precipitation falls from the sky. They analyze their measurements to make a weather report.

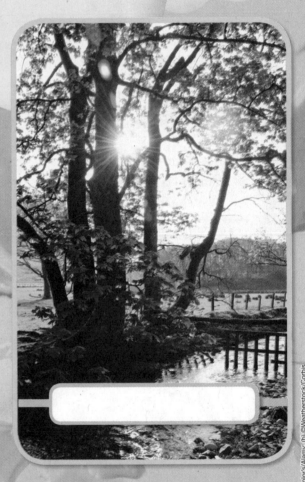

Label the kind of weather shown in each photo on these pages. Then select one of the photos, and write a caption for it in the space below.

_____

_____

_____

Weather reports tell you what the weather will be like. They help you plan your day. For example, if the weather is cloudy and cold, you need to wear warm clothing to go outside. But if the weather is sunny and warm, you could wear a T–shirt and sandals.

Weather reports are helpful in other ways. Planes cannot fly in severe weather, so airports use weather reports to help schedule flights. Weather reports also help farmers care for their crops. They need to water their crops in dry weather. They need to protect their crops from freezing in cold weather.

Watching the **Weather**

You likely have used a thermometer before. Some of the tools shown on these pages might not be as familiar as a thermometer. But all are used to measure weather.

1

2

Meteorologists use tools to study the weather. You can use some of these tools, too, at home or at school.

- Weather balloons are used to carry weather tools high up into the atmosphere. Instruments attached to the balloon measure temperature, wind speed, and other weather conditions.

- A *wind vane* measures wind direction. It points in the direction from which the wind blows. Wind direction can be given as *N* for north, *S* for south, *E* for east, *W* for west, or as a combination such as *NE* for northeast.

- An **anemometer** measures wind speed. It has cuplike arms that spin when the wind blows. Wind speed is measured in kilometers per hour (km/hr).

- A **barometer** measures air pressure. It has a sealed metal chamber that expands and contracts when air pressure changes. Air pressure may be measured in inches of mercury (in. Hg) or in millibars (mb).

- A *hygrometer* measures the amount of water vapor in the air, or **humidity**.

The higher the temperature, the more water vapor air can hold. The amount of water vapor in the air compared to what it can hold at a given temperature is called *relative humidity*. Relative humidity is given as a percentage.

Which Tool Is Which?

Look at the pictures on these pages. Identify the tool next to each number, and explain what it measures. Record your answers in the chart below.

	Tool	What It Measures
1		
2		
3		
4		
5		

3

4

5

Lying Low, Reaching High

You might see a cloud in the sky and think it looks like a fluffy dog. How would you go about classifying all the different clouds in the sky?

Active Reading As you read these two pages, underline two characteristics used to classify clouds.

Clouds have different shapes and form at different heights in the atmosphere. Shape and height are two characteristics used to classify clouds.

Based on their shapes, clouds can be classified as stratus, cirrus, or cumulus.

- *Stratus* [STRAT•uhs] clouds form flat layers that cover most of the sky. They may signal rain.

- *Cirrus* [SIR•uhs] clouds are thin, white, and feathery. They are often signs of fair weather.

- *Cumulus* [KYOO•myuh•luhs] clouds are puffy and white. They may have flat bases. They can signal fair weather or stormy weather.

Stratus clouds form low in the sky. They look like a low, gray blanket. Fog is a kind of stratus cloud that forms near the ground.

Do the Math!
Estimating Fractions

Meteorologists look at the clouds in the sky to estimate cloud cover. Estimate the fraction of cloud cover in this model of the sky.

_____

_____

Cloud Identification Chart

High Clouds
Cirrostratus
6,000 m
Cirrocumulus
Altostratus
Middle Clouds
Altocumulus
2,000 m
Cumulus
Stratocumulus
Cumulonimbus
Stratus
Low Clouds
Nimbostratus

The chart on this page shows how clouds can also be classified by their heights.

- Low clouds are those formed below about 2,000 m (6,500 ft). Temperatures at this height are not very cold, so the clouds are mostly made of water droplets.

- Middle clouds are formed between 2,000 and 6,000 m (6,500 and 20,000 ft). Temperatures here can be cold, so the clouds are sometimes made of ice crystals. Altostratus [al•toh•STRAT•uhs] and altocumulus [al•toh•KYOO•myuh•luhs] are examples of middle clouds.

- High clouds are formed above 6,000 m (20,000 ft). High clouds are often made of ice crystals because of the cold temperatures at these heights.

Notice that the tall cumulonimbus [kyoo•myuh•loh•NIM•buhs] cloud stretches from low heights to high heights. This kind of cloud has a flat top, and it often produces thunderstorms.

Cumulus clouds are usually made of water droplets. They resemble cotton puffs and often form at lower elevations. Sometimes they grow very tall and wide.

Cirrus clouds often form high in the atmosphere, where temperatures are cold. They are made up of ice crystals. They are often a sign that the weather is about to change.

It's Pouring
Solids and Liquids

Some precipitation falls as gentle flakes of snow.
Some precipitation falls as big drops of water.
Why isn't all precipitation the same?

As you read these two pages, underline the sentences that may help you contrast different kinds of precipitation.

Precipitation is solid or liquid water that falls from clouds to Earth's surface. Whether precipitation is solid or liquid may depend on the air temperature. Air temperature changes with the seasons, with elevation, and with location. Rain, snow, sleet, and hail are kinds of precipitation.

- *Rain* is liquid precipitation that falls through warm or cool air. It is the most common kind of precipitation.

- *Snow* is solid precipitation that falls through cold air.

- *Sleet* is precipitation that freezes near the ground. It often begins as rain or snow.

- *Hail* is solid precipitation made of layers of ice. It usually falls during thunderstorms.

Measuring Rain

Look at the picture of the rain gauge. It shows the amount of rain that fell in an area. How much rain fell?

_____

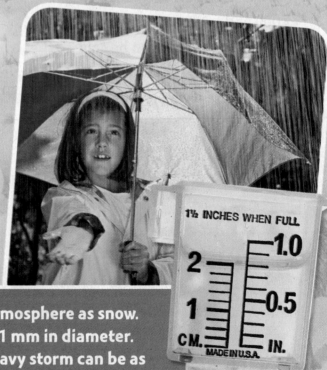

Rain can start out high in the atmosphere as snow. A typical drizzle drop is about 0.1 mm in diameter. A raindrop that falls during a heavy storm can be as large as 6 mm in diameter. A rain gauge measures the depth of rain that falls in an area.

1½ INCHES WHEN FULL

1.0
2
0.5
1
CM.   IN.
MADE IN U.S.A.

Sleet is made up of small pellets of ice. It may form when snow partially melts as it falls through a warm layer of air and freezes in a cold layer of air near the ground.

Hail forms inside large thunderclouds. First, wind carries raindrops high into the colder part of the cloud. The raindrops freeze and then fall through the lower, warmer part of the cloud. There, a new layer of moisture sticks to the hail particles, and wind carries them up again. This cycle repeats and the hail particles grow larger until they fall to the ground.

Snow forms when water vapor in the atmosphere turns directly into a solid. Like raindrops, when snow crystals become too large for air currents to keep them up, they fall to Earth. Snow falls in cold temperatures.

When you're done, use the answer key to check and revise your work.

Write the term that matches each photo and caption.

1. This kind of cloud is usually found high in the sky. It is often made of ice crystals and signals fair weather.

   _____

2. This kind of cloud is found low in the sky. It often forms flat layers and produces rainy weather.

   _____

3. This kind of cloud is often found low in the sky. It has a flat base and can signal fair or rainy weather.

   _____

Summarize

Use the terms below to fill in the graphic organizer about precipitation.

rain gauge   precipitation   snow   rain   air temperature   hail   sleet

4. _____

Measured using a

5. _____

Affected by

10. _____

Types of

6. _____

7. _____

8. _____

9. _____

124

Name _____

Word Play

1 Write the word that each clue below describes. If you need help, use the word bank. Then find the words in the word search.

1. A measure of the amount of water vapor in the air

   _____

2. State of the atmosphere at a given place and time

   _____

3. Tool that measures air pressure

   _____

4. Tool that measures wind speed

   _____

5. Thin, white, and feathery cloud

   _____

6. Cloud that forms near the ground

   _____

7. Precipitation made of layers of ice

   _____

O	D	H	U	E	Y	N	V	W	J	A
W	E	A	T	H	E	R	R	M	C	M
T	W	I	K	O	K	A	D	A	Z	S
C	N	L	H	U	M	I	D	I	T	Y
U	D	O	Z	D	S	N	O	W	K	C
M	Q	R	B	A	L	Q	L	N	M	I
U	A	N	E	M	O	M	E	T	E	R
L	B	A	R	O	M	E	T	E	R
U	R	Q	O	Z	D	Q	R	P	E	U
S	K	P	K	S	T	R	A	T	U	S
A	L	F	O	G	L	H	O	Y	K	P

Challenge: What other weather-related words can you find in the word search?

_____

_____

_____

_____

barometer	weather	humidity	fog
cirrus	hail	anemometer	

Apply Concepts

2 Complete the scene by drawing the type of precipitation that is most likely to fall based on the given air temperature. Label each scene with the type of precipitation.

25 °C

0 °C

−10 °C

_____   _____   _____

3 In the space below, draw the type of cloud that signals thunderstorms. Write a description of the cloud and the type of precipitation it produces.

_____

_____

_____

_____

4 Draw a circle around the weather tool you would use to measure air pressure. Draw an X over the weather tool you would use to measure wind speed. Draw a square around the weather tool you would use to measure wind direction.

Take It Home!

Share what you have learned about weather with your family. Go outside and look at the clouds. Describe the kinds of clouds that you see. Explain what kind of weather they usually signal.

SC.5.E.7.3 Recognize how air temperature, barometric pressure, humidity, wind speed and direction, and precipitation determine the weather in a particular place and time.
SC.5.E.7.7 Design a family preparedness plan for natural disasters and identify reasons for having such a plan.

Lesson **4**

Essential Question

How Do Weather Patterns Help Us Predict Weather?

Engage Your Brain!

Find the answer to the following question in this lesson and record it here.

What do you think will happen when the dark cloud moves over this place?

_____

_____

_____

_____

Active Reading

Lesson Vocabulary

List the terms. As you learn about each one, make notes in the Interactive Glossary.

_____   _____

_____   _____

Signal Words: Details

This lesson gives many details about predicting weather. Active readers look for signal words to identify examples and facts about a topic. Some words and phrases that signal details are *for example, also,* and *in fact.*

Windy Weather

You can't see air. But you can feel it each time the wind blows. What exactly is wind, and why does it blow?

Active Reading As you read this page, circle common, everyday words that have a different meaning in science.

Air is made of matter. It has mass and volume. It presses on you from all sides. To understand wind, you must know more about air pressure. **Air pressure** is the weight of the atmosphere on Earth's surface.

The sun does not heat all parts of Earth's surface evenly. This uneven heating of Earth's surface causes differences in air pressure. The differences in air pressure cause air to move. **Wind** is moving air. In general, wind blows from areas of high pressure to areas of low pressure.

Lows

What are two characteristics of air in a low pressure area?

_____

_____

_____

Air Pressure

Local Winds Land heats up more quickly than water does. This means that during the day, the air above the land is warmer and has a lower density than the air above the water. Because of these differences, the warm air over the land rises and cool air over the water moves inland to replace it. This is called a *sea breeze*.

At night, the land loses heat faster than the water does. The cool air over the land has a greater pressure than the warm air over the water. So, the cool air moves out to sea to replace the rising warm air. This is called a *land breeze*.

The weight of air particles at the top of the atmosphere presses down on the air particles underneath. So, air pressure is greater near Earth's surface than high above it.

Temperature can affect air pressure. In cold temperatures, where air particles move close together and sink, the air pressure is high. In warm temperatures, where air particles move apart and rise, the air pressure is low. Across Earth's surface, air moves from high-pressure to low-pressure areas.

Battling Bodies of Air

When you take a shower,
the air inside the bathroom becomes warm and wet.
When you open the bathroom door, the warm,
wet air meets cool, dry air. You've made a front!
Read on to find out more about fronts and
how they affect weather.

Active Reading As you read these two pages, draw boxes around each type of front that is described.

Meteorologists call a large body of air that has the same temperature and moisture properties throughout an **air mass**. The properties of an air mass depend on where it forms. An air mass that forms over warm land will be warm and dry. An air mass that forms over cold water will be cold and wet.

In the United States, winds often blow from west to east. The winds carry air masses from one place to another. Sometimes, two air masses with different properties meet. The boundary between the two air masses is called a **front**.

Different fronts bring different types of weather. A cold front forms where a cold air mass moves under a warm air mass. Severe weather often forms along cold fronts.

Sunny skies and cooler air that can be wet or dry usually follow a cold front. A warm front forms where a warm air mass moves over a cold air mass. Light rains and snow showers are common along warm fronts. Behind a warm front, warmer temperatures and cloudy skies are common.

How Will the Weather Change?

Look at the map to the right. In which direction is the cold front moving, and what kind of weather might it bring?

_____

_____

_____

Warm air is lifted steeply upward along a cold front. Water vapor in the air cools and condenses into large cumulonimbus clouds. Hailstorms are possible.

Warm air rises and cools slowly along a warm front. Cloudy skies can extend over large areas. Steady rain or snow can fall.

LEGEND
⚫▲▲ cold front
⚫⚫⚫ warm front

Weather forecasters use symbols to show fronts. The triangles and half-circles on these symbols point in the direction the front is moving.

Mapping the Weather

A flashing red hand on a traffic signal means *don't walk.* You use symbols each time you cross a busy street. Weather forecasters use symbols, too, to show weather conditions.

Active Reading As you read these two pages, circle clue words or phrases that signal a detail such as an example or an added fact.

Maps are useful tools. A **weather map** is a map that uses symbols to show weather data. You already know the symbols for cold fronts and warm fronts. Weather maps also use symbols to show areas of high pressure (H) and areas of low pressure (L). They might also show temperature, cloud cover, and wind direction for different places.

How do meteorologists get the data they need to make weather maps? They use weather tools such as thermometers, barometers, and anemometers. These tools are placed in weather stations. A *weather station* is a structure that has tools for measuring and recording weather data at a given location. Weather stations are found all across the United States.

Meteorologists also get weather data from other sources. Satellites high above Earth send back information about cloud cover and storms. Doppler radar uses radio waves to track storms. Meteorologists look for patterns in the data they collect. For example, high pressure often brings fair weather. Low pressure often brings stormy weather. A weather report is based on the patterns that meteorologists find in the data they collect.

Predicting the Weather

Use the weather map on the right to describe the weather for the city of Denver and to predict how it will change .

_____

_____

_____

_____

Weather maps can be used to help predict the weather. The map key shows what the symbols on the weather map represent.

ATLANTIC OCEAN

L

L

Rapid City
31°/22°F

H

Chicago
38°/25°F

New York
40°/29°F

San Francisco
49°/43°F

Salt Lake City
55°/42°F

Denver 43°/36°F

Nashville
52°/47°F

Los Angeles
62°/57°F

Phoenix
73°/67°F

Tulsa
49°/37°F

Atlanta
65°/58°F

Odessa 47°/40°F

PACIFIC OCEAN

New Orleans
70°/67°F

Gulf of Mexico

Miami
78°/69°F

LEGEND

▲▲▲	Cold front
●●●	Warm front
• •	Rain
✳	Snow
△	Hail
○	Sunny
◑	Partly cloudy
●	Cloudy
H	High pressure
L	Low pressure

weather satellite

Meteorologists use satellites, Doppler radar, computer models, and weather stations to make weather reports. Using all of these tools, meteorologists are able to accurately track and predict the weather.

Doppler radar

weather station

When Disaster Strikes

Tornadoes. Hurricanes. Blizzards. Sometimes, the weather can turn dangerous. What should you do to stay safe when bad weather strikes?

Active Reading As you read these two pages, circle two sentences that describe how to stay safe during a disaster.

A hurricane is a low-pressure storm. Its center, or eye, is calm. But wind speeds around the eye can be as fast as 250 km/hr. The strong winds cause much of the damage that a hurricane brings.

Thunder is crashing overhead. You look outside. You see a whirling column of air that stretches from a dark cloud to the ground. It's a tornado! Tornadoes, hurricanes, and blizzards are types of severe weather.

- A *tornado* has a funnel shape. Its strong winds can toss cars into the air. It can form from violent thunderstorms.

- A *hurricane* is a strong storm that forms over warm ocean water. When a hurricane moves over land, it can cause flooding, tornadoes, and thunderstorms. It is the most powerful storm of all.

- A *blizzard* is a strong winter storm. Blizzards have high winds and heavy snowfall.

Preparedness plans help people stay safe when disasters strike. Before and after a disaster, volunteers help provide assistance for people in need. They might help to sandbag riverbanks to prevent flooding or deliver water and food to those who need it.

Meteorologists track severe weather. They rank the storms by how strong the winds are or how much damage the storms might cause. They put out warnings so that people can seek shelter before a storm hits.

If possible, you should always go indoors when a storm is near. To prepare for severe weather, you can help your family put together an emergency kit. Your kit should have water, flashlights, batteries, canned food, first-aid supplies, and a radio. Listen to the radio for storm warnings.

Do the Math!
Solve Word Problems

The table shows how much water people of different ages should drink each day. Suppose a family wants to be sure they have enough water in case a natural disaster strikes. The family includes a mother, a father, a 10-year-old son, and a 6-year-old daughter. About how many gallons of water should they store to cover their needs for 3 days?

Remember: 16 cups equal 1 gallon.

Age Range	Amount of Water Needed Each Day
1 to 3 years	4 cups
4 to 8 years	5 cups
9 to 13 years	8 cups
14 years to adult	10 cups

_____

_____

_____

Sum It Up!

When you're done, use the answer key to check and revise your work.

Read the summary statements. Then match each statement with the correct picture.

A

B

C

D

1

1. During the day, cool, dense air from the ocean moves inland, replacing warm air over the land.

2. A cold air mass moves under a warm air mass.

3. During the night, cool, dense air over land moves out to sea, replacing warm air over the ocean.

4. A warm air mass moves gently over a cold air mass.

Summarize

Fill in the Venn diagram about air pressure by writing the correct number in each category.

5. Shown as *L* on a weather map

6. Brings fair weather

7. Measure of the weight of the atmosphere on Earth's surface

8. Shown as *H* on a weather map

9. Brings stormy weather

High Pressure Low Pressure

Both

Name _____

Word Play

1 Complete the crossword puzzle. Use the word bank if you need help.

Across

1. Body of air with the same properties throughout
5. Structure that houses weather tools
6. Boundary between two different air masses
7. Map that shows weather conditions

Down

2. Measure of the weight of the atmosphere on Earth's surface
3. Breeze that blows from the sea to the land
4. Moving air

wind	front	air mass	weather station
weather map	air pressure	sea breeze	

Apply Concepts

2 The symbols below show weather data for a place. Write what each symbol stands for. Predict the kind of weather a place near the *H* will have.

_____

_____

_____

_____

_____

3 Fill in the graphic organizer below to show how meteorologists get data to predict the weather.

Meteorologists get weather data from

weather stations

4 Label the kinds of severe weather shown in the pictures below.

_____   _____   _____

5 Heated air inside a hot-air balloon causes it to rise into the sky. When the air cools, the balloon returns to the ground. When is the hot-air balloon behaving like an air mass in a high-pressure area? In a low-pressure area?

_____

_____

_____

_____

6 Label each picture with the type of air mass that would form over it.

_____   _____

_____   _____

7 Mountain and valley breezes are similar to land and sea breezes. During the day, the sun heats up a mountain's side more quickly than the valley below. In the picture below, draw arrows to show wind direction during the day.

8 Put a check mark (√) next to each item that should be part of an emergency kit.

Items	Emergency Kit
1. air conditioner	
2. portable radio	
3. electric blanket	
4. bottled water	
5. first-aid supplies	

Take It Home!

Share with your family what you've learned about preparing for bad weather. Work with a family member to make a safety plan. Gather supplies for an emergency kit. Review the plan with family members.

SC.5.N.1.1 ... plan and carry out scientific investigations.... SC.5.N.1.6 Recognize and explain the difference between personal opinion/interpretation and verified observation. SC.5.E.7.3 Recognize how air temperature, barometric pressure, humidity, wind speed and direction, and precipitation determine the weather in a particular place and time.

Name _____

Essential Question

How Can We Observe Weather Patterns?

Set a Purpose

Why is it helpful to observe the weather?

_____

_____

_____

Think About the Procedure

Why should the chosen location for your weather station be sheltered from the sun?

_____

_____

_____

Why would it be useful to measure the weather conditions at the same time every day?

_____

_____

_____

_____

Record Your Data

Day	Weather Observations
	Weather Predictions

Draw Conclusions

How can we observe weather patterns?

_____

_____

_____

_____

Analyze and Extend

1. Describe weather patterns in your data.

_____

_____

_____

_____

2. Which weather conditions were most likely to change before the weather changed?

_____

_____

_____

_____

3. What were your weather predictions? On which weather pattern did you base them?

_____

_____

_____

_____

4. Were your predictions accurate? Explain.

_____

_____

_____

_____

5. What would have made your weather predictions more accurate?

_____

_____

_____

_____

6. Think of other questions you would like to ask about weather patterns and predictions.

_____

_____

_____

_____

142

SC.5.E.7.5 Recognize that some of the weather-related differences, such as temperature and humidity, are found among different environments.... SC.5.E.7.6 Describe characteristics ... of different climate zones as they relate to latitude, elevation, and proximity to bodies of water.

Lesson 6

Essential Question

What Factors Affect Climate?

Engage Your Brain!

Find the answer to the following question in this lesson and record it here.

Giraffes live in warm places. How can there be snow near a giraffe's home?

_____

_____

_____

_____

Active Reading

Lesson Vocabulary

List each term. As you learn about each one, make notes in the Interactive Glossary.

_____   _____

_____   _____

Visual Aids

A map adds information to the text that appears on the page with it. Active readers pause their reading to study maps and decide how their information adds to the text.

Climate vs. Weather

During the summer, the weather might be sunny one day and cloudy the next. But for most places, temperatures in the summer stay warm. The weather changes, but the overall weather pattern stays the same.

Active Reading As you read the next two pages, draw a star next to what you consider to be the most important sentence, and be ready to explain why.

Your area has certain weather patterns during the year. These patterns make up the climate where you live. **Climate** is the long-term weather patterns of a place.

Climate is different from weather. *Weather* describes what the atmosphere is like at a given time and place. For example, on average, a desert might get only a few centimeters of rain each year. The desert has a dry climate. But the weather in the desert might be rainy one day and dry the next.

Scientists find the climate of an area by averaging weather conditions over a long period of time. They study an area's temperature, wind speed, wind direction, cloud cover, air pressure, and amount of precipitation. They find the average of these conditions for each month or year. They look at 30 years or more of data to determine the climate of an area.

Do the Math!
Analyze Data

Use the data in the table to make a line graph. Then compare all the graphs to answer the questions below.

1. During which months in 2005 was Fargo's precipitation more than 20 mm below its long-term average?

_____

_____

2. During which months in 2005 was Fargo's average temperature closest to its long-term average? Which month is most different?

_____

_____

_____

_____

_____

Fargo's Average Monthly Precipitation in 2005

Fargo's Long-term Average Monthly Precipitation

Fargo's Long Term Average Monthly Temperature

Fargo's Average Monthly Temperature in 2005

Average Monthly Temperature for Fargo, North Dakota, in 2005			
Month	Average Temp. °C	Month	Average Temp. °C
Jan	−13.0	July	22.0
Feb	−10.0	Aug	20.0
Mar	−2.0	Sept	14.0
Apr	7.0	Oct	7.0
May	14.0	Nov	−2.0
June	18.0	Dec	−8.0

Hot, Cold, and Medium

Is it hot year-round where you live? Or is it cold? What is the climate where you live? Look through these pages and find out!

Active Reading As you read these two pages, underline the sentence that describes the temperature in each climate zone.

Places can be grouped into different climate zones. A **climate zone** is an area that has similar average temperatures and precipitation throughout. Three of Earth's climate zones are *tropical, temperate,* and *polar.*

Tropical climates are generally warm. They occur near the equator. The **equator** is the imaginary line that divides Earth into its northern and southern hemispheres, or halves.

Temperate climates are found in middle latitudes, between the tropical and the polar climate zones. **Latitude** is a measure of how far north or south a place is from the equator.

Polar climates are generally the farthest from the equator. They have cold temperatures year-round and low amounts of precipitation.

Temperate climate zones have moderate temperatures and varying precipitation. For most of the year, the temperature ranges from 10 °C to 18 °C. They usually have four distinct seasons. Much of the United States is found in this zone.

Polar climate zones are generally covered in ice and snow year-round. They are found near the poles, where the sun is never high in the sky. The temperature rarely rises above 10 °C and there is little precipitation. Few plants and animals live in this zone.

Comparing Climates Zones

Fill in the Venn diagram below to compare and contrast tropical and temperate climate zones.

Tropical Zone   Both   Temperate Zone

Tropical climate zones are near the equator. There, the sun is directly overhead nearly all year. The sun's position causes intense heating of Earth's surface. Generally, the temperature is greater than 18 °C. The amount of precipitation varies greatly in this zone. We can find lush, diverse forests in this climate zone.

Why Climates Differ

Why does it rarely snow in Florida? Why isn't Alaska warm year-round? What things make one climate different from another?

Active Reading As you read this page, draw one line under a cause. Draw two lines under the effect.

Different factors affect the kind of climate a place has. These factors include distance from the equator, elevation, proximity to bodies of water, and landforms.

Most places that are close to the equator have warmer climates than places that are farther away. But if a place has a high elevation, it will have a cool climate even if it is on the equator. That's why snowy mountaintops can be found in tropical places.

Oceans and large lakes affect climate, too. Water heats up and cools down more slowly than land does. So places near the coast often are cooler in summer and warmer in winter than places far from the ocean. Landforms, such as mountains, can affect the rain pattern of large areas.

Gulf of Mexico

Pacific Ocean

The different colors on the oceans show water temperature. The warmest water is colored red, and the coolest is blue. The *Gulf Stream* is a warm ocean current. It flows up from near the equator, along the east coast of North America, and across the Atlantic Ocean toward northern Europe. It deeply affects the temperature and precipitation amounts of nearby coastal areas.

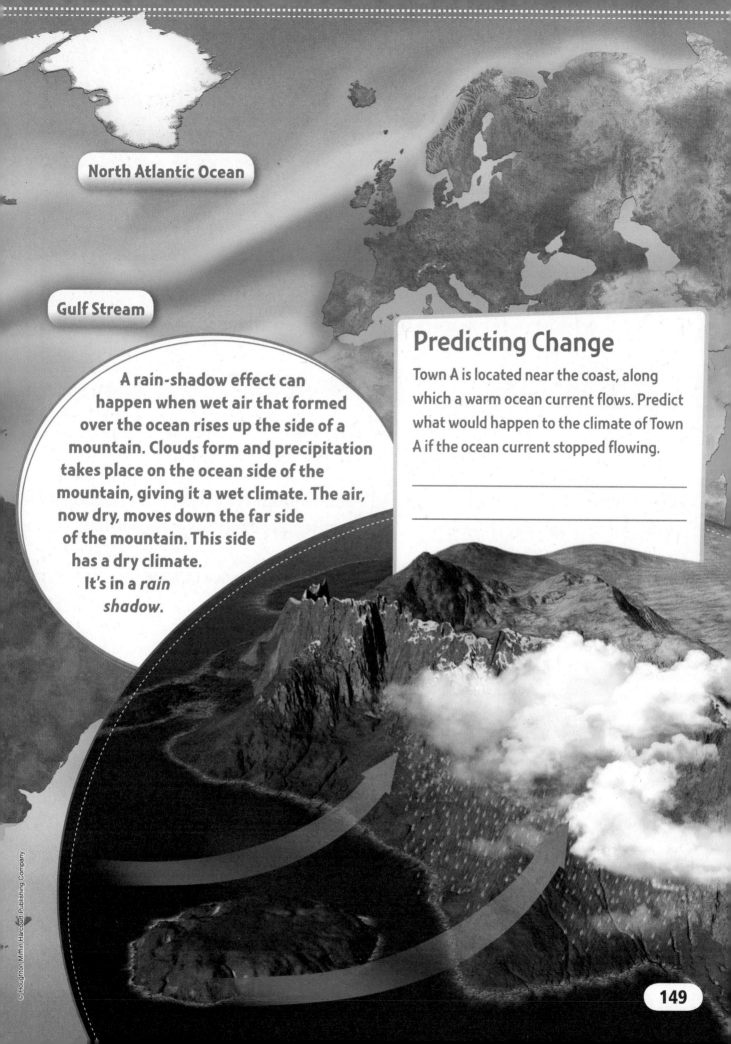

North Atlantic Ocean

Gulf Stream

A rain-shadow effect can happen when wet air that formed over the ocean rises up the side of a mountain. Clouds form and precipitation takes place on the ocean side of the mountain, giving it a wet climate. The air, now dry, moves down the far side of the mountain. This side has a dry climate. It's in a *rain shadow*.

Predicting Change

Town A is located near the coast, along which a warm ocean current flows. Predict what would happen to the climate of Town A if the ocean current stopped flowing.

_____

_____

Climate and the Environment

Why do polar bears live in cold places, while elephants live in warm places? How does climate affect the living and nonliving things in a place?

Active Reading As you read this page, find and underline examples of how climate affects living and nonliving things.

Climate affects where organisms can live. A polar bear has a thick layer of fat that keeps it warm in the polar climate where it lives. Maple trees have broad leaves to capture sunlight during the warm summer months. They shed their leaves during the cold, dry winter to prevent water loss.

Climate also affects the nonliving parts of the environment. Over time, wind-driven waves can reshape a continent's coastline. Rain, wind, and changes in temperature can cause rock to break. The broken bits of rock can mix with dead plant and animal matter to form soil.

Polar bears

Desert: A desert is a dry environment. Temperatures may vary greatly in deserts. It can be very hot during the day and cold at night. Living things in deserts need to be able to survive on little water. Cactuses have a waxy coating that helps them store water.

Swamps: Swamps can be covered by fresh water, salt water, or both. Swamps occur in places where the ground cannot soak in all the precipitation or runoff that reaches the area. Temperatures may be very hot in swamps for part of the year. Many types of plants and animals live in swamps.

Tropical rain forests: Tropical rain forests are found in warm, wet climates. They receive nearly the same amount of sunlight year-round. Vegetation covers most of the land in tropical rain forests. It provides food and shelter for many animals.

What effects would a drier climate have in a swamp environment?

_____

_____

_____

_____

When you're done, use the answer key to check and revise your work.

Complete the outline below to summarize the lesson.

1

I. Climate

    A. **1** _____

    B. determined by the long-term average
       precipitation and temperature

II. Main climate zones

    A. **2** _____

       1. warm year-round

       2. can be wet or dry

       3. found near the equator

    B. Temperate

       1. **3** _____

       2. different amounts of precipitation

       3. found in middle latitudes

    C. Polar

       1. usually little precipitation

       2. **4** _____

       3. found in high latitudes

III. **5** _____

    A. bodies of water

    B. landforms

    C. elevation

    D. distance from the equator

Summarize

Fill in the missing words to tell how scientists determine the climate of a place.

Climate is different from 6. _____ , which describes what the atmosphere is like at a

given time and place. Scientists find the climate of a place by averaging weather conditions over a

7. _____ period of time.

They study an area's temperature, wind speed, wind direction, cloud cover, air pressure, and amount

of 8. _____ .

They find the 9. _____ of these conditions for each month of the year. They look at

10. _____ years or more of data to find the climate of a place.

Answer key: 1. the long-term weather patterns of a place 2. Tropical 3. moderate temperatures 4. cold year-round 5. Factors that affect climate 6. weather 7. long 8. precipitation 9. average 10. 30

Name _____

Word Play

1 Use the clues to unscramble the words in the box. Use the word bank if you need help.

1. qaroeut: the imaginary line that divides Earth into the northern and southern hemispheres, or halves	
2. ertmpeate emlciat: has moderate temperatures	
3. taliecm noze: an area with the same kind of climate conditions	
4. dutlatei: distance of a place from the equator	
5. lopricta itleamc: is warm year-round	
6. rewaeth: state of the atmosphere at a certain time and place	
7. ropal atmlcie: is cold year-round	
8. catmile: long-term weather patterns of a place	

latitude	temperate climate	climate zone	polar climate
climate	equator	tropical climate	weather

Apply Concepts

2 The pictures below show different kinds of clothing to wear in the fall. In which climate zone would you wear each piece of clothing? Write your answers on the lines under the pictures.

_____ _____ _____

3 Correctly label each statement below with a *C* if it refers to climate and a *W* if it refers to weather.

a. In Antarctica, the average yearly temperature is below freezing. _____

b. Cherrapunji, India, may be the rainiest place on Earth. _____

c. It hasn't rained for two weeks in Macon, Georgia. _____

d. Today's air temperature was the highest this week. _____

4 In the picture below, add arrows to show how air moves to form a rain shadow. Add labels showing where you would find a dry climate and a wet climate.

5 Label the climate zones in the map below.

A _____

B _____

C _____

6 The graph below shows the long-term average monthly temperature of a place. In which climate zone is this place likely to be found? Explain.

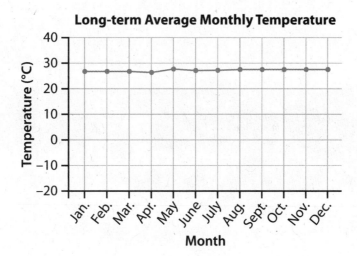

Long-term Average Monthly Temperature

_____

_____

7 Suppose the climate of a rain forest changes. Its temperature is now always near or below freezing, but its precipitation remains high. Draw and describe what this place would look like after a few years.

_____

_____

_____

8 The picture shows a landform. Label where the climate will be the coolest and where it will be the warmest on the landform.

Share what you have learned about climate with your family. Find out about the kinds of homes people build in different climates. Work with a family member to make a model of a home in a different climate.

SC.5.E.7.2 Recognize that the ocean is an integral part of the water cycle and is connected to all of Earth's water reservoirs via evaporation and precipitation processes.

Careers *in* Science

10 THINGS YOU SHOULD KNOW ABOUT Hydrologists

1 Hydrology is the study of the quality and movement of water. A hydrologist is a person who uses hydrology in their everyday work.

2 The word *hydrology* comes from the Greek words *hydro* meaning "water" and *logos* meaning "study".

3 To make sure it is safe, hydrologists test the water you drink for pollutants.

4 Hydrologists need to know how soils and rocks may affect water quality.

5 They also care about the quality of the water in rivers, streams, and oceans.

6 Hydrologists can help decide where to dig wells for underground water.

7 A hydrologist can help farmers figure out how to get water for their crops.

8 Hydrologists help design dams to produce electricity and prevent floods.

9 They can use their knowledge to help predict floods and droughts.

10 A hydrologist can help design sewers and drainage systems.

Show What You Know About Hydrologists

Answer these five questions about hydrologists.

1 What part of a hydrologist's work do you find most interesting?

_____

_____

_____

2 What do hydrologists study?

_____

_____

_____

3 How do hydrologists help us?

_____

_____

_____

4 Write the question that goes with the answer below.

_____

_____

_____

Answer: They want to make sure water is safe to drink.

5 Write and answer your own question about hydrologists.

_____

_____

_____

_____

Multiple Choice

Identify the choice that best answers the question.

SC.5.E.7.3, SC.5.N.1.1

1 Deanna measured the temperature and humidity every afternoon for four days. She recorded the results in the table below.

Day	Temperature	Relative humidity (%)
Monday	28 °C (82 °F)	90
Tuesday	27 °C (81 °F)	79
Wednesday	24 °C (75 °F)	70
Thursday	28 °C (82 °F)	69

Which day could Deanna conclude was the most hot and humid?

(A) Monday   (C) Tuesday

(B) Wednesday   (D) Thursday

SC.5.E.7.3, SC.5.N.1.1

2 Kendell wants to determine if there is a trend in air temperature changes during April. Which of the following procedures should he follow?

(F) Measure the temperature every hour for 1 day.

(G) Measure the temperature at noon every day in April.

(H) Measure the temperature at the same time each Monday.

(I) Measure the temperature on the first and last day of April.

SC.5.E.7.4

3 Most of the clouds in photograph of a mountain scene are cirrus clouds. Where do cirrus clouds form?

(A) around mountains   (C) near the ground

(B) at high elevations   (D) over the oceans

SC.5.E.7.3

4 The table below describes some weather conditions at two different weather stations.

	Station 1	Station 2
Temperature	10 °C (50 °F)	20 °C (68 °F)
Precipitation	3 cm	2 cm
Wind	3 km/hr west	8 km/hr east
Cloud cover	overcast	mostly cloudy

Which statement is correct?

(F) Station 1 is experiencing more rain than station 2.

(G) Both stations are experiencing freezing conditions.

(H) Station 1 is experiencing stronger winds than station 2.

(I) Both stations have wind traveling in the same direction.

SC.5.E.7.1

5 The diagram below shows the water cycle.

At which point does precipitation happen?

(A) 1

(B) 2

(C) 3

(D) 4

SC.5.E.7.4

6 Which of the following is a cumulus cloud?

Ⓕ

Ⓖ

Ⓗ

Ⓘ

SC.5.E.7.3

7 The following diagram shows a location where two air masses meet.

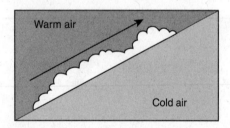

What is the weather like at this type of air boundary?

Ⓐ cloudy and rainy   Ⓒ clear and warm

Ⓑ clear and cold   Ⓓ windy and cold

SC.5.E.7.3

8 Jeffrey notices that the air pressure is rising. Based on this observation, which type of weather does Jeffrey expect?

Ⓕ unstable weather   Ⓗ windy weather

Ⓖ stormy weather   Ⓘ fair weather

SC.5.E.7.3

9 The following diagram shows the pattern of air movement in a coastal area.

Which type of wind is illustrated in the diagram?

Ⓐ valley breeze   Ⓒ land breeze

Ⓑ sea breeze   Ⓓ mountain breeze

SC.5.E.7.6

10 Darnell read that the central part of Argentina has a climate that is very similar to that of the central part of the United States.

What information on the map provides the best explanation for the climates' similarities?

Ⓕ Both countries are located to the east of the Pacific Ocean.

Ⓖ There are large mountains in the western parts of both countries.

Ⓗ The central parts of both countries are about the same distance from the equator.

Ⓘ Both countries are very large compared to many of the countries in the Americas.

160 Unit 3

SC.5.E.7.3

11 Scientists study many factors that allow them to predict weather. Which factor **most directly** affects the movement of air?

(A) air pressure   (C) precipitation

(B) relative humidity   (D) temperature

SC.5.E.7.5

12 Although each place on Earth has its own climate, they can be grouped based on certain overall characteristics. What are the key factors that scientists use to determine the climate of a particular place?

(F) temperature and precipitation

(G) length of seasons and precipitation

(H) distance from the ocean and altitude

(I) types of living things and temperature range

SC.5.E.7.2

13 Oceans receive freshwater from precipitation and rivers. Yet ocean levels do not change very much from these actions. Why are ocean levels not greatly affected?

(A) Water is constantly seeping underground in the ocean.

(B) Water is constantly evaporating over the ocean's surface.

(C) Water is constantly flowing back into rivers from the oceans.

(D) Water is constantly deposited back on land through ocean wave action.

SC.5.E.7.1

14 Tara is studying the water cycle. She knows that in order for evaporation to happen, there needs to be a source of energy that generates heat. What is the main source of energy that powers the water cycle?

(F) sun   (H) clouds

(G) oceans   (I) water vapor

SC.5.E.7.5

15 Jamie sketched the following picture of the landscape he saw while he was on vacation. It included cacti and barren rock.

What can you conclude about what kinds of plants can grow in this climate?

(A) Only plants that grow very rapidly can grow in this climate.

(B) Only plants that need frequent, heavy rainfalls can grow in this climate.

(C) Only plants that can survive with very little water can grow in this climate.

(D) Only plants that can handle both extreme heat and cold can grow in this climate.

SC.5.E.7.1

16 The figure below shows how a puddle changes during the day.

What process is taking place ?

(F) condensation   (H) evaporation

(G) precipitation   (I) runoff

SC.5.N.1.1, SC.5.E.7.1, SC.5.E.7.2

17 Ms. Janick's class wants to measure how quickly water evaporates. They measure the level of some water in a glass for 4 days and record the levels. Which graph shows that the water evaporated over time?

Ⓐ

Ⓑ

Ⓒ

Ⓓ

SC.5.N.1.1, SC.5.N.1.5, SC.5.E.7.1, SC.5.E.7.2

18 Christina has a glass of water. Michael has a fruit juice drink. Both drinks are at room temperature, and both students add ice to their drinks. Condensation begins to form on the outside of Christina's glass before Michael's. How could they state their observations as a problem to design an experiment?

Ⓕ What is condensation?

Ⓖ How does ice cause condensation to form in water?

Ⓗ Does the temperature of the air influence condensation?

Ⓘ Does the type of liquid influence the rate at which condensation forms?

SC.5.E.7.3

19 A scientist is describing weather conditions in an area. At 12:00 p.m., he reports that the temperature is 18 °C (65 °F). At 5:00 p.m., the temperature is 15 °C (59 °F). What could explain the difference between the two temperatures that the scientist reported?

Ⓐ Temperature usually increases from morning to afternoon.

Ⓑ Weather conditions, including air temperature, can change quickly.

Ⓒ Thermometers can give only one accurate temperature reading per day.

Ⓓ He used a thermometer in the morning and a barometer in the afternoon.

SC.5.E.7.6

20 Where in a tropical climate are you **most likely** to find cooler weather and snow?

Ⓕ at the top of a tall mountain

Ⓖ at sea level near a cold ocean current

Ⓗ in cloudy places near the center of the continent

Ⓘ at the base of a mountain range that blocks air flow

The Nature of Matter

Big Idea 8

Properties of Matter

Big Idea 9

Changes in Matter

Miami Beach, FL

I Wonder Why

Why are some kinds of sand better than others for making sand castles?
Turn the page to find out.

Here's Why Sand is made of many kinds of matter, including pieces of rock and shell. Wet sand has different properties than dry sand. The water in moist sand helps hold together the tiny pieces of rock and shell.

Track Your Progress

Essential Questions and Florida Benchmarks

Big Idea 8 — *Properties of Matter*

Big Idea 9 — *Changes in Matter*

Now I Get the Big Idea!

SC.5.P.8.1 Compare and contrast the basic properties of solids, liquids, and gases, such as mass, volume, color, texture, and temperature.

Lesson **1**

Essential Question

What Are Solids, Liquids, and Gases?

Engage Your Brain!

As you read the lesson, look for the answer to the following question and record it here.

Bottled water and the snow from this snow machine are both water. How are these forms of water different?

_____

_____

_____

_____

Active Reading

Lesson Vocabulary
List the terms. As you learn about each one, make notes in the Interactive Glossary.

_____   _____

_____   _____

_____   _____

Compare and Contrast

Many ideas in this lesson involve comparisons and contrasts—how things are alike and different. Active readers stay focused on comparisons and contrasts when they ask themselves, How are these things alike? How are they different?

What's the Matter?

This book is made of matter, and so are you. You might think that matter can be seen and felt. But did you know that air is matter also? What is matter?

Active Reading As you read these two pages, draw two lines under each main idea.

The large pencil has more matter than the smaller pencils. It has more mass and more volume.

Breathe in and out. Can you feel air hitting your hand? You can't see air, and you can't grab it. Yet air is **matter** because it has mass and it has volume. Matter cannot be created or destroyed. It might change form, but it is still matter.

Mass is the amount of matter in something. Each of the tiny particles that make up matter has mass, even though the particles are so small you cannot see them. **Volume** is the amount of space something takes up. When air is blown into a balloon, you can see that it has volume.

Name That Matter

Look at the matter in this picture.

1. What matter is soft and sticky?

_____

2. What matter is hard and sharp?

_____

Odor

Texture

Matter Has Properties

You might say that apple juice is gold in color, tastes sweet, and pours easily. These are properties of the juice, which means they are characteristics used to describe or identify it. All matter has properties.

All the properties shown on this page are physical properties. You can observe a physical property without changing the matter into a new substance. For example, texture is how something feels. In observing that sandpaper has a rough texture, you don't change the sandpaper.

Color

Comparing Stones

Complete the Venn diagram by comparing and contrasting the properties of the two stones.

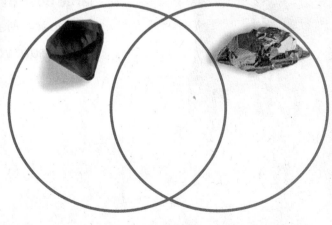

More Properties

Color, texture, and odor are just a few physical properties. What are some other properties of matter?

Active Reading As you read these two pages, circle common, everyday words that have a different meaning in science.

Temperature

Temperature is a measure of the energy of motion of the particles in matter. Melted glass has a very high temperature. Temperature can be measured by using a thermometer.

Volume

The food in the small bowl has less volume than the food in the large bowl because it takes up less space. Many tools can be used to measure volume.

Mass

A bowling ball and a basketball have about the same volume. The bowling ball has a greater mass because it contains more matter. Mass can be measured by using a balance.

Density

Density is found by dividing the mass of an object by its volume. The density of the gas in this balloon is less than the density of the air around it. That is why the balloon "floats" in air.

Do the Math!
Use Division

Use the data to find the density of each of these foods.

Determining Densities of Foods			
Food	Mass	Volume	Density
gelatin	75 g	100 mL	
pudding	90 g	100 mL	
whipped cream	50 g	100 mL	

Liquids

A **liquid** is a substance that has a definite volume but does not have a definite shape. The particles in a liquid move slower than the particles in a gas, and they slide by each other.

States of Matter

Another physical property of matter is its state. Solid, liquid, and gas are the most common states of matter on Earth.

Active Reading As you read these two pages, draw boxes around the names of the three things that are being compared.

Gases

A **gas** is a substance that does not have a definite shape or volume. The particles in a gas move very quickly and are far apart from each other.

Matter is made of tiny particles. The particles in solids, liquids, and gases have different amounts of energy. The amount of energy affects how fast the particles move and how close together they are.

The shape and volume of something depends on its state. Because each particle in a gas is affected little by the other particles, gas particles are free to move throughout their container. Gases take both the shape and the volume of their container.

Particles in a liquid cannot move as freely. A sample of a liquid keeps the same volume no matter what container it is in. However because the particles slide by each other, a liquid takes the shape of its container.

The particles in a solid do not move from place to place, so solids keep the same shape and volume.

Solids

A **solid** is a substance with a definite shape and volume. The particles in a solid are very close to each other. They don't move from place to place. They just vibrate where they are.

The bubbles in the tank are a _____.

The water is an example of a _____.

The castle is a _____.

A Matter of Temperature

On a hot day, an ice cube melts. This change is caused by a change in temperature. When matter changes state, the type of matter is not changed.

Active Reading As you read these two pages, draw one line under a cause. Draw two lines under the effect.

When matter takes in or releases energy, its temperature changes. When enough energy is taken in or released, matter can change state.

When a gas releases energy, its temperature goes down until it *condenses,* or changes to a liquid. When a liquid releases energy, its temperature goes down until it *freezes,* or changes to a solid.

When a solid takes in energy, its temperature rises until it *melts*, or changes to a liquid. When a liquid takes in energy, its temperature rises until it *evaporates*, or changes to a gas. Evaporation and boiling are similar—both turn liquids into gases. Evaporation is slower and happens only at a liquid's surface. Boiling is faster and happens throughout the liquid.

When a solid absorbs enough energy, the solid melts, changing to a liquid.

When a liquid absorbs enough energy, the liquid *boils*, or rapidly changes to a gas.

When a gas releases enough energy, the gas condenses, changing to a liquid. Particles of water vapor condense and form raindrops and dew.

When a liquid releases enough energy, the liquid freezes, changing to a solid. A raindrop that freezes becomes a snow flake. Dripping water that freezes can form icicles.

The temperature at which a certain type of matter freezes or melts is the same. The temperature at which a type of matter condenses or boils is also the same. For water, the melting and freezing points are 0 °C. The condensation and boiling points are 100 °C. Evaporation can happen at temperatures below the boiling point.

Lava is hot, melted rock that erupts from a volcano. Lava releases energy as it cools and becomes solid rock.

▶ Complete this graphic organizer.

As a solid takes in energy, its temperature _____. Eventually, it will _____, changing to a _____.

If the liquid takes in enough _____, it will _____, changing to a _____.

Properties of Solids, Liquids, and Gases

Each different material has its own unique properties. However, properties can change depending on the state of the material.

Active Reading As you read these two pages, find and underline facts about each state of matter.

Each state of matter has different physical properties. Liquids and gases both flow, moving from place to place. Gases can expand, taking up more space, or compress, taking up less space. Solids have definite textures.

Liquid water flows much more quickly than honey.

Liquids
All liquids flow from one place to another. Different liquids may flow at different rates.

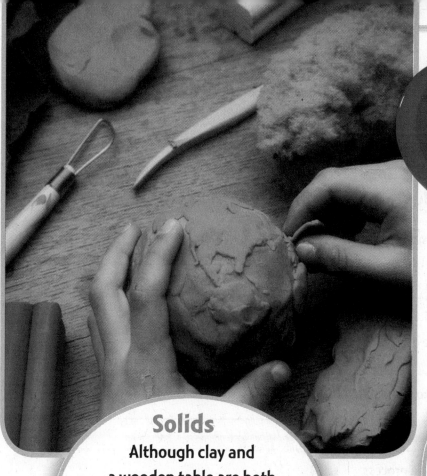

Solids

Although clay and a wooden table are both solids, each one feels different. All solids have a shape, but the shape of some solids can be changed easily.

Gases

A lot of gas has been compressed in this tank. It is under high pressure. Compressed gas from the tank expands, filling many balloons.

▶ Complete this main-idea-and-details graphic organizer.

Main Idea
_____

Liquids	Gases	_____
Motor oil and milk _____ at different rates.	When you push on the sides of a balloon, the gas inside is _____.	Glass and sandpaper have different _____.

Sum It Up!

When you're done, use the answer key to check and revise your work.

Read the summary statements below. Each one is incorrect. Change the part of the summary in blue to make it correct.

1. A property is a characteristic of matter that is used to determine the state of the matter.

_____

2. A sample of ice has a volume of 1.0 mL and a mass of 0.9 g. The density of the ice is 1.1 g/mL.

_____

3. The particles in a solid are close together, but they can slide past each other.

_____

4. A solid changes to a liquid during a process known as freezing.

_____

5. Solids and liquids can be compressed when put under pressure.

_____

6. The mass of an object can be measured by using a measuring cup.

_____

Summarize

Read the properties below. Write *S* for solid, *G* for gas, and *L* for liquid. Some properties may have more than one answer.

7. Has a definite texture and shape _____

8. Can melt _____

9. Can freeze _____

10. Can boil _____

11. Takes the volume of its container _____

12. Can condense _____

13. Can flow _____

14. Takes the shape of its container _____

15. Has a definite volume _____

Answer Key: 1. describe or identify matter **2.** 0.9 g/mL **3.** liquid **4.** melting **5.** Gases **6.** balance **7.** S **8.** S **9.** L **10.** L **11.** G **12.** G **13.** L, G **14.** L, G **15.** S, L

Brain Check

Name _____

Word Play

1 Use the clues below to fill in the words in the puzzle.

1. To squeeze a gas into a smaller space
2. A physical property that describes how something feels
3. The state of matter that keeps its shape and volume when it is placed in a different container
4. The measure of how much thermal energy is in the particles of matter
5. Anything that has mass and volume
6. What happens to a liquid when it releases enough energy
7. Calculated by dividing mass by volume
8. The state of matter that has particles that slide by each other
9. The amount of space something takes up
10. The state of matter that expands to fill its container

Read down the squares with red borders. The word you find will to complete the riddle below.

Perry the porcupine's portrait perfectly portrayed his pestering personality and prickly __ __ __ __ __ __ __ __ __ __ __.

Apply Concepts

2 Tell what property each of the following tools is used to measure.

_____   _____   _____

3 Complete these descriptions of the different states of matter.

		Solids
_____ _____	_____ Particles are closer together and move past each other.	Particles are very close and vibrate in place.
Examples: air; helium in balloons; oxygen in a tank	Examples: _____ _____	Examples: _____ _____

4 Fill in the name of the processes (such as freezing) that are represented.

(a) _____   (b) _____

SOLID → (a) → LIQUID → (b) → GAS

(c) _____   (d) _____

Take It Home!

Play a game of 20 Questions with members of your family. Have them choose a simple item that you can see in the room. Try to guess what the item is by asking yes/no questions about the item's properties.

SC.5.P.9.1 Investigate and describe that many physical and chemical changes are affected by temperature.

Essential Question

How Does Matter Change?

Engage Your Brain!

As you read the lesson, look for the answer to the following question and record it here.

A piece of iron can change in different ways. How is iron bending different from iron rusting?

_____

_____

_____

Active Reading

Lesson Vocabulary

List the terms. As you learn about each one, make notes in the Interactive Glossary.

_____

_____

_____

Main Idea and Details

Detail sentences give information about a topic. The information may be examples, features, characteristics, or facts. Active readers stay focused on the topic when they ask, What fact or information does this sentence add to the topic?

© Houghton Mifflin Harcourt Publishing Company (t)Image Source/SuperStock

Classifying Change

▲ Slicing apples and cracking eggs are physical changes.

When an apple pie cooks, chemical changes occur. Cooked apples do not have the same properties as a raw apple.

Matter has properties, but matter also undergoes changes. How many different ways does matter change?

Active Reading Each visual on these two pages has an empty bubble. Write a *C* if the visual shows a chemical change. Write a *P* if it shows a physical change.

Matter has physical properties that can be observed without changing the type of matter. Matter can also change in ways that do not affect the type of matter. These changes are called **physical changes**.

When you sharpen a pencil, the pencil goes through a physical change. The wood shavings and bits of graphite don't look like a pencil any more. But the wood is still wood, and the graphite is still graphite.

▲ Slicing a pie is another physical change.

▲ The properties of the ash and gases that form when wood burns are different from the properties of wood.

▲ When iron rusts, it undergoes a chemical change.

Matter has other properties that cannot be observed without changing the identity of the matter. These properties are chemical properties. For example, you don't know if a type of matter will burn unless you burn it. When matter burns, it changes identity.

In the same way, **chemical changes** result in a change in the identity of matter. When a strawberry rots, it undergoes chemical change. The rotten strawberry's properties are quite different from those of a fresh strawberry. A chemical **reaction** is the process in which new substances are formed during a chemical change.

When you eat apple pie, chemical changes in your body digest the food.

▶ Place a *P* by each physical change and a *C* by each chemical change.

Change	Type
Bacteria decompose leaves.	
A newspaper turns yellow in sunlight.	
Water evaporates.	
Gasoline burns in a car engine.	

181

Swelling
and Shrinking

Why do you think many car owners use one tire pressure in summer and another one in winter? When temperature differs, volume often differs.

Most matter expands when the temperature goes up and contracts when the temperature goes down. Some kinds of matter expand and contract more than others. People may run hot water over the metal lid of a glass jar. This expands the lid so that it's easier to take off the jar.

One exception is water. It expands when it freezes. Because ice takes up more volume than the same amount of liquid water, ice is less dense than water. That's why ice floats in a glass of water. In winter, ice first forms at the surface of a lake.

> One of water's unique properties is that it expands when it freezes.

Frozen Water
Volume = 1.09 L

Liquid Water
Volume = 1.00 L

Sometimes water flows into cracks in rocks and freezes. The expanding water makes the cracks in the rock larger and breaks large rocks into smaller pieces.

Expansion Joints

▶ Explain why bridges have expansion joints in them.

_____

_____

_____

_____

◀ This photo shows the same balloon at two different temperatures. The size of a sample of gas depends on its temperature. The gas in a balloon expands when it is warmed. The gas compresses when it is cooled.

Temperature = –80 °C
Volume = 1.9 L

Temperature = 35 °C
Volume = 3.0 L

Tampering with Temperature

When a burner on a stove is really hot, it glows red. A change in color is just one way temperature can affect matter.

Active Reading As you read this page, underline examples of how temperature affects physical changes in matter.

Some physical changes, such as tearing a piece of paper, are not affected by temperature. Other physical changes happen faster or slower at different temperatures. How quickly a change occurs is called the rate of change.

For example, ice on a lake will melt if the air temperature is above 0 °C. It will melt even faster if the air temperature is warmer. In the same way, water condenses more quickly on the outside of a very cold soft drink can than it does on a cool can.

Hot! Hot! Hot!
As iron is heated, it glows red or yellow.

WOW! This metal rod has been heated to more than 500 °C (932 °F).

OUCH! The filament of a light bulb is made of a metal called tungsten. It is glowing because it is heated to 2,500 °C!

Do the Math!
Graph Data

The data table shows how long it takes identical ice cubes to melt when placed in equal amounts of water at different temperatures. Make a line graph of these data.

Temperature of water (°C)	Melting time of ice (sec)
14	450
19	300
27	170
42	140
48	90
70	25

When grass and the air around it cool at night, water vapor in the air might condense, forming dew. As morning sunlight warms the air, the dew evaporates. In this photograph, the grass in the shade is wet but the grass in the sun has dried.

Faster or Slower?

Temperature affects the rate at which chemical changes occur, too. Read to find out how.

cold water

warm water

An effervescent antacid tablet reacts more quickly with warm water than it does with cold water.

Increasing temperature often speeds up the rate of a chemical change. For example, increasing oven temperature speeds up the chemical changes that occur when a cake bakes or a potato cooks.

Decreasing temperature usually slows down the rate of chemical change. This is why food stays fresh longer when it is kept cool. Also, unused batteries stay charged longer when kept in the refrigerator.

The chemical changes that make food spoil are slowed down by keeping the food in the refrigerator.

186

Fevers

You feel awful. Your head hurts, and you have a fever. Why might having a fever be a good thing?

When you have a fever, your temperature rises above your normal body temperature (about 37 °C). A low fever is between 38 °C and 39 °C. A high fever is greater than 40 °C. Low fevers help the body fight disease. High fevers can cause severe problems.

Temperature can increase for many reasons. For example, certain bacteria have materials that your brain identifies as harmful. The brain sends out signals that cause an increase in the chemical changes that produce energy. Your temperature increases. Bacteria cannot survive at this higher temperature.

Do the Math!
Use a Number Line

On the number line below, plot the following values in °C.
a. normal body temperature
b. a slight fever
c. a high fever

36   38   40   42   44   46

Sum It Up!

When you're done, use the answer key to check and revise your work.

The outline below is a summary of the lesson. Complete the outline.

I. Matter undergoes changes.

    A. One type of change is a (1) _____.

        1. Matter does not change identity.

        2. Example: (2) _____

    B. (3) _____

        1. Matter changes identity.

        2. Example: (4) _____

II. Temperature affects matter.

    A. When temperature increases,

        1. the speed of a chemical change (5) _____.

        2. the rate of melting and boiling (6) _____.

        3. matter may become larger, or (7) _____.

    B. When temperature decreases,

        1. the speed of a chemical change (8) _____.

        2. the rate of freezing or condensing (9) _____.

        3. all matter can become smaller, or (10) _____.

Tell whether each change is a physical change or a chemical change.

(11) _____   (12) _____   (13) _____

Brain Check

Name _____

Word Play

1 It's easy to get tongue-tied when talking about how matter changes. Look at the statements below. Switch the red words from one sentence to another until each statement makes sense.

A. In a chemical change, the identity of matter does not change.

_____

B. Water will melt faster on a very cold soft drink can than it will on a cool soft drink can.

_____

C. Another name for a chemical change is a chemical property.

_____

D. Ice will condense more slowly in cold water than in warm water.

_____

E. In a physical change, the identity of the matter changes.

_____

F. Most types of matter expand when the temperature is decreased.

_____

G. A reaction of matter will stay the same during a physical change.

_____

H. When water freezes, it contracts.

_____

Challenge The words in the boxes below are jumbled. Put them in the correct order to make a meaningful sentence.

changes are rusting and chemical burning
_____
_____

red is heated when it turns iron
_____
_____

2 Each of the pictures shows a change. Write a *P* by the pictures that show physical changes and a *C* by the pictures that show chemical changes.

3 Make a list of physical changes and chemical changes that you observe or see the effects of in your school.

Physical Changes

_____

_____

_____

_____

_____

_____

_____

_____

Chemical Changes

_____

_____

_____

_____

_____

_____

_____

_____

4 What would make each of the following processes happen faster? On each line, write *increase in temperature* or *decrease in temperature*.

Ice cream melting	Boiling water to cook potatoes
_____	_____

Water condensing on the outside of a glass	Water freezing overnight on a street
_____	_____

5 Explain what is happening in these pictures. Tell whether the changes are physical or chemical.

_____

_____

_____

_____

_____

_____

6 Why is it important to follow the instructions on this jar of food?

_____

_____

_____

_____

_____

_____

7 Draw an example of a chemical reaction. Then explain what is happening in your drawing.

_____

_____

_____

_____

_____

_____

8 Explain why a sidewalk has built-in cracks every few feet.

_____

_____

_____

_____

_____

9 Explain what happens in a campfire.

Wood is made of cellulose, lignin, and other substances.

↓

The wood is set on fire, and a _____ change occurs.

↓

The cellulose and lignin are changed into other substances, including _____ and _____.

Take It Home! Ask an adult to help you practice taking the temperature of someone in your family. Determine whether any of your family members have a fever. Explain to family members why people get fevers.

SC.5.N.1.3 Recognize and explain the need for repeated experimental trials. **SC.5.N.2.2** ... evidence produced by ... investigations should be replicable by others. **SC.5.P.9.1** Investigate and describe that many physical and chemical changes are affected by temperature.

Name _____

Essential Question

How Can Temperature Change Matter?

Set a Purpose
What will you learn from this experiment?

_____

_____

State Your Hypothesis
Write your hypothesis, or testable statement.

_____

_____

_____

Think About the Procedure
Why do you need to add equal amounts of yeast, sugar, and water to each balloon?

_____

_____

_____

How will you be sure that you measure the distance around each balloon in the same way?

_____

_____

_____

_____

Record Your Data
In the space below, make a table in which you record your results.

Draw Conclusions

Plot your data on a line graph.

What conclusion can you draw?

_____

_____

_____

Analyze and Extend

1. Why might you want to repeat this experiment several more times and compare your results to those in other groups?

_____

_____

_____

_____

2. How do the results of this experiment help you understand what happens when bread bakes?

_____

_____

_____

_____

3. Why do you think food spoils faster when it is not refrigerated?

_____

_____

_____

_____

4. Think of other questions you would like to ask about how temperature relates to the rate of a chemical reaction.

_____

_____

_____

_____

_____

_____

SC.5.P.8.2 Investigate and identify materials that will dissolve in water and those that will not and identify the conditions that will speed up or slow down the dissolving process.
SC.5.P.8.3 Demonstrate and explain that mixture of solids can be separated based on observable properties of their parts such as particle size, shape, color, and magnetic attraction.

Essential Question
What Are Mixtures and Solutions?

Engage Your Brain!

As you read the lesson, look for the answer to the following question and record it here.

How are a smoothie and a salad alike? How are they different?

_____

_____

_____

_____

Active Reading

Lesson Vocabulary
List the terms. As you learn about each one, make notes in the Interactive Glossary.

_____

_____

Problem and Solution
Ideas in this lesson may be connected by a problem-solution relationship. Active readers mark a problem with a *P* to help them stay focused on the way information is organized. When multiple solutions are described, they mark each solution with an *S*.

Matter Mix-Up

A box of colored pencils. A basket of footballs, tennis balls, and hockey pucks. A toy box full of toys. All these things are mixtures. But what is a mixture?

This fruit salad is a mixture of different pieces of fruit.

Look at the mixtures on these pages. They have a few things in common. First, two or more substances or objects were combined. The fruit salad has several types of fruit. The laundry pile has several types of clothing. Second, each type of matter in a mixture keeps its own identity. The peach in the fruit salad is the same type of matter as it was before it was mixed into the fruit salad. The jeans in the laundry pile are still jeans.

By now, you've probably figured out that a **mixture** is a combination of two or more substances that keep their identities. The parts of a mixture don't undergo a chemical change. Making a mixture is a physical change.

A carbonated beverage is a mixture of water, gases, and other ingredients.

These clothes are all jumbled together. How do you know this pile of laundry is a mixture?

_____

_____

_____

Find a Solution!

In some mixtures, it's easy to see the individual pieces that are mixed together. In other mixtures, small parts are very evenly mixed. What are these special mixtures?

Active Reading As you read these two pages, underline lesson vocabulary words each time they are used.

Each bite of fruit salad contains different combinations of fruit. You can separately taste peaches and different kinds of berries. But what do you notice when you drink a glass of lemonade? Every sip tastes the same. This is because lemonade is a solution. A **solution** is a mixture that has the same composition throughout.

When food coloring is added to water, the two liquids evenly mix, forming a solution.

198

A solution forms when one substance *dissolves* in another. When something dissolves, it breaks up into particles so tiny they can't be seen even with a microscope. These particles then evenly mix with the other part of the solution. Not everything dissolves. If you put a rock and salt in water, the rock won't dissolve, but the salt will.

Solutions are commonly liquids, such as the mixture of the different liquids that make up gasoline. But not all solutions are liquids. Air is a solution of different gases. Tiny particles of nitrogen, oxygen, and other gases are evenly mixed in air. Brass is an example of a solid solution formed from solid copper and solid zinc.

A mixture of sand and water forms where waves wash over the sand. Such a mixture is not a solution.

Ocean water itself is a solution. It contains several different dissolved substances.

What makes a solution different from other mixtures?

_____

_____

Separating Mixtures

Suppose you really don't like olives. How are you going to get them off that deluxe pizza your friend ordered? Sometimes you need to separate the components of a mixture.

Active Reading As you read this page, put brackets [ ] around the sentence that describes the problem and write *P* next to the sentence. Underline the sentence that describes the solution and write *S* next to it.

Mixtures are not always easy to separate. But since mixing is a physical change, each component in a mixture keeps most of its physical properties. Physical properties such as color, size, melting point, boiling point, density, and ability to dissolve can be used to separate mixtures. Separating a mixture can be very simple. Or it can involve several, complex steps when one method is not enough.

▶ What property was used to separate the items on this tray?

_____

Density

Every substance has its own density. A less-dense substance will float on a denser substance. Objects will float in water if they are less dense than water. They will sink if they are denser than water.

When One Isn't Enough

sieve/mesh screen

A sieve or mesh screen has holes that matter can pass through. Matter that is smaller than the holes passes through the mesh screen while matter that is larger than the holes stays above the mesh screen.

magnetic force

A magnet attracts matter that contains iron, separating it from the other parts of the mixture.

filtration

A filter works like a mesh screen with very tiny openings, or pores. Only the smallest bits of matter—like water particles and dissolved particles of salt—can pass through the pores.

evaporation/boiling

Boiling is when a liquid rapidly changes to a gas at the boiling point of the liquid. Evaporation also changes a liquid to a gas, but it occurs at temperatures below the boiling point. During these processes, only the liquid particles leave the solution. Dissolved particles stay behind.

A magnet takes away bits of iron.

Water is added. Then the filter removes the soil.

The water is boiled away. Only salt is left behind.

Recycling Mixtures

Does your family recycle? We all know that it saves energy and protects natural resources to recycle plastic, metal, and glass. The first step in recycling is to separate all those items in the recycling bin!

Most items turned in for recycling must be sorted, or separated before they can be recycled. As with other mixtures, this mixture is separated according to the physical properties of the items in the bin.

Steel cans are easy to separate. A big magnet can remove them from the mixture. Most other items have to be separated by hand. Plastics are separated according to the recycling number for that type of plastic. This number is found in a small triangle on the bottom of the item.

All types of paper are sorted out and placed in bundles. Aluminum is separated and crushed. After glass is separated from the mixture, it is again separated by color. Then all these items are sent to places that recycle them so they can be made into new products.

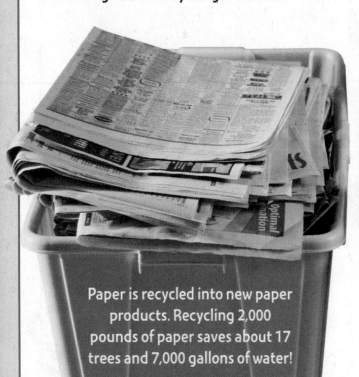

Paper is recycled into new paper products. Recycling 2,000 pounds of paper saves about 17 trees and 7,000 gallons of water!

Plastic that is not used for new containers has other uses. One use is in plastic lumber, which can be used to build decks and railings.

Do the Math!
Make a Graph

One community's garbage contains these things. Each section of the circle graph represents one of these materials. Label each section with the correct name and percent.

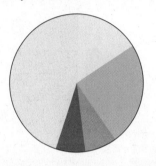

Our Community's Recycling	
Percent	**Material**
45%	Non-recyclables
24%	Paper
16%	Glass
8%	Aluminum
5%	Plastics
2%	Food

Newspaper

Many schools collect items for recycling, especially paper.

Brown Glass

Green Glass

Different colors of glass have different uses. Most colorless glass is recycled into new glass containers.

When you're done, use the answer key to check and revise your work.

Write *S* if the photo and caption describe a mixture that is a solution. Write *M* if they describe a mixture that is NOT a solution.

_____ (1) When you combine ingredients to make a sandwich, each ingredient keeps its identity. You could easily separate them.

_____ (2) Soft drinks are made by dissolving a gas and other ingredients in water. The dissolved particles are much too small to be seen.

_____ (3) The solid bits of orange pulp do not dissolve in the liquid. Because the pulp particles are large, they will eventually settle out.

_____ (4) Particles of several different gases make up air. Air on one side of a room is just like the air on the other side.

Summarize

Fill in the missing words to tell how to separate mixtures.

To sort the items in your junk drawer, you'd use observable (5) _____

such as size, color, shape, and (6) _____ attraction. But how would you separate

table sugar, sand, and pebbles? Because the pebbles are (7) _____

than the grains of sugar and sand, you could remove them using a sieve, or mesh (8) _____.

You could then add water and shake until the sugar (9) _____.

If you poured this mixture through a coffee (10) _____ into a beaker, the

(11) _____ would be left on the filter, but the sugar solution would pass

through. Adding heat would cause the water to (12) _____ , leaving solid sugar

behind.

© Houghton Mifflin Harcourt Publishing Company

Answer Key: 1. M 2. S 3. M 4. S 5. properties 6. magnetic 7. larger 8. screen 9. dissolves 10. filter 11. sand 12. evaporate or boil

Name _____

Word Play

1 Complete the crossword puzzle. Use the words in the box if you need help.

Across

1. Another name for a mesh screen
4. Type of change that doesn't involve the formation of a new kind of matter
5. Tool that attracts objects that contain iron
6. What an object that is less dense than water will do when placed in water
7. Object used to separate very small particles from a mixture
8. The amount of matter in a given volume

Down

1. A physical property; for example, round, square, rectangular, or flat
2. Process by which a liquid changes slowly to a gas
3. Kind of mixture that has the same composition throughout
5. A combination of two or more substances that keep their individual identities

| sieve | shape | evaporation | solution* | physical |
| magnet | mixture* | float | filter | density |

* Key Lesson Vocabulary

Apply Concepts

2 Circle the substances below that are solutions.

brass trumpet

trail mix

shells

sandwich

drink from a mix

3 Make a list of solid mixtures in your classroom.

_____   _____

_____   _____

_____   _____

_____   _____

_____   _____

4 Draw and label a diagram to show how you would separate each mixture.

5 Answer these questions about recycling in terms of what you know about mixtures.

a. How would you increase the amount of garbage that is recycled at your school?

_____

_____

_____

_____

b. Why is sorting important when recycling?

_____

_____

c. Draw a line connecting each piece of garbage with the can it should be thrown in.

(milk jug)   (soup can)   (envelope)   (cardboard box)

(soda can)   (water bottle)   (broken pencil)

[Garbage]   [Plastic]   [Aluminum and Tin]   [Paper]

6

Salt seems to disappear when it is poured into water. Use the terms *mixture*, *solution*, and *dissolve* to explain what happens.

_____

_____

_____

7 Tell how you would use one or more of these tools to separate the mixtures.

Rice from dried soup mix

_____
_____
_____
_____
_____

Salt from saltwater

_____
_____
_____
_____
_____

Nails from gravel

_____
_____
_____
_____
_____

8 Tell what would happen if you stirred each of these cups faster.

_____ _____
_____ _____
_____ _____
_____ _____
_____ _____
_____ _____

Water and Sugar

Water and Sand

Share what you have learned about mixtures with your family. With a family member, identify examples of mixtures at mealtime, or in places in your home.

Name _____

SC.5.N.1.1 ... plan and carry out scientific investigations.... **SC.5.N.1.4** Identify a control group and explain its importance in an experiment. **SC.5.P.8.2** Investigate and identify materials that will dissolve in water and those that will not and identify the conditions that will speed up or slow down the dissolving process.

Essential Question

What Affects the Speed of Dissolving?

Set a Purpose
What will you learn from this experiment?

_____

_____

_____

_____

State Your Hypothesis
Write your hypothesis, or testable statement.

_____

_____

_____

_____

Think About the Procedure
Why do you need to rinse the containers between steps?

_____

_____

_____

Would it affect the conclusions for this activity if two different groups stirred at different rates?

_____

_____

_____

_____

Record Your Data
Record your results in the data table below.

Time It Takes to Dissolve	
Treatment	**Time (sec)**
No Stirring	
Stirring Slowly	
Stirring Quickly	
Coarse Salt	
Table Salt	
Cold Water	
Warm Water	

Draw Conclusions

Make a bar graph to display the data in which you tested how stirring affects the rate of dissolving.

(blank graph box)

What conclusion can you draw?

_____

_____

_____

Analyze and Extend

1. You're adding sugar to a glass of iced tea. How might you speed up how quickly the sugar dissolves?

_____

_____

_____

2. Minerals dissolve in river water. Would you expect minerals to dissolve faster in a fast-moving river or one that moves slowly? Why?

_____

_____

_____

3. A water softener is a device that uses salts to remove certain substances from water. Most home water softeners use salt pellets or rock salt, both of which are chunks of salt. Why wouldn't you want to use table salt in a softener?

_____

_____

_____

_____

4. Think of other questions you would like to ask about the rate of dissolving a solid in water.

_____

_____

_____

_____

_____

_____

Lesson **6**

© Houghton Mifflin Harcourt Publishing Company ©OJ/Alamy

Essential Question

What Is the Atomic Theory?

Engage Your Brain!

As you read the lesson, look for the answer to the following question and record it here.

This building in Brussels, Belgium, is called the Atomium. Why do you think it was given that name?

_____

_____

_____

Active Reading

Lesson Vocabulary
List the terms. As you learn about each one, make notes in the Interactive Glossary.

_____   _____

_____   _____

Visual Aids
A diagram adds information to the text that appears on the page with it. Active readers pause their reading to review the diagram and decide how the information in it adds to what is provided in the text on the pages.

A Teeny Tiny Theory

DEMOCRITUS

→ **Atoms**

Elements

Compounds

From the time of Democritus, scientists have studied matter and proposed theories about it. What do we now think about what makes up matter?

Active Reading As you read the next page, draw a line from each part of the atom diagram to the sentences that describe it.

Suppose you could break a silver chain into smaller and smaller pieces. The pieces would become so small that you couldn't see them without a microscope. How small could the pieces get before they were no longer silver? The answer—one silver atom. An **atom** is the smallest unit of a pure substance that has the properties of that substance.

The **atomic theory** is a scientific explanation of the structure of atoms and how they interact with other atoms. Democritus first suggested that the smallest part of matter is an atom. Over the years, theories that scientists made about atoms have changed as scientists learn more about atoms.

Gold is one type of matter.

Gold brick

Flakes of gold

Atoms are the building blocks of all matter.

Current atomic theory states that an atom is mostly empty space. At its center, there is a small, dense core called the nucleus. The nucleus is surrounded by electrons.

Proton

A *proton* is a positively charged particle found in the nucleus of an atom.

Neutron

Neutrons are also particles found in the nucleus, but a neutron has no charge.

Electron

Electrons are negatively charged particles that speed through an area around the nucleus called the electron cloud.

Gold atoms

▶ Draw an arrow pointing to a single gold atom.

▶ Use the Venn diagram to compare and contrast electrons and protons.

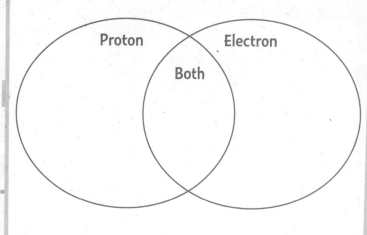

Proton   Electron

Both

27   28   29   30

Ni

110   111   112   113   114   115   116

Mt   Ds   Rg   Uub   Uut   Uuq   Uup   Uuh

It's Elementary!

Copper, oxygen, and mercury have one thing in common. They are all elements. Exactly what is an element?

Active Reading As you read these two pages, draw a large *E* next to the names of five elements that are described.

There are many kinds of matter. An **element** is the type of matter made of just one kind of atom. All atoms of an element have the same number of protons. For example, boron is an element. Every atom of boron contains exactly five protons. No other element has atoms with exactly five protons.

What's so special about protons? Electrons are far from the nucleus, so they can be gained or lost. Also, different atoms of the same element can contain different numbers of neutrons. Protons stay the same.

Atoms

→ **Elements**

Compounds

Neon

Protons: 10

Uses: neon signs, helium-neon lasers, television tubes, refrigerant

Mercury

Protons: 80

Uses: laboratory instruments, thermostats, dental fillings, pesticides

Elements are substances that can't be broken into simpler substances.

Chlorine

Protons: 17

Uses: disinfecting water; making paper, paints, plastics, and dyes

Silver

Protons: 47

Uses: jewelry, silverware, photography, welding solder, mirrors

Copper

Protons: 29

Uses: plumbing, coins, electrical wires, making brass and bronze

Draw and Label a Carbon Atom

Use the information provided to draw and label a carbon atom.

Protons: 6

Neutrons: 6

Electrons: 6

Putting It All Together

There are more than 100 elements, but you can see that there are many more types of matter than that. What are these other types?

Active Reading As you read this page, draw boxes around the names of the two things that are being compared.

Atoms

Elements

→ Compounds

Many atoms go through chemical change with a different type of atom and form compounds. A **compound** is a substance formed by at least two types of atoms that are chemically combined.

The properties of a compound are often different from the properties of the elements that form it. For example, atoms of carbon and oxygen will react, forming the compound carbon dioxide. This compound has its own properties that are different than those of carbon and oxygen.

Hydrogen Atoms + Oxygen Atom = Water

Sodium Atoms + Chlorine Atoms = Salt

Compounds are made of atoms of at least two different elements.

Firework Colors

Orange	Yellow	Red
calcium chloride	sodium nitrate	lithium carbonate

1 calcium	**1 sodium**	**2 lithium**
2 chlorine	**1 nitrogen**	**1 carbon**
	3 oxygen	**3 oxygen**

Some of the colors in fireworks come from compounds. For example, calcium chloride, which contains one calcium atom for every two chlorine atoms, results in an orange color.

Fructose is often called fruit sugar. For every 6 atoms of carbon in the compound, there are 12 hydrogen atoms and 6 oxygen atoms.

Do the Math!
Use Fractions

Add the total number of atoms in fructose. In lowest terms, what fraction of fructose consists of:

1. carbon atoms? _____

2. hydrogen atoms? _____

3. oxygen atoms? _____

09	110	111	112	113	114	115	116
Mt	Ds	Rg	Uub	Uut	Uuq	Uup	Uuh

When you're done, use the answer key to check and revise your work.

1 Label the parts of this atom.

Ⓐ _____

Ⓑ _____

Ⓒ _____

Ⓓ _____

2 Sequence the following from smallest to largest.

_____ Ⓐ atom   _____ Ⓑ proton   _____ Ⓒ compound   _____ Ⓓ nucleus

3

Fill in the blanks.

An atom is the smallest particle of an Ⓐ _____ that has its properties. Our current

Ⓑ _____ is the result of the ideas of many scientists over

many years. Scientists currently theorize that atoms contain a dense core that is called the

Ⓒ _____ . It contains positively charged particles called Ⓓ _____,

and Ⓔ _____ , which have no charge. Particles called Ⓕ _____

move around the center of the atom. The identity of an element is determined by the number of

Ⓖ _____ in one atom of the element. When atoms of different elements join

together, Ⓗ _____ form.

Word Play

1 For each jumbled term, unscramble the letters to form a term from this lesson. Use the clues to help you.

a. tasmo

_ _ _ _ _○

The smallest particles of an element

b. ueotnrn

_ _○_ _ _ _ _

The particle in an atom that has no charge

c. retelocn

_ _ _ _ _○_ _

Moves around the outside of an atom

d. omdocpun

_ _ _ _○_ _ _ _

Formed from at least two types of chemically combined atoms

e. onropt

_ _○_ _ _ _

The positively charged part of the nucleus

f. mitoca rohety

_ _ _ _ _○_ _ _ _ _ _ _

Changed through history as scientists learned more about atoms

h. cnluseu

_ _ _ _○_ _ _

The dense, central part of an atom

i. nemtele

○_ _ _ _ _ _

Contains only one kind of atom

Riddle Put the circled letters into the riddle in the order they are circled.

What did the chemistry teacher get for her birthday?

the element of _ _ _ _ _ _ _ _ _ _

Apply Concepts

2 Draw and label a diagram of a nitrogen atom.
It should have 7 protons, 7 neutrons, and 7 electrons.

3 Use the terms *atom* and *element* to explain what makes silver and gold different.

_____

_____

4 Complete the table.

Compound	Atoms	Fraction of each type of atom
methane	5 total: 1 carbon, 4 hydrogen	
propane	11 total: _____	3/11 carbon, 8/11 hydrogen
hydrogen peroxide	4 total: 2 hydrogen, 2 oxygen	
carbon dioxide	3 total: _____	1/3 carbon, 2/3 oxygen

Take It Home! Check the ingredient lists on labels of several household products. Find the names of two different compounds. Use reference books or the Internet to find out what elements are in the compounds.

SC.5.P.8.4 Explore the scientific theory of atoms (also called atomic theory) by recognizing that all matter is composed of parts that are too small to be seen without magnification.

People in Science

Meet the Atomic All-Stars

Marie Curie

Marie Curie worked as a scientist in France. She discovered that some elements are radioactive. That means energy radiates, or comes out, of the elements. In 1903, Marie Curie became the first woman ever to win a Nobel Prize. In 1911, she won another. She is one of the most famous female scientists of all time.

Some of Marie Curie's early work on radioactivity studied this type of uranium mineral known as pitchblende.

Inés Triay

Inés Triay is a scientist who works with radioactive materials, too. She works to clean up dangerous wastes that are produced when radioactive elements are used in nuclear power plants. In 2009, President Barack Obama assigned Triay to an important job in the U.S. Department of Energy. She is head of the team that properly disposes of nuclear waste.

The symbol on this sign warns of radioactivity that could be dangerous to your health.

RADIOACTIVE

Complete a Timeline

Fill in the boxes with information about Marie Curie and Inés Triay. For each entry you add, draw a line to the correct location on the timeline.

1898 Marie Curie discovers two new radioactive elements, called radium and plutonium.

1896 Marie Curie's teacher, Henri Becquerel, first discovers radioactivity.

1908 Hans Geiger invents a tool now called the "Geiger counter." It measures radioactivity.

1951 For the first time, electricity is generated using radioactive elements.

1934 Marie Curie dies from a disease caused by radiation. No one knew that radioactivity can be very bad for human health.

1979 Two scientists, Godfrey Hounsfield and Allan McLeod Cormack, win the Nobel Prize in Medicine for the C.T. scan machine. It uses small amounts of radiation and takes pictures of the inside of the human body.

Think About It!

How did Marie Curie's work lead to improved health care?

Name _____

Multiple Choice

Identify the choice that best answers the question.

SC.5.P.9.1

1 Joseph put water, sugar, and yeast into a balloon. Then he put the balloon in a warm place for 1 hour. Which of the following is most like the change happening in Joseph's balloons?

 Ⓐ

 Ⓒ

Ⓑ

Ⓓ

SC.5.P.9.1, SC.5.N.1.3

2 Daniel put water, sugar, and yeast into a balloon. Then he measured the mass of the balloon. He put the balloon in a warm place for 2 hours. Then he measured the mass again. He repeated his experiment three times to get more data. Predict how the mass of the balloon changed.

Ⓕ same mass   Ⓗ more mass
Ⓖ less mass   Ⓘ no more mass

SC.5.P.8.1

3 Which of these correctly describes a change in state of water?

Ⓐ liquid water ➜ melts ➜ solid water
Ⓑ liquid water ➜ boils ➜ water vapor
Ⓒ solid water ➜ condenses ➜ liquid water
Ⓓ water vapor ➜ evaporates ➜ liquid water

SC.5.P.9.1

4 When an egg is cracked and put in a hot pan, it flows easily. After it cooks for a minute, the egg becomes solid.

Why does the egg change?

Ⓕ Breaking the shell is a physical change in the egg that makes it solid.

Ⓖ Breaking the shell is a chemical change that makes the egg become solid.

Ⓗ Heating the egg on the stove causes the egg to evaporate and become solid.

Ⓘ Adding heat causes a chemical change in the molecules of the egg that makes it solid.

SC.5.P.9.1

5 The volume of a given mass of gas is one of its physical properties that can change. Which graph shows how the volume of a gas changes as the temperature of the gas increases?

Ⓐ

Ⓒ

Ⓑ

Ⓓ

SC.5.P.9.1

6 Stacey tried to remove a metal lid from a glass jar, but the lid was too tight. Her mother held the jar so that the lid was in hot water for a minute. Then, Stacey was able to turn the lid easily. How did the hot water make the lid easier to remove?

(F) Heating the glass jar made it expand, so the lid turned easily.

(G) As the metal lid was heated, it expanded so that it was not as tight.

(H) Water on the metal lid made it easier to hold, so it was easier to turn.

(I) The water corroded the metal, so it did not hold as tightly to the glass.

SC.5.P.9.1

7 Which of these statements best describes the effect of temperature on chemical changes?

(A) Chemical changes generally happen faster at higher temperatures.

(B) Chemical changes generally happen slower at higher temperatures.

(C) Chemical changes are not affected by a change in temperature.

(D) Chemical changes happen only if the temperature is very hot.

SC.5.P.8.4

8 What does the modern atomic theory state?

(F) All matter is made up of atoms.

(G) All atoms are made up of hundreds of smaller particles.

(H) Atoms of different elements are exactly the same.

(I) Atoms of different kinds combine to form different elements.

SC.5.P.8.2, SC.5.N.1.1

9 Kym has set up an experiment with four beakers, each filled with 100 mL of water at four different temperatures. She plans to time how long it takes for 1 tsp of sugar to dissolve at each temperature. To determine if there is a trend, she will add the sugar to each beaker of water without stirring, wait for it to dissolve, then plot her results on a graph. Which of the following graphs would most likely show the results of Kym's experiment?

(A) **Graph A**

(B) **Graph B**

(C) **Graph C**

(D) **Graph D**

SC.5.P.8.2, SC.5.N.1.1

10 Claire is studying how quickly sugar dissolves in warm and cold water. First, she dissolves a 4 g sample of raw sugar, as shown in the following figure, in both warm and cold water. Then, she dissolves a 4 g sample of white sugar, as shown in the following figure, in both warm and cold water.

Raw sugar   White sugar

In which of the following solutions would the sugar dissolve the slowest?

   F   raw sugar, cold water

   G   raw sugar, warm water

   H   white sugar, cold water

   I   white sugar, warm water

SC.5.P.8.2

11 Mrs. Lopez is a chemist who is studying salt crystals. She wants to slow the rate at which the crystals dissolve in a solution of water. What could she do to slow the dissolving rate?

   A   Crush the salt.   C   Cool the solution.

   B   Heat the solution.   D   Stir the solution.

SC.5.P.8.2

12 Mia made punch for a school picnic. She added sugar, strawberries, raspberries, and mint leaves to soda water. Which of these will dissolve in the soda?

   F   sugar   H   raspberries

   G   strawberries   I   mint leaves

SC.5.P.8.3

13 Nadia has a mixture of oil and water. She wants to separate the mixture. How can she do this?

   A   by using a magnet to attract the oil

   B   by pouring the mixture through a sieve

   C   by evaporating the water from the mixture

   D   by letting the oil float to the top and skimming it off

SC.5.P.8.3

14 A container holds a mixture of glass shards and iron filings. What is the best way to separate the glass shards from the iron filings?

   F   Use a magnet.

   G   Heat the mixture.

   H   Sort them by size.

   I   Separate them by shape.

SC.5.P.8.1

15 The states of matter differ in many ways, including shape and volume. The following three figures show the particles in a solid, a liquid, and a gas.

   1   2   3

Which of the following correctly identifies the state of matter?

   A   3: gas   C   2: solid

   B   1: liquid   D   2: liquid

SC.5.P.9.1

16 This diagram shows what happens when water changes state.

Gas →1→ Liquid →2→ Solid
Gas ←3← Liquid ←4← Solid

Which statement correctly explains some of the temperature changes shown in the diagram?

(F) Temperature increases in steps 1 and 2.

(G) Thermal energy decreases in steps 1 and 2.

(H) Energy of molecules decreases in steps 3 and 4.

(I) Motion of molecules decreases in steps 3 and 4.

SC.5.P.8.1

17 There are three main states of matter: liquid, solid, and gas. Which statement describes the shape of a solid?

(A) It has its own shape.

(B) It does not have shape.

(C) It takes the shape of its container.

(D) It changes shape with temperature.

SC.5.P.8.1

18 There are different characteristics for each of the states of matter. Which statement describes a difference between liquids and solids?

(F) Temperature can change a solid to a liquid, but it cannot change a liquid to a solid.

(G) Solids have a definite volume and liquids do not have a definite volume.

(H) The particles in a solid are much closer together than the particles in a liquid.

(I) Solids take on the shape of their containers and liquids maintain their own shapes.

SC.5.P.8.1

19 The table gives the mass and volume of four unknown solids.

Sample	Mass (g)	Volume (mL)	Density
1	125	3	
2	324	9	
3	234	2	
4	540	8	

Which is the correct explanation of how to find the density?

(A) Divide the volume by the mass.

(B) Divide the mass by the volume.

(C) Multiply the volume by the mass.

(D) Add the mass and volume and divide by 2.

SC.5.P.8.4

20 Franklin drew the following pictures of two metal objects.

He knows that the can on the left is made up of the element aluminum. The wire on the right is made up of the element copper. Which of the following can he conclude about the atoms in the two objects?

(F) No two atoms are alike in either object.

(G) Both have atoms that are shaped like cylinders.

(H) The atoms in the can and the wire are identical to each other.

(I) The atoms in the can are different from the atoms in the wire.

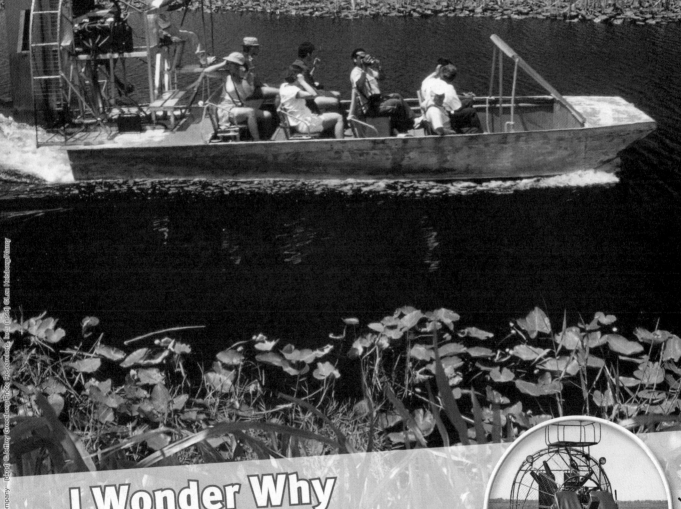

UNIT 5
Forms of Energy

Big Idea 10

Forms of Energy

I Wonder Why
In the Florida Everglades, airboats skim quickly across the water. Why do airboats need gasoline to run? *Turn the page to find out.*

Here's Why Energy is needed to make the fan spin to push the boat across the water. This energy comes from gasoline. Without gasoline to burn, the boat's engine wouldn't work.

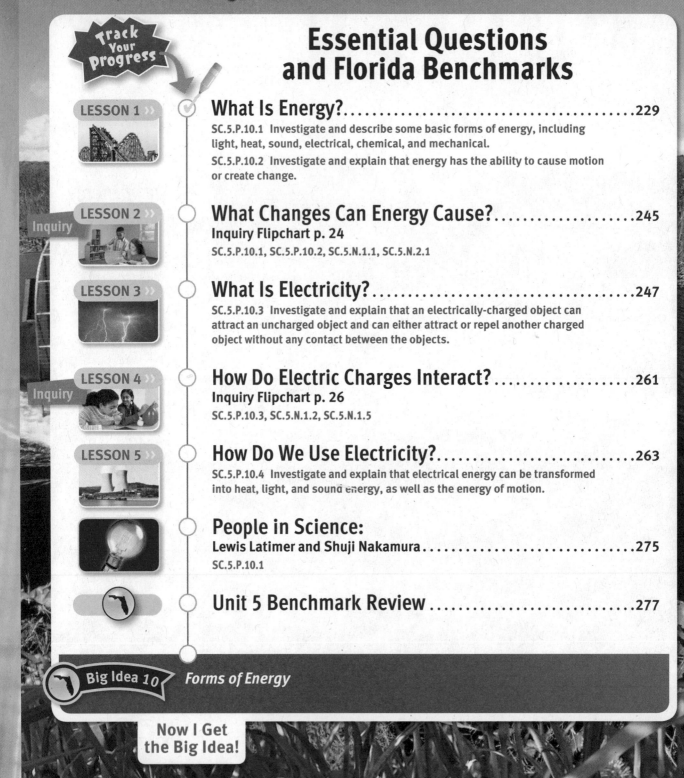

Track Your Progress

Essential Questions and Florida Benchmarks

Big Idea 10 *Forms of Energy*

Now I Get the Big Idea!

SC.5.P.10.1 Investigate and describe some basic forms of energy, including light, heat, sound, electrical, chemical, and mechanical. SC.5.P.10.2 Investigate and explain that energy has the ability to cause motion or create change.

Lesson 1

Essential Question

What Is Energy?

Engage Your Brain!

As you read the lesson, figure out the answer to the following question. Write the answer here.

What kinds of energy are represented in this picture?

_____

_____

_____

_____

Active Reading

Lesson Vocabulary

List the terms. As you learn about each one, make notes in the Interactive Glossary.

_____   _____

_____   _____

_____   _____

Compare and Contrast

Many ideas in this lesson are about ways that things are alike or different. Active readers stay focused on comparisons and contrasts by asking how things are alike and how they are different.

Energy
All Around
· · · · ·

What does a melting scoop of ice cream
have in common with a kicked soccer ball?
The ice cream and the ball both change in
some way. What causes these changes?

As you read this page, underline
important details about energy.

▶ A soccer ball won't
move unless something
gives it energy. Energy
changes the ball's motion. Circle the thing
in the picture that gave the ball energy.

Think about all the ways that you use
energy. **Energy** is the ability to cause
changes in matter. Energy is involved when
matter moves or changes its shape. A
change in temperature also involves energy.

Energy can transform, or change, from
one form into another. The boy in the
picture is using energy to run. The energy
came from food that he ate.

When the boy kicks the ball, his foot
transfers energy to the ball. The moving
ball transfers energy again. Energy moves
to particles in the air and on the ground.
These tiny particles begin to move faster.

The ball stops moving after it has
transferred all its energy. Energy is never
used up. It just changes from one form to
another.

The tiny particles that make up solid ice cream move slowly. Energy from the sun causes a change in their motion. The particles move faster. The ice cream melts and becomes a liquid.

▶ What caused this ice cream to melt?

_____

_____

_____

▶ For each statement, write *T* for true or *F* for false.

◯ 1. Energy can cause a change in matter.

◯ 2. Energy can change from one form to another.

◯ 3. Energy can be used up and destroyed.

◯ 4. Energy can be transferred from one object to another.

The Ups and Downs of Energy

Does an object that is not moving have any energy? Let's find out!

As you read this page, circle the sentences that tell how potential energy and kinetic energy are different.

Does a book sitting on a shelf have energy? Yes! Someone gave it energy by lifting the book to the shelf. The energy is now stored in the book. The energy an object has because of its position or condition is called **potential energy** (PE).

If the book falls off the shelf, it begins moving. Its potential energy changes to the energy of motion. The energy an object has because of its motion is called **kinetic energy** (KE).

When the roller coaster car is at the top of a hill, most of its energy is potential energy due to its position. Gravity will change this PE to KE as the car starts downhill.

When you compress a spring or stretch a rubber band, your energy is stored in the object as potential energy. The potential energy changes to kinetic energy when you release the spring or rubber band.

Position isn't the only way that energy can be stored. A match head has potential energy stored in chemical bonds between its particles. Striking the match releases the stored energy as heat and light. A charged battery also contains potential energy. A battery dies when all of its potential energy has been transformed to electrical energy.

Potential Energy	Kinetic Energy

As the car moves downhill, its PE changes to kinetic, or moving, energy. At the bottom of the hill, the car's energy is kinetic. This KE becomes PE as the roller coaster car travels up the next hill.

▶ Fill in the three bubbles on the roller coaster track. Write *KE* if a coaster car at that position would have mostly kinetic energy. Write *PE* if it would have mostly potential energy.

▶ When does a roller coaster car have the most kinetic energy?

_____

_____

_____

_____

Loud, Soft, Hot, Cold

The kinetic energy of a moving roller coaster car is easy to see. How can you sense energy in tiny particles of matter that are too small to see?

Active Reading As you read these two pages, underline the sentences that tell you how sound energy and thermal energy are alike.

When a trumpet makes noise, it vibrates, or moves back and forth. The trumpet transfers energy to tiny particles of air. Each particle of air moves back and forth, bumping into other particles. The sound travels outward.

▶ Draw an arrow to show the direction that sound waves are traveling.

If someone knocks on your door, the particles in the door vibrate. They bump into particles in the air on your side of the door. The sound travels through the door and through the air to you as a sound wave.

Sound energy is —

- a form of energy that is carried as waves in vibrating matter.

- a type of kinetic energy, because particles of matter are moving.

- the cause of all the sounds you hear.

234

Another type of energy that involves moving particles is thermal energy. *Thermal energy* is the total kinetic energy of the particles that make up a substance.

Thermometers measure thermal energy. You sense thermal energy as temperature. The more thermal energy an object has, the greater its temperature. Thermal energy helps you to stay warm, to cook your food, and to heat water for washing or bathing.

▶ In a hot-air balloon, the burning of propane produces thermal energy. This energy raises the temperature of the air particles inside the balloon to _____ °C.

▶ This thermometer shows normal body temperature, which is _____ °C (98.6 °F).

▶ The air at the top of this icy mountain has very little thermal energy. Its temperature is _____ °C.

Do the Math!
Use Number Lines

Draw a number line. On the line, place the three temperatures (in °C) shown in the pictures on this page. Then add a point for normal room temperature, 22 °C.

See a Sea of Energy

The sun is the source of the light energy entering the cave.

Your ears use sound energy to hear. What kind of energy allows your eyes to see?

Active Reading As you read, draw boxes around the descriptions of light energy and electrical energy.

Suppose you are using a flashlight in a dark room. You drop the flashlight and it breaks. What can you see? Nothing! Your eyes need light energy to work.

Light energy is a form of energy that can travel through space. Light can also pass through some types of matter, such as air or glass. Light energy travels as waves.

You can see light energy. Some objects give off light. You see all other objects when light reflects, or bounces off, from them and enters your eyes.

▶ List three sources of light.

_____

_____

_____

You see the cave walls when light bounces off them and reaches your eyes.

Electrical energy changes to light energy in a flashlight.

Objects that give off light energy often give off heat. But the two types of energy are different. You can tell them apart by the way you sense the energy. Your skin senses heat, but it cannot sense light energy. Your eyes sense light energy.

Flashlights and television sets produce light. To do this, they use another type of energy, called electrical energy. **Electrical energy** is energy caused by the movement of electric charges. When you use electricity, you are using electrical energy.

Electrical energy can change to other types of energy you can use. Electrical energy changes to thermal energy in a toaster or a stove. Cell phones and stereo speakers use electrical energy to produce sound. In lamps and spotlights, electrical energy changes to light energy.

Computers and other devices that are plugged in use electrical energy.

▶ List three objects that use electrical energy.

_____

_____

_____

Energy in Machines and Food

•••••

You have learned about machines that use electrical energy. Some machines don't need to be plugged in. What forms of energy do they use?

Many objects, such as a ball thrown in the air, have both kinetic and potential energy. **Mechanical energy** (ME) is the total energy of motion and position of an object. As a ball drops, its potential energy decreases as its kinetic energy increases. Its mechanical energy, though, stays constant. The relationship among these forms of energy is shown by the following equation.

Mechanical Energy = Kinetic Energy + Potential Energy

A machine uses mechanical energy to do work. For example, a fan plugged into the wall uses electrical energy. It changes that energy into the mechanical energy of the spinning fan blades. The spinning fan uses the mechanical energy to do work—moving the air in a room.

▶ Describe how energy in gasoline is transformed in a lawn mower.

_____

_____

_____

_____

_____

_____

© Houghton Mifflin Harcourt Publishing Company (bkgd) ©Stewart Cohen; (t) ©Comstock/Getty Images

238

Have you ever felt as if you were going to "run out of energy"? The energy your body uses comes from the food you eat. Food contains a kind of potential energy called chemical energy. **Chemical energy** is energy that is stored in matter and that can be released by a chemical reaction.

When your body needs energy, it breaks down food and releases potential chemical energy from it. If you use that energy to run or jump, it changes into kinetic energy. Your body also uses chemical energy stored in food to produce thermal energy. This keeps your body at a steady temperature.

Cars use chemical energy in liquid fuel such as gasoline. A flashlight uses the chemical energy stored in a battery to produce light. Some stoves change chemical energy to thermal energy by burning a gas called propane.

▶ Winding the key on the toy increases the toy's _____ energy.

▶ Our bodies use the _____ energy in food to move and stay warm.

▶ The hands on this watch move because the watch has _____ energy.

239

Spotlight on Energy

A stage production requires different kinds of energy. How many are being used on this stage?

Active Reading As you read these pages, draw a box around each type of energy.

Some stage shows use fire, sparklers, and explosions. These elements turn stored chemical energy into light, heat, and sound energy.

Musicians use mechanical energy to play instruments. The instruments make sound energy that the audience hears as music.

These performers are high above the stage. They have a lot of potential energy due to their position.

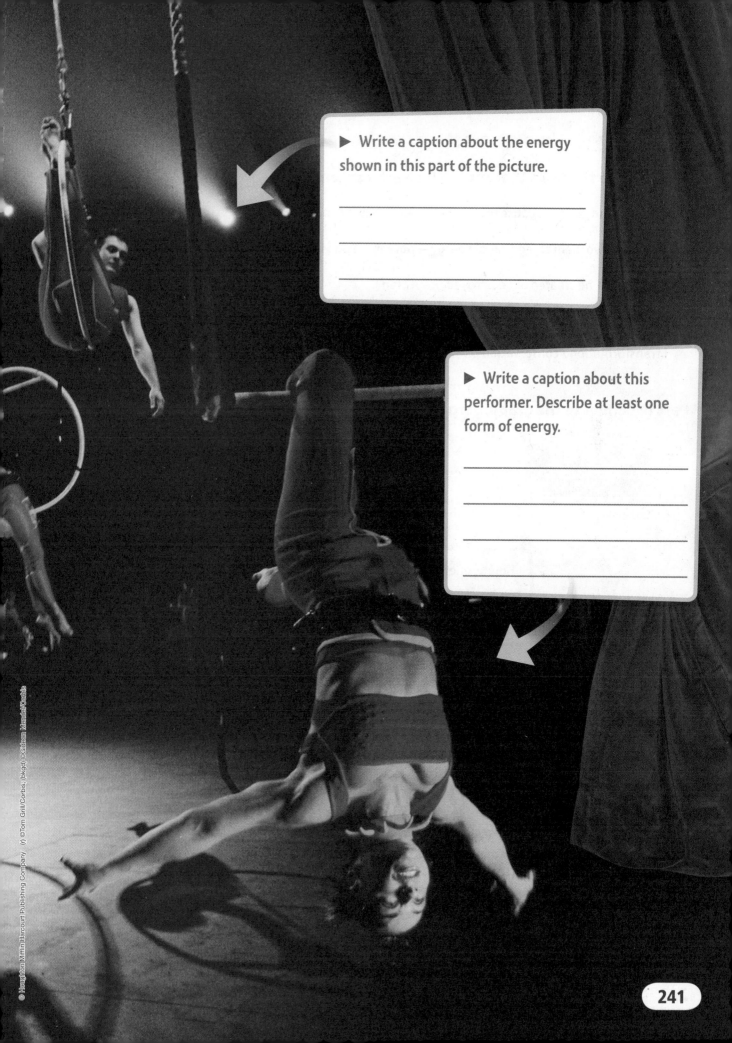

▶ Write a caption about the energy shown in this part of the picture.

_____

_____

_____

▶ Write a caption about this performer. Describe at least one form of energy.

_____

_____

_____

_____

Sum It Up!

When you're done, use the answer key to check and revise your work.

Part I: Circle the word that completes each sentence.

A. Energy is the ability to cause motion or create (matter / change).

B. There are two main categories of energy—potential and (thermal / kinetic).

C. Energy can't be created or (destroyed / captured).

D. Energy can change from one form to another, which is called energy (transformation / conservation).

Part II: Complete the graphic organizer below.

ENERGY

Potential energy is energy stored in an object because of its position or condition.

Kinetic energy is the energy of motion.

A. _____ energy is energy that can be released by a chemical reaction.

B. _____ energy is the total kinetic energy of the particles in matter.

C. _____ energy is the form of energy that you can see.

F. _____ energy is the combination of the potential and kinetic energy an object contains.

E. _____ energy is energy caused by movement of electrical charges.

D. _____ energy travels as waves through vibrating matter.

© Houghton Mifflin Harcourt Publishing Company

Answer Key: Part I: A. change B. kinetic C. destroyed D. transformation Part II: A. Chemical B. Thermal C. Light D. Sound E. Electrical F. Mechanical

Name _____

Word Play

1 Use the clues and the word bank to fill in the puzzle.

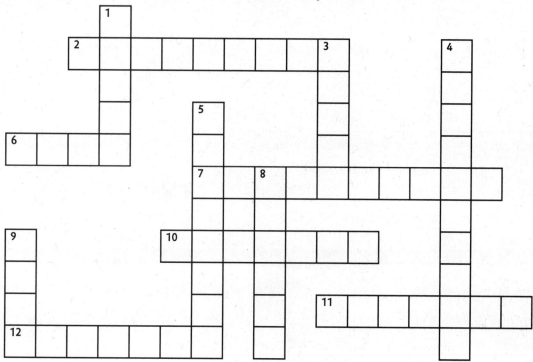

Across

2. Stored energy due to position or condition
6. A substance that contains useful chemical energy
7. Energy caused by the movement of electric charges
10. Energy of motion
11. To move back and forth
12. Energy of moving particles of matter

Down

1. Form of energy you can hear
3. Form of energy you can see
4. Total potential and kinetic energy of an object
5. Energy that can be released by a chemical reaction
8. Ability to cause changes in matter
9. What your body feels thermal energy as

mechanical*	chemical*	electrical*	sound	light	energy*
potential*	kinetic*	thermal	vibrate	food	heat

* Key Lesson Vocabulary

Apply Concepts

2 Complete the matching game. The first one is done for you.

Light Energy (E) (3)	A. The total kinetic energy of the particles in matter	
Thermal Energy ◯◯	B. Energy caused by motion of electric charges	
Sound Energy ◯◯	C. Energy that is stored in matter and can be released during a chemical reaction	
Electrical Energy ◯◯	D. Energy carried as waves of vibrating matter	
Mechanical Energy ◯◯	E. Energy that travels as a wave and that you are able to see	
Chemical Energy ◯◯	F. Sum of an object's potential and kinetic energy	

3 Use the terms *potential energy* and *kinetic energy* to tell what is happening to the skier.

_____

_____

_____

_____

_____

4 Identify the types of energy present or produced in each lettered part of the picture.

a. _____

b. _____

c. _____

Take It Home! When you go home, ask your family to help you list all the kinds of energy you use around your house. Try to find at least one example of each type of energy you learned about in this lesson.

SC.5.N.1.1 ... plan and carry out scientific investigations of various types.... **SC.5.N.2.1** ... science is grounded in empirical observations that are testable.... **SC.5.P.10.1** Investigate and describe some basic forms of energy.... **SC.5.P.10.2** Investigate and explain that energy has the ability to cause motion or create change.

Name _____

Essential Question

What Changes Can Energy Cause?

Set a Purpose
How will this investigation help you observe changes in matter?

_____

_____

_____

_____

State Your Hypothesis
Write your hypothesis, or testable statement.

_____

_____

_____

Think About the Procedure
How hot do you predict the solar cookers will become?

_____

_____

_____

What variable will you change in this experiment?

_____

_____

_____

_____

Record Your Data
Draw a data table, and record your temperature measurements.

Draw Conclusions

Was your hypothesis supported? Why or why not?

_____

_____

_____

_____

Analyze and Extend

1. What was the purpose of the aluminum foil? How would your results differ if you had made the cooker just from the poster board? Explain.

_____

_____

_____

_____

_____

2. How might a solar cooker be useful in places where there is no electricity?

_____

_____

_____

3. How could you improve your solar cooker to make it heat faster?

_____

_____

_____

_____

4. The setup for an experiment is shown below. What problems do you see with the way the experiment is designed?

_____

_____

_____

_____

_____

_____

5. What other questions would you like to ask about using solar energy? What investigations could you do to answer the questions?

_____

_____

_____

_____

_____

_____

_____

_____

SC.5.P.10.3 Investigate and explain that an electrically-charged object can attract an uncharged object and can either attract or repel another charged object without any contact between the objects.

Essential Question

What Is Electricity?

Engage Your Brain!

As you read the lesson, look for the answer to the following question and record it here.

What causes the girl's hair to stand out from her head?

_____

_____

_____

_____

Active Reading

Lesson Vocabulary

List the terms. As you learn about each one, make notes in the Interactive Glossary.

_____

_____

Main Ideas

The main idea of a paragraph is the most important idea. The main idea may be stated in the first sentence, or it may be stated elsewhere. Active readers look for main ideas by asking themselves, What is this section mostly about?

All Charged UP

You can charge a battery. A football player may charge downfield. How is an electric charge different?

Active Reading As you read these two pages, underline the main idea on each page.

What do you, this book, and your desk have in common? You are all made of atoms. Atoms are the building blocks of all matter. An atom is made of even tinier particles called protons, neutrons, and electrons.

The main difference between protons, electrons, and neutrons is their electric charge. *Electric charge* is a property of a particle that affects how it behaves around other particles.

- Protons have a positive charge (+1).

- Electrons have a negative charge (-1).

- Neutrons are neutral. They have no charge.

When an atom has equal numbers of protons and electrons, the positive charges and negative charges cancel each other. The atom itself has no charge.

Legend

- = neutron
- = proton
- = electron

Each of these atoms
has equal numbers of
protons and electrons.
Both atoms are neutral.

An electron from
the atom on the left
moves to the atom on
the right.

The atom on the left
now has a charge of +1.
The atom on the right
has a charge of –1.

Atoms sometimes gain or lose electrons. Such a gain or loss causes an atom to have an unequal number of positive and negative charges. For example, if an atom with four protons and four electrons gains an electron, the atom will have a charge of –1.

If a neutral atom loses an electron, the number of protons will no longer balance the number of electrons. The atom will have a charge of +1.

▶ Draw an atom with three protons, four neutrons, and four electrons.

What is the charge of the atom?

_____

Opposites Attract

Have you ever had a "bad hair day"? Your hair sticks out in all directions and won't lie flat. What causes that?

Active Reading As you read this page, circle the definitions of *attract* and *repel*. On the next page, draw a box around the sentence with the main idea.

Particles with the same charge repel, or push away from, one another. Particles with opposite charges attract one another, or pull together.

© Houghton Mifflin Harcourt Publishing Company ©Doug Martin/Photo Researchers, Inc.

Do the Math!
Positive and Negative Numbers

Fill in the missing squares.

Original Charge on an Object	Electrons Gained or Lost	Final Charge on the Object
+300	Gains 270	
−300	Loses 525	
−270		−500

In the dryer, atoms in clothing gain and lose electrons. Each piece of clothing becomes charged. The positively charged surfaces attract the negatively charged surfaces. As a result, the clothes stick together.

Electric charges can build up on objects. This buildup of charges is called **static electricity**. Objects with opposite electric charges attract each other. Objects with the same charge repel each other.

When you brush your hair, electrons move from each strand of hair to the brush. Soon all the strands are positively charged. Having the same charge causes the strands to repel one another and stick out.

A charged object can also attract a neutral object. If you rub a balloon on your hair, the balloon picks up extra electrons. They give it a negative charge. When you bring the balloon near a wall, electrons in a small section of the wall are repelled and move away. This leaves a positive charge at the surface of the wall. The balloon sticks to the wall.

Lightning Strikes

Thunderstorms can be scary. Lightning strikes can be deadly. What is lightning, and how can you stay safe during a thunderstorm?

Active Reading As you read these two pages, underline the main idea on each page.

Static electricity is a buildup of charges on an object. The word *static* means "not moving." Charges stay on an object until it comes close to an object with a different charge.

As you walk across a carpet, electrons move from the carpet to you. Because electrons repel each other, they spread out all over your body. When you touch something, the electrons jump from your finger to the object. This jumping is called an electrostatic discharge. You feel it as a tiny shock.

ZAP!
Electrons jump from a person with a negative charge.

▶ Complete this cause-and-effect graphic organizer.

Cause: An object with a negative charge is placed near an object with a positive charge.	→	Effect: _____ _____ _____

Not all electrostatic discharges cause small shocks. Some result in huge shocks. During a thunderstorm, tiny raindrops or ice particles bump into each other. These collisions cause an electric charge to build in the clouds.

Positive charges form at the top of a cloud and on the ground. Negative charges form near the bottom of a cloud. When the difference in charge between a cloud and the ground is great enough, there is a huge electrostatic discharge that we call lightning.

A lightning spark can jump between two clouds, between a cloud and air, or between a cloud and the ground. The temperature inside a lightning bolt can reach 50,000 °F. That's hotter than the surface of the sun!

Lightning Safety

- Stay inside during thunderstorms.

- Turn off electrical appliances and stay away from windows.

- If you can't get inside a safe structure, wait in a car with a metal top for the storm to pass.

- Know the weather forecast. If you will be outdoors, have a plan in case a thunderstorm develops.

Objects that lightning strikes can catch on fire. A tree struck by lightning may split.

▶ Draw a cloud above the ground. Then draw positive and negative charges to show what causes lightning.

Current Events

You can control electrons by making them flow through a wire in the way water flows in a river.

When electric charges have a path to follow, as they do in the wire below, they move in a steady flow. This flow of charges is called an electric current.

insulator

copper wire

electrons

In this copper wire, electrons are moving through the wire.

Chemical reactions in a battery can provide the energy that causes the electrons to flow. An electricity generating station is another source of electric current.

▶ What do the blue dots on this wire represent, and what is it called when they flow?

_____

_____

_____

These homes are all connected by wires to an electricity generating station.

Static electricity may be fun and exciting to watch. On the other hand, moving charges are more useful. Electrons can be made to move through a wire. They make up an electric current. You can use an electric current to do many kinds of useful work. We use electric currents for cooking food, lighting a room, and producing sound.

A battery is one source of electric current. Most of the electricity used in schools, homes, and businesses does not come from batteries. Instead, it is provided by an electricity generating station, or energy station.

There are many types of electricity generating stations. They all turn other forms of energy into electrical energy. Wires carry this energy from the station to every outlet in your home. These wires may be on poles above ground or buried below ground.

Never climb or play near wires, and never dig in the ground where wires are present.

▶ List three devices that use electric current from batteries and three that use regular house current.

Batteries: House Current:

_____   _____

_____   _____

_____   _____

Sum It Up!

When you're done, use the answer key to check and revise your work.

The outline below is a summary of the lesson. Complete the outline.

I. Electric Charges

    A. Each of the three types of particles that make up atoms has a different charge.

        1. Protons have a positive charge.

        2. _____

        3. _____

    B. Atoms can gain or lose electrons.

II. Static Electricity

    A. Definition: the buildup of electric charge on an object

    B. Objects with charges interact with each other.

        1. Like charges repel.

        2. _____

III. Electrostatic Discharge

    A. Definition: the jumping of electrons from one object to another

    B. Examples

        1. Getting shocked after walking across a rug

        2. _____

IV. Electric Current

    A. Definition: _____

    B. Sources

        1. _____

        2. Electricity generating stations

Answer Key: I. A. 2. Electrons have a negative charge. I. A. 3. Neutrons have no charge. II. B. 2. Opposite charges attract. III. B. 2. Lightning IV. A. the flow of electrons through a wire. IV. B. 1. Batteries

Name _____

Word Play

1 Fill in the blank in each sentence. Then find the words in the blanks in the word search.

a. Two positive charges _____ each other.

b. A positive charge and a negative charge _____ each other.

c. The buildup of electric charge on an object is _____ electricity.

d. The steady flow of electric charges along a path is electric _____.

e. A proton has a _____ charge.

f. A neutron is _____ because it has no charge.

g. An electron has a _____ charge.

h. Electricity is produced at a generating _____.

```
C  N  E  G  A  T  I  V  E
U  F  R  E  P  E  L  R  V
R  I  G  H  T  E  N  I  I
R  N  A  T  T  R  A  C  T
E  G  C  I  T  A  T  S  I
N  E  U  T  R  A  L  L  S
T  I  G  H  T  N  I  N  O
S  T  A  T  I  O  N  G  P
```

Find the letters you didn't circle in the word search. Write them in order from left to right in the blanks below.

Riddle: What do you call a very scary electrostatic discharge?

_ _ _ _ _ _ _ _ _ _ _   _ _ _ _ _ _ _ _ _

Apply Concepts

2 List the three particles that make up an atom. Describe the charge of each particle.

Parts of an Atom	
Particle	Charge

Where are these particles found in an atom?

_____

_____

_____

3 Draw an atom with 9 protons, 10 neutrons and a charge of –1. Label each part in your drawing.

4 Explain why the balloons are sticking to this cat.

_____

_____

_____

_____

5 Look at the pairs of objects below. The charge of each object is shown. Tell how each pair will interact. Write *attract*, *repel*, or *nothing*.

+22	–34	_____
0	+130	_____
–40	–81	_____
0	0	_____

6 Complete the sequence graphic organizer.

A wool sock and a cotton shirt _____ against each other in a dryer.

↓

Electrons move from the wool to the _____ . .

↓

The two pieces of clothing have _____ charges and they _____ each other.

7 List three ways in which electric current helps you do work, and describe the energy transformation that takes place.

_____

_____

_____

_____

_____

_____

_____

_____

_____

8 Explain why the event in the drawing takes place.

_____

_____

_____

_____

_____

_____

_____

9 Match each drawing with its description. Circle the drawings that show sources of current that people use every day.

electric current	static electricity	electrostatic discharge	battery

10 Suppose you are playing soccer at a park and you hear thunder that sounds far away. Describe some things you should and should not do to stay safe.

_____

_____

_____

_____

_____

_____

Take It Home!

Do your clothes stick together when they come out of the dryer? If so, how could you prevent this from happening? If not, why don't they stick together? When you put on a sweater, does it ever stick to your hair? Does this happen throughout the year, or only at certain times?

SC.5.N.1.2 Explain the difference between an experiment and other types of scientific investigation. **SC.5.N.1.5** … authentic scientific investigation frequently does not parallel the steps of "the scientific method." **SC.5.P.10.3** Investigate and explain that an electrically-charged object can attract an uncharged object and can either attract or repel another charged object without any contact between the objects.

Name _____

Essential Question

How Do Electric Charges Interact?

Set a Purpose
What do you think you will observe during this activity?

_____

_____

_____

_____

Think About the Procedure
Why do you rub one balloon but not the other in Step 2?

_____

_____

_____

_____

Why do you rub both balloons in Step 3?

_____

_____

_____

_____

Why is this activity not an experiment?

_____

_____

_____

_____

Record Your Observations
Draw diagrams to show what happened during Steps 2 and 3. Label the diagrams.

261

Draw Conclusions

What caused the balloons to behave as they did in Steps 2 and 3?

_____

_____

_____

_____

_____

Analyze and Extend

1. What do you think happens when you rub a balloon with a wool cloth?

_____

_____

_____

2. What happens when objects with opposite charges are near each other? Give an example that you have seen in your everyday activities.

_____

_____

_____

3. What happens when objects with similar charges are near each other? Give an example that you have seen.

_____

_____

_____

_____

4. Look at the drawings of balloons below. In each pair, the drawing shows the charges on one balloon. Look at the way each pair of balloons is interacting, and draw the charges on the second balloon.

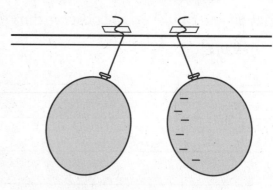

5. What other questions would you like to ask about using electric charges? What investigations could you do to answer your questions?

_____

_____

_____

_____

_____

_____

_____

SC.5.P.10.4 Investigate and explain that electrical energy can be transformed into heat, light, and sound energy, as well as the energy of motion.

Essential Question

How Do We Use Electricity?

Engage Your Brain!

As you read, figure out the answer to the following question and record it here.

How would this scene have been different in 1910?

_____

_____

_____

Active Reading

Lesson Vocabulary
List the terms. As you learn about each one, make notes in the Interactive Glossary.

_____

_____

_____

Signal Words: Sequence
Signal words show connections between ideas. Words that signal sequence include *now, before, after, first,* and *next.* Active readers remember what they read because they look for signal words that identify sequence.

Electricity
Has Many Uses

Suppose you had lived in 1900 rather than today. The pictures show how different your day might have been.

Active Reading As you read this page, write *before* or *after* in the box next to each object to indicate the sequence.

Does a clock radio wake you up in the morning? Do you use an electric toothbrush or hair dryer? How do you cook your breakfast?

Electrical appliances do work. They perform useful tasks by converting electrical energy into other forms of energy, such as sound, thermal, and mechanical energy. Some appliances run on batteries. Others are plugged into a socket, which provides greater electrical energy. Think about the appliances you use each day. How would your day change if there were no electricity?

The only light came from candles or oil-burning lamps. Now we can turn on lamps with the flick of a switch.

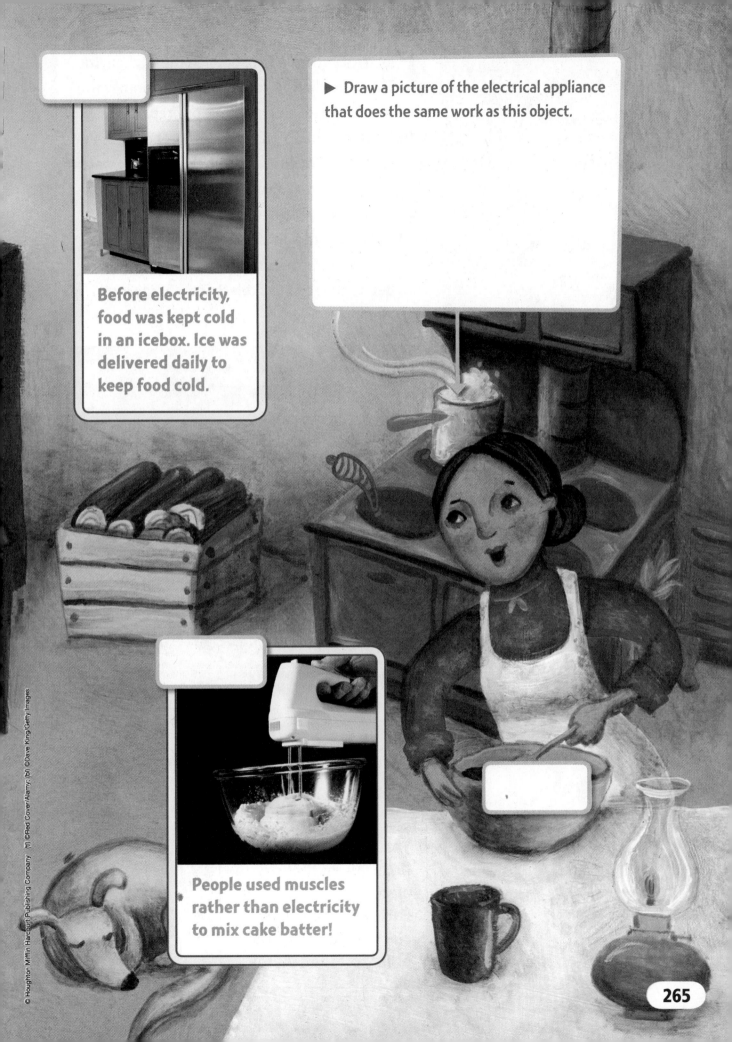

Before electricity, food was kept cold in an icebox. Ice was delivered daily to keep food cold.

▶ Draw a picture of the electrical appliance that does the same work as this object.

People used muscles rather than electricity to mix cake batter!

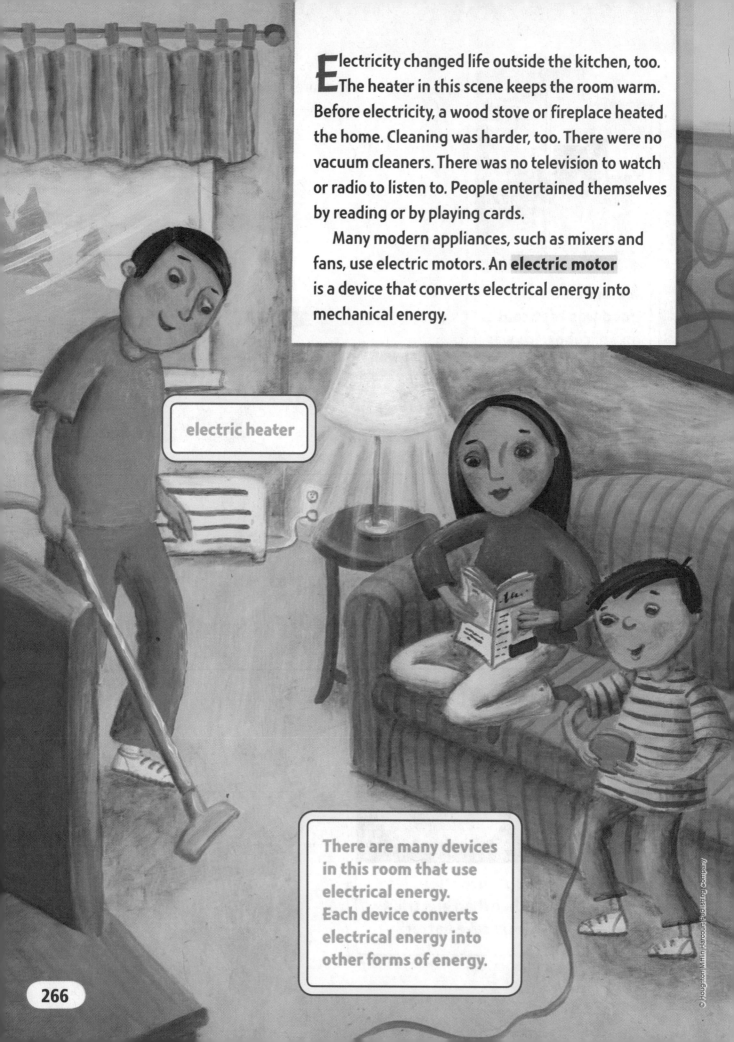

Electricity changed life outside the kitchen, too. The heater in this scene keeps the room warm. Before electricity, a wood stove or fireplace heated the home. Cleaning was harder, too. There were no vacuum cleaners. There was no television to watch or radio to listen to. People entertained themselves by reading or by playing cards.

Many modern appliances, such as mixers and fans, use electric motors. An **electric motor** is a device that converts electrical energy into mechanical energy.

electric heater

There are many devices in this room that use electrical energy. Each device converts electrical energy into other forms of energy.

Then and Now

Match the objects that do the same kind of work. Draw a picture of the missing appliance. Then describe the energy change that takes place in each electrical appliance.

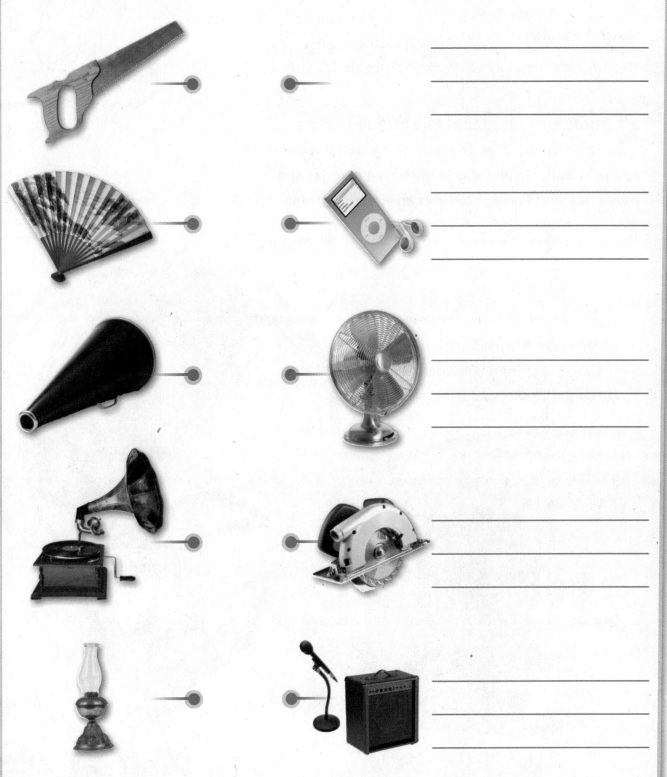

Electromagnets

Electricity and magnetism are related.
One can produce the other.

Active Reading As you read this page, circle the sentence that explains how magnetism produces an electric current.

Suppose you slide a coil of wire back and forth around a bar magnet. When the ends of the wire are attached to a light bulb, the bulb lights! Moving a magnet and a wire near each other produces an electric current.

Turning the handle on the device below turns a coil of wire inside three U-shaped magnets. Electricity flows through the wire and lights the lamp.

Hand-cranked
light bulb

Modern hand-
cranked flashlight

If magnets produce electricity, can electricity make magnets? Yes! Wrapping a coil of current-carrying wire around an iron nail makes the nail a magnet. You can use it to pick up small iron objects such as paper clips. A device in which current produces magnetism is called an **electromagnet**.

Huge electromagnets are used in junk yards. They separate iron and steel objects from other objects. The operator swings the electromagnet over a pile of junk. He turns on the current. All the iron pieces jump to the magnet. The operator then swings the magnet over a container and turns off the current. The magnetism stops, and the iron drops into the container.

Electromagnets have become very important and useful. Every electric motor today contains at least one electromagnet. You can also find electromagnets in telephones, doorbells, speakers, and computers. Doctors can use electromagnets to make pictures of the inside of the body.

► In the first box, write the cause of the action in the second box. Then figure out what that effect can cause, and fill in the third box.

	An electric current flows through the wire.	

Conserving Electricity

You've probably been asked to conserve, or use less, electricity. Why is conserving electricity important?

Active Reading As you read, underline a sentence that tells how you can conserve energy.

hydroelectric dam

Electricity generating stations, also known as energy stations, may use water, coal, or atoms to produce the electricity you use.

Inside a hydroelectric [hy•droh•ee•LEK•trik] dam, the mechanical energy of falling water is used to turn generators, which change mechanical energy into electrical energy.

windmills

Windmills have been used to grind grain or pump water. Today, wind turbines generate electricity.

Suppose you spin a magnet inside a coil of wire. A current flows through the wire. You've made a **generator**, a device that converts kinetic energy to electrical energy. Huge generators in energy stations change kinetic energy into electricity. The electricity travels through wires to homes, schools, and businesses.

Some energy stations use falling water or wind to turn generators. Other energy stations convert solar energy to electricity. These resources will never run out. They are called renewable resources.

Most energy stations burn coal or other fuels to heat water. The water rises as steam, which turns the generator. Coal is a limited resource. It will eventually run out. That's why it is important to conserve, or use less, electricity. For example, you can turn off the lights when you leave a room or use a towel instead of a hair dryer.

Do the Math!
Solve a Problem

Sam's electric bill was $200 for the month of June. The air conditioner accounts for $\frac{1}{2}$ of the bill, and the water heater accounts for $\frac{1}{5}$ of the bill. How much did it cost to run each appliance in June?

Use information in the summary to complete the graphic organizer.
When you're done, use the answer key to check and revise your work.

Summarize

Electrical appliances use electrical energy to do work and perform useful tasks. Some of these appliances, such as a flashlight or an MP3 player, get electricity from batteries. Others must be plugged into a wall socket. Electrical appliances convert electrical energy into other forms of energy, such as thermal energy, sound energy, and light energy. Many appliances, such as washing machines and fans, contain an electric motor, which converts electricity into the energy of motion. An electric current may also be used to make an electromagnet. Generators in energy stations contain electromagnets. The generators produce electric current, which travels through wires to homes, schools, and businesses. It is important to conserve electricity because some of the resources energy stations use will eventually run out.

1 Main Idea: Electrical appliances use electrical energy to

_____

_____

2 Detail: Some appliances work on batteries. Others must be

_____

_____

_____

_____

3 Detail: Electrical appliances convert

_____

_____

_____

_____

4 Detail: Conserving electricity is important because

_____

_____

_____

_____

© Houghton Mifflin Harcourt Publishing Company

Answer Key: 1. do work and perform useful tasks. **2.** plugged into a wall socket. **3.** electrical energy to other forms of energy, such as thermal, sound, light, and mechanical energy. **4.** resources used by energy stations may run out.

Name _____

Word Play

1 Unscramble each of the clues to form a word or a phrase from the word bank. Copy each letter in a numbered cell to the cell below with the same number.

TECGARLOETNEM [ ][ ][ ][ ][ ][ ][ ][ ][5][ ][ ][ ]

RECLICTE ROOTM [ ][8][ ][ ][ ][ ]   [ ][ ][ ][ ][ ]

TORRAGEEN [ ][4][ ][ ][ ][ ][ ][ ]

ONECREVS [ ][ ][2][ ][ ][ ][ ]

REECUSROS [ ][ ][ ][1][ ][ ][ ][ ]

GANSEITMM [ ][ ][10][7][ ][ ][3][ ][ ]

CICLETERTIY [6][ ][ ][ ][ ][9][ ][ ][ ][ ][11]

Word Bank
conserve
electricity
electric motor
electromagnet
generator
magnetism
resources

This lesson is about [1][2][3][4][5]   [6][7][8][9][10][11].

Apply Concepts

2 Draw a common electrical appliance. Then explain how it changes electrical energy to other forms of energy and what kind of work it does.

_____

_____

_____

_____

3 Draw an *X* over each appliance that changes electrical energy to mechanical energy.

Circle each appliance that changes electrical energy to thermal energy.

Draw a square around each appliance that changes electrical energy to sound energy.

Draw a triangle around each appliance that changes electrical energy to light energy.

4 What is the device in this drawing called? What would happen if you put this device near a pile of iron nails? Why?

_____

_____

_____

5

A. What are some resources used to generate electricity in electricity generating stations?

_____

_____

_____

B. Describe three ways that you can conserve electricity.

_____

_____

_____

_____

Take It Home!

Discuss with your family some specific ways that you could conserve electricity. You might talk about ways to use less electricity or about things you can do by hand rather than using an electrical appliance.

People in Science

Meet two Scientists Whose Work Shines Bright

Lewis Latimer

Lewis Latimer was born in 1848. His parents were slaves who had fled to a new life of freedom in Massachusetts. Lewis Latimer worked for Thomas Edison, a pioneer in making light bulbs. But Lewis Latimer made some key improvements. In 1882, he invented a new way to make filaments needed for early light bulbs. He also wrote one of the world's first books explaining electric lighting to the public.

Shuji Nakamura

Shuji Nakamura is a Japanese inventor born in 1954. Working in a small electronics company in 1993, Shuji Nakamura made a discovery. He invented the first successful blue light-emitting diode, or LED. The blue LED made today's bright white LED lights possible. These new LED lights use much less energy than a regular bulb. They can last about 100 times longer, too. Using these lights helps the environment.

Lighting the Way

Fill in the boxes with information about Lewis Latimer and Shuji Nakamura. For each entry you add, draw a line to the correct location on the timeline.

1780 Aimé Argand makes major improvements to the oil lamp.

1879 Thomas Edison's company begins selling incandescent light bulbs, which give off light when a filament inside the bulb heats up.

1923 The first neon lights in the United States are sold.

1938 The first commercial fluorescent lamps become available for purchase.

1960 The first working laser was demonstrated.

1976 Compact fluorescent bulbs were developed.

Think About It!

Lighting has changed a lot since the days of oil lamps. Why do you think people continue to develop new ways to produce light?

Benchmark Review

Name _____

Multiple Choice

Identify the choice that best answers the question.

SC.5.P.10.3

1 Carlita hangs two balloons from a desk. When they hang normally, they are close together but they do not touch. Carlita rubs both balloons with a wool cloth. What happens when she lets the balloons hang near one another?

(A) They push one another apart.

(B) They touch one another and pop.

(C) They touch one another and stick together.

(D) They are close together but do not touch.

SC.5.P.10.3, SC.5.N.2.1

2 The balloons shown below are part of Eric's investigation into positive and negative charges. He rubbed both balloons with a wool cloth.

What must be true of the balloons?

(F) They have the same charge.

(G) They have opposite charges.

(H) Neither of them has a charge.

(I) One of them has a charge and the other does not.

SC.5.P.10.3

3 Olivia is combing her hair. After a while, she notices that the comb attracts the hairs on her head as shown below.

Which explanation best describes why the hairs are attracted to the comb?

(A) Combing the hairs caused them to lose their static charge.

(B) Combing the hairs caused the comb to lose its static charge.

(C) Combing the hairs gave them a charge that is opposite the charge on the comb.

(D) Combing the hairs gave them a charge that is the same as the charge on the comb.

SC.5.P.10.2

4 Maria is working on an art project. She needs a rusty iron nail for her artwork, so she places a shiny, new nail outside in a wet location. How will the air and water change the nail?

(F) It will dry out the nail.

(G) It will cause the nail to cool down.

(H) It will make the nail decrease in volume.

(I) It will cause the nail to chemically change.

SC.5.P.10.1

5 Which figure shows light energy?

(A)

(B)

(C)

(D)

SC.5.P.10.2, SC.5.N.1.1, SC.5.N.1.4

6 Three different groups of students made solar cookers. They wanted to see which of the cookers could make a pot of baked beans the hottest in 3 hours. Which of the following is one of the things they should do in their experiment?

(F) Use different types of beans in each cooker.

(G) Put the cookers in places with different amounts of sunlight.

(H) Use a thermometer to test each pot of beans at the end of 3 hours.

(I) Have a student taste the beans from the different cookers and say which was hottest.

SC.5.P.10.3

7 An electron has a negative charge. What is true about the charge of a particle that is attracted to an electron?

(A) It is neutral.

(B) It is positive.

(C) It is negative.

(D) It is repulsive.

SC.5.P.10.3

8 What effect will one positive charge have on another positive charge?

(F) They repel each other from a distance.

(G) They attract each other from a distance.

(H) They repel each other only when they touch.

(I) They attract each other only when they touch.

SC.5.P.10.1

9 The picture shows a three-pronged plug. One of the flat prongs carries current from the supply that enters the electrical outlet, and the other returns the current to the service panel of the building.

What would be a correct prediction for the purpose of the round prong?

(A) It also carries current from the outlet.

(B) It carries any extra current away, preventing a shock.

(C) It increases the amount of electric current entering the outlet.

(D) It decreases the amount of electric current entering the outlet.

SC.5.P.10.3

10 You rub two balloons on your hair on a dry day. Your hair is attracted to both balloons. Then, you bring the balloons near one another. How would you describe what happens to the balloons?

(F) They repel one another.

(G) They attract one another.

(H) They neither attract nor repel one another.

(I) Opposite charges make one balloon become larger and one become smaller.

SC.5.P.10.3

11 Imagine you bring a negatively charged rod near a piece of metal. What happens within the metal?

(A) Protons in the metal move toward the rod.

(B) Electrons in the metal move toward the rod.

(C) Protons in the metal move away from the rod.

(D) Electrons in the metal move away from the rod.

SC.5.P.10.4

12 When an electric current runs through a doorbell buzzer, a mechanism inside vibrates back and forth and makes the doorbell work. Which energy transformation occurs when someone pushes the button on a doorbell?

(F) electrical energy into heat energy and sound energy

(G) electrical energy into motion energy and sound energy

(H) motion energy into electrical energy and sound energy

(I) motion energy and sound energy into electrical energy

SC.5.P.10.4

13 Joe had two toy cars. One car had a spring which he wound up before the car would move. The other car did not have a spring, but it needed a battery to work. How are the two cars different?

(A) The two cars transform different kinds of energy into motion.

(B) One car works only on a level surface, and the other can move up a ramp.

(C) There is no difference between the two cars because they both move forward on a surface.

(D) The two cars both transform electrical energy into motion, but they get the electrical energy in different ways.

SC.5.P.10.4

14 When Tishana left her bedroom, she flipped the light switch. The light bulb on her lamp stopped giving off light. What caused the light bulb to go out?

(F) The filament in the bulb stopped moving, so it could not make light.

(G) The electric current stopped, so no more electrical energy was converted into light.

(H) The bulb became cooler, so the light bulb stopped converting heat energy into light.

(I) The electric current stopped, so light energy could not be converted into electrical energy.

SC.5.P.10.1

15 The illustration below shows a large dam that is used to produce electricity. Water flows from the lake behind the dam to the river below the dam. It passes through turbines that are connected to electric generators.

Which energy transformation occurs in the hydroelectric power plant?

(A) heat energy into electrical energy

(B) energy of motion into electrical energy

(C) electrical energy into energy of motion

(D) energy of motion and sound energy into electrical energy

SC.5.P.10.1

16 Ellen is putting new batteries in her flashlight. Which type of energy is stored in the batteries?

(F) chemical

(G) kinetic

(H) light

(I) thermal

SC.5.P.10.2

17 Which is **not** something that energy can do?

(A) be completely used up

(B) cause an object to move

(C) change an object's temperature

(D) change into other forms of energy

SC.5.P.10.1

18 One type of energy is the result of waves that travel through matter and cause particles in the matter to vibrate. Which type of energy is it?

(F) chemical

(G) kinetic

(H) potential

(I) sound

SC.5.P.10.1

19 A thermometer shows that the temperature in a room has increased. Which type of energy of the air in the room has increased?

(A) chemical   (C) electrical

(B) sound   (D) thermal

SC.5.P.10.1

20 The picture below shows a burning candle. A candle burns because of energy stored in the particles of wax.

Which type of energy changes take place when the candle burns?

(F) Chemical energy changes into thermal energy and light energy.

(G) Electrical energy changes into light energy and chemical energy.

(H) Kinetic energy changes into potential energy and thermal energy.

(I) Potential energy changes into kinetic energy and light energy.

Working with Electricity

Big Idea 11

Energy Transfer and Transformations

I Wonder Why

This laboratory is at Thomas Edison's home in Fort Myers, FL. Why did Edison want to study electricity? *Turn the page to find out.*

Here's Why Edison, a great inventor, realized that there were many uses for electricity. He was the first to build an energy station that supplied electricity to homes, schools, and businesses.

Track Your Progress

Essential Questions and Florida Benchmarks

Big Idea 11 *Energy Transfer and Transformations*

Now I Get the Big Idea!

SC.5.N.1.1 ... plan and carry out scientific investigations.... **SC.5.N.2.1** ... science is grounded in empirical observations that are testable.... **SC.5.P.11.1** Investigate and illustrate the fact that the flow of electricity requires a closed circuit (a complete loop). **SC.5.P.11.2** Identify and classify materials that conduct electricity and materials that do not.

Name _____

Essential Question

What Is an Electric Circuit?

Set a Purpose
What will you learn from this investigation?

_____

_____

_____

_____

Think About the Procedure
Did the order in which you arranged the parts make a difference? Explain.

_____

_____

_____

_____

Was the procedure an experiment? Why or why not?

_____

_____

_____

_____

Record Your Data
In the space below, draw your circuit that worked. Label each part, and describe how the parts were connected.

Place a check mark next to the materials that enabled the bulb to light up.

Paper clip   ____

Wood craft stick   ____

Pencil lead   ____

Draw Conclusions

How can you build a circuit?

_____

_____

_____

_____

_____

Analyze and Extend

1. Why is it helpful to have a switch in a circuit?

_____

_____

_____

_____

2. Why would a circuit not work when a wire is replaced with a cotton string?

_____

_____

_____

3. Look at the first part of the word _circuit_. Why do you think what you built is called a circuit?

_____

_____

_____

4. Look at the drawing below. Draw lines to show how three wires could be connected to make the bulbs light up.

5. Each part of a circuit has a different job. Write the name of the part that performs each job below.

- Source of current _____

- Carries current _____

- Turns circuit on and off _____

- Changes electrical energy to light _____

6. What other questions would you like to ask about electric circuits? What investigations could you do to answer the questions?

_____

_____

_____

_____

_____

_____

284

Essential Question

What Are Electric Circuits, Conductors, and Insulators?

Engage Your Brain!

Find the answer to the following question and record it here.

This picture shows the inside of a robot. What do the dark lines have to do with the robot's operation?

_____

_____

_____

_____

Active Reading

Lesson Vocabulary

List the terms. As you learn about each one, make notes in the Interactive Glossary.

_____   _____

_____   _____

_____

Compare and Contrast

When you compare things, you look for ways in which they are alike. When you contrast things, you look for ways in which they are different. As you read each page, look for ways in which the things described are alike and different.

It's Shocking!

Working around electric utility lines is dangerous! How does a line worker avoid getting hurt?

Active Reading Draw a box around the sentences that contrast conductors and insulators.

Even on a hot day, a worker who repairs electric utility lines is bundled up in protective clothing. The thick gloves, the bulky boots, and the hard plastic hat are very heavy. But they help to keep the worker from being electrocuted!

The rubber and plastic used in protective clothing do not allow the flow of electric charge. A material that resists the flow of electric charge is called an **insulator**.

Electric charges flow easily through metals and some liquids. A material that readily allows electric charges to pass through it is called a **conductor**.

The worker's clothing is made of insulators. They keep electric charges from passing through him if he accidentally touches the wrong wires.

The parts that you hold on a plug, as well as the covering of the wire, are insulators. The metal prongs that go into the outlet are good conductors.

Electrical appliances work when electric charges flow through them. The parts that carry electric charges are made of conductors. Insulators are wrapped around the conductors, making the appliances safe to handle.

▶ Label the parts by writing *conductor* or *insulator*.

▶ Why are insulators used?

_____

_____

_____

_____

_____

_____

_____

A Path to Follow

The wiring in a lamp doesn't change. So why isn't the light on all the time?

When you go to school and back home, your path is a loop. An electric **circuit** is a path along which electric charges can flow. For an electrical device to work, the circuit must form a complete loop. This type of circuit is called a *closed circuit*. There are no breaks in the path.

What happens if a loose wire gets disconnected? The path is broken, and charges cannot flow. This type of circuit is called an *open circuit*. Many circuits have a switch. A switch controls the flow of charges by opening and closing the circuit.

buzzer

What's Wrong?

The buzzer in this circuit is not working. Trace the circuit with your finger, and describe what's wrong with the circuit.

_____

_____

Fix the picture so that the buzzer works.

switch

288

Open Circuit

When the switch in a circuit is open, the circuit isn't complete. Electric charges cannot flow, so the light stays off.

Closed Circuit

The switch is now closed. Electric charges can flow through the circuit, and the bulb lights up.

▶ The filament in this light bulb is a tiny wire that is part of the circuit. If the filament breaks, the circuit is _____.

filament

Who Needs a Map?

To travel from point A to point B, you usually take the shortest route. What if one of the roads on that route is blocked? Simple! You just take another road. But what would happen if there were only one road from point A to point B?

Active Reading Underline the sentences that compare series circuits and parallel circuits.

Series Circuits

In a series circuit, electric charges must follow a single path. The charged particles move from the battery's positive terminal to its negative terminal.

▶ Draw an arrow showing how charges flow in this circuit.

If one light bulb in a series circuit burns out, all of the lights go out because the circuit is broken.

Suppose that the television and all the lights in a room are part of the same circuit. What would happen if one of the light bulbs burned out? It would depend on how the circuit is wired.

A **series circuit** has only one path for electric charges to follow. If any part of the path breaks, the circuit is open. Nothing works!

A circuit with several different paths for the charges to follow is called a **parallel circuit**. If one part of the circuit breaks, the charges can still flow along the other parts.

Color a Complex Circuit

1. Look at the circuit below. Color the bulb or bulbs that should be lit.
2. Draw an *X* on the switch that is open. Draw an arrow above the closed switch.

Parallel Circuits

In this parallel circuit, electric charges can flow through both the top loop and the bottom loop.

If one part of a parallel circuit breaks, only that part of the circuit stops working.

Circuit Overload!

You sometimes hear about house fires caused by overloaded electrical wiring. How can you use electrical appliances safely?

<u>television</u>
3 amps

<u>hair dryer</u>
12.5 amps

As electric charges flow through conductors, they produce heat. Insulation protects the materials around it from the heat—up to a point! If too much heat builds up, the insulation can melt. As protection against fires, a fuse or a circuit breaker is added to each circuit. Fuses and circuit breakers are switches that work automatically. They open if charge flows too quickly through a circuit. The flow stops and the wires cool, preventing a fire.

WOW!

This wire got so hot that it melted the insulation around it. It could have started a fire.

Circuit overload occurs when too many devices in a circuit are turned on. Each device needs a certain flow of electrical charge, which is called current. Current is measured in amperes, or amps (A).

Circuit breakers open when the number of amps is greater than a certain value. Suppose the value for a breaker is 15 A. In this case, all the devices you use at the same time must require no more than 15 A.

Never plug in more appliances than a circuit is designed to handle!

With power strips like this one, it's possible to plug many devices into a single wall outlet. **That could be a big mistake!**

Should You Plug It In?

Draw a line connecting the hair dryer to one of the outlets in the power strip. Then connect the other devices you could use at the same time without overloading a 15-amp circuit breaker.

lava lamp
0.5 amp

laptop computer
1.5 amps

clothes dryer
42 amps

This panel contains circuit breakers. Each breaker allows a certain number of amps of electric current to pass through one circuit.

Do the Math!
Solve Word Problems

1. How many times more amps does a television need than a lava lamp?

_____

2. Circuit breakers are made in increments of 5 amps. What size breaker would you need for a circuit with a television, two laptops, and a lava lamp?

_____

When you're done, use the answer key to check and revise your work.

On each numbered line, fill in the vocabulary term that matches the description.

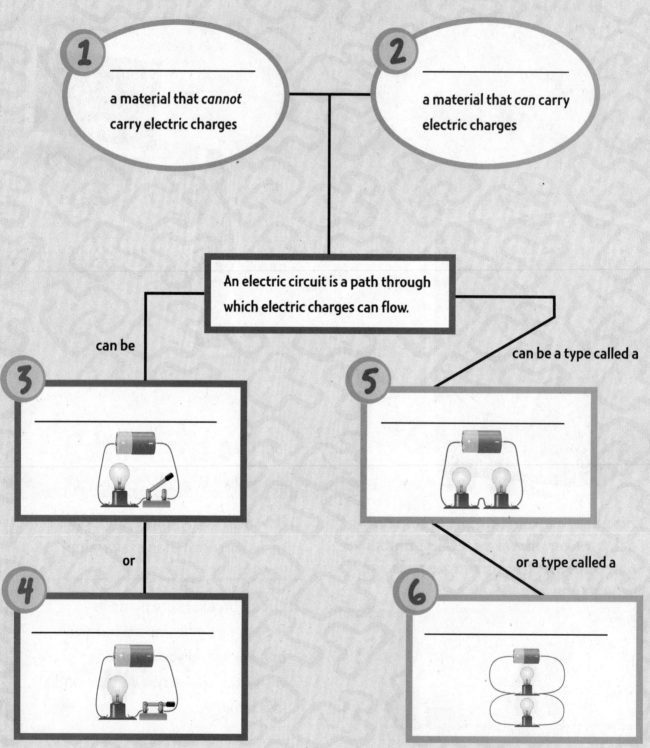

1
_____
a material that *cannot* carry electric charges

2
_____
a material that *can* carry electric charges

An electric circuit is a path through which electric charges can flow.

can be

3
_____

can be a type called a

5
_____

or

4
_____

or a type called a

6
_____

294

Name _____

Word Play

1 Unscramble the scrambled word in each sentence. Write the unscrambled word after the sentence. The first one is done for you.

a.	In some circuits, electrical energy is transformed into light energy by a light **lubb**.	(B) U L B 6
b.	The wires in a circuit are made of a material that is a **doortuccn**.	_ _ _ _ _ _ _ _ _ ◯ 10
c.	A path that electricity can follow is an electric **icurict**.	_ _ _ ◯ ◯ _ _ 4 5
d.	A circuit in which electric charges can follow several different paths is called a **rallpale** circuit.	_ ◯ _ _ _ _ _ _ 8
e.	If a wire is disconnected, the circuit is an **enop** circuit.	_ _ ◯ _ 9
f.	The covering on electric plugs and around wires is made of an **rainulost**.	◯ _ _ _ _ _ _ _ ◯ 2 7
g.	A circuit in which all the devices are connected in a single path is a **ressie** circuit.	_ _ ◯ _ _ _ 3
h.	When a light is on, it is part of a **scolde** circuit.	◯ _ _ _ _ _ 1

Solve the riddle by writing the circled letters above in the correct spaces below.

Riddle: What is another name for a clumsy electrician?

A _ _ _ C _ I _   B _ E _ K _ _ _
  1 2 3 4 5   6 7 8 9 10

Apply Concepts

2 Draw an open series circuit with two light bulbs, a battery, and a switch.

3 Explain what an overloaded circuit is. How can you prevent having an overloaded circuit?

_____

_____

_____

_____

_____

_____

_____

4 Write the word _conductor_ or _insulator_ on each of the lines. Then infer which type of material is inside the holes in the outlet. Explain.

_____

_____

_____

5 Suppose you are building a series circuit with a battery and a small light bulb and you run out of wire. What common objects could you use to connect the battery to the light bulb? Explain.

_____

_____

_____

6 Name each lettered part of the circuit, and explain what the part does.

A _____

B _____

C _____

D _____

7 Many appliances in your home use electrical energy. What other forms of energy are produced when the appliances are turned on? Name at least three different appliances and the types of energy they produce.

_____

_____

_____

_____

8 Study each of the following circuits.

- Make a check mark to show whether the circuit is open or closed.

- Draw the missing parts needed to make the open circuits work.

- Write whether the circuit is a series circuit or a parallel circuit.

☐ open
☐ closed

_____

☐ open
☐ closed

_____

☐ open
☐ closed

_____

☐ open
☐ closed

_____

Take It Home!

Discuss with your family what you have learned about circuits. Gather some electrical devices and explain how they use electricity. Try flipping some switches in your home, and explain whether they are series circuits or parallel circuits.

Ask an Electrician

Q. Do electricians make electricity?

A. No. Electricity is made in generating stations and carried to buildings through wires. Electricians work with wires to make sure the electricity moves safely.

Q. Don't electricians worry about electric shocks when they work?

A. Electricians must always turn off electricity to the wires they are working on. Electricity can be dangerous and safety is an important part of the job.

Q. What kind of training do you need to be an electrician?

A. Most electricians learn from experienced electricians while they are attending classes. During this period, they are called an apprentice.

Now It's Your Turn!

What question would you ask an electrician?

_____

_____

_____

Untangle the Wires!

For each circuit, explain what would happen when the switch at the bottom is closed.

Red: _____

Purple: _____

Green: _____

Orange: _____

Blue: _____

Multiple Choice

Identify the choice that best answers the question.

SC.5.P.11.1

1 A circuit diagram uses symbols to represent each part of the circuit. Look at the circuit diagram and the key shown below.

Light bulb

Battery

— Wire

What is the purpose of the wire in the circuit?

Ⓐ to use the electric current

Ⓑ to connect the components

Ⓒ to provide a source of electrical energy

Ⓓ to change the circuit from open to closed

SC.5.P.11.1, SC.5.N.1.1

2 During planning for an investigation, Harini draws four ways that she could connect a battery, a paper clip, a light bulb, and some wire. Which arrangement would light the bulb?

SC.5.P.11.1

3 Study the circuit below. When the switch is closed, all three light bulbs are lit.

What will happen if Bulb A burns out?

Ⓐ Bulbs B and C will continue to shine.

Ⓑ Bulbs B and C will stop shining.

Ⓒ Bulbs B and C will shine more brightly.

Ⓓ Bulbs B and C will shine less brightly.

SC.5.P.11.1

4 Gary built the circuit shown below.

Light bulb

Switch

Buzzer 1

What happened when Gary closed the switch?

Ⓕ The bulb lit, and the buzzer sounded at the same time.

Ⓖ Nothing happened because light bulbs and buzzers must be in different circuits.

Ⓗ Nothing happened because there was no source of electrical energy in the circuit.

Ⓘ Nothing happened because the circuit needed to have two switches.

SC.5.P.11.2, SC.5.N.2.1

5 Jayden uses various objects to complete a circuit. He compares how bright a bulb glows using each object. His results are shown below.

Object	Glow
nail	very bright
crayon	dim
eraser	very dim
pencil lead	bright

Which object is the **best** electrical conductor?

(A) nail

(B) eraser

(C) crayon

(D) pencil lead

SC.5.P.11.1

6 Which of the following will cause electric charges to no longer flow through a circuit?

(F) A wire is replaced with a conductor.

(G) A switch is flipped, causing the circuit to become closed.

(H) The circuit is changed so that the wires do not make a complete loop.

(I) The wires are changed so that a series circuit becomes a parallel circuit.

SC.5.P.11.1

7 The plastic coating was removed from the end of the wire shown below.

Copper wire

What is the purpose of the plastic coating?

(A) to carry electric current in a circuit

(B) to make the wire more flexible

(C) to insulate people or objects from the electric current in the wire

(D) to make it easier to tell when the wire is carrying electric current

SC.5.P.11.1

8 The circuit below consists of a battery, a light bulb, and three switches. All of the switches are open, and the light bulb is off.

Which combination of switches could be closed and cause the light bulb to remain off?

(F) X and Y

(G) Y and Z

(H) X and Z

(I) X, Y, and Z

SC.5.P.11.2

9 Study the materials in the table below.

Insulators	Conductors
air	gold
cloth	iron
silver	copper
bronze	glass
rubber	aluminum

Which are placed in the wrong column?

(A) air, copper, and glass

(B) iron, glass, and rubber

(C) bronze, glass, and iron

(D) silver, bronze, and glass

SC.5.P.10.4

10 A doorbell circuit includes a source of current, a bell, a button that switches the current on and off, and wires. What energy transformation occurs when the doorbell rings?

(F) electrical energy into light energy

(G) electrical energy into sound energy

(H) chemical energy into light energy

(I) mechanical energy into electrical energy

Forces and Motion

Big Idea 13

Forces and Changes in Motion

Daytona, FL

I Wonder Why

Why do the tires on the Daytona 500 cars look so much different than tires on a regular car? *Turn the page to find out.*

Here's Why The tires on race cars are smooth so they have a lot of contact with the track. Friction between the tires and the track helps keep the cars from sliding as they make fast turns.

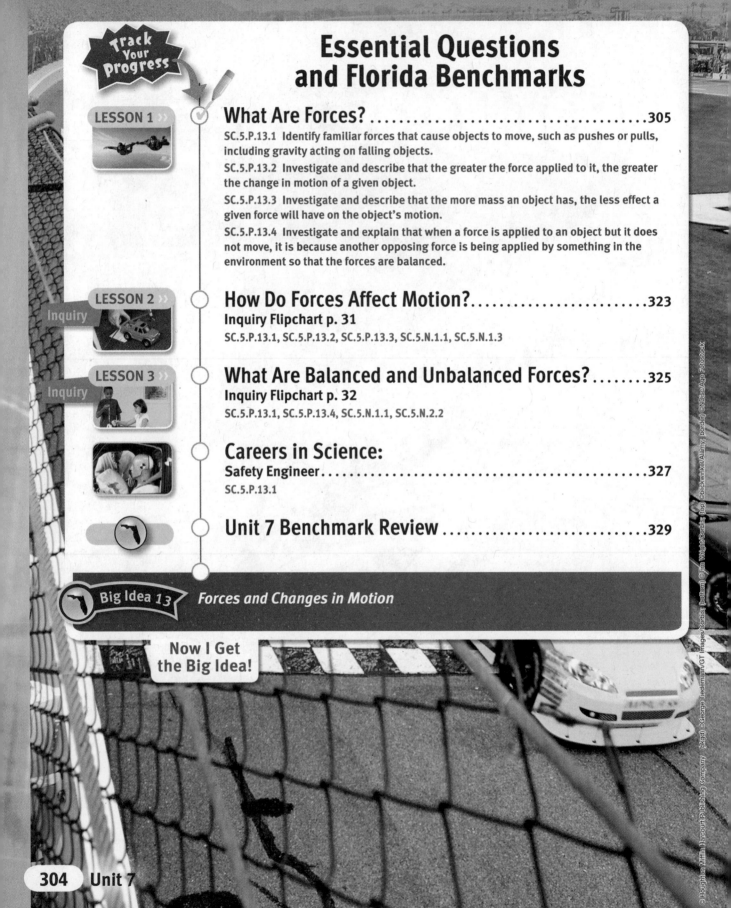

Track Your Progress

Essential Questions and Florida Benchmarks

Big Idea 13 *Forces and Changes in Motion*

Now I Get the Big Idea!

SC.5.P.13.1 Identify familiar forces that cause objects to move.... SC.5.P.13.2 ... the greater the force applied to it, the greater the change in motion of a given object. SC.5.P.13.3 ... the more mass an object has, the less effect a given force will have on the object's motion. SC.5.P.13.4 ... when a force is applied to an object but it does not move, ... another opposing force is being applied ... so that the forces are balanced.

Lesson 1

Essential Question

What Are Forces?

Engage Your Brain!

As you read the lesson, figure out the answer to the following question. Write the answer here.

What forces are acting on this cyclist? Are all the forces balanced?

_____

_____

_____

_____

_____

_____

Active Reading

Lesson Vocabulary

List the terms. As you learn about each one, make notes in the Interactive Glossary.

_____   _____

_____   _____

_____

Cause and Effect

Some ideas in this lesson are connected by a cause-and-effect relationship. Why something happens is a cause. What happens as a result of something else is an effect. Active readers look for effects by asking themselves, What happened? They look for causes by asking, Why did it happen?

PUSHING and Pulling

You pull on a door to open it. You lift up a backpack. You push on the pedals of a bike to go faster. What is the relationship between force and motion?

Active Reading As you read this page, underline the effects a force can have on an object.

The horse and the road it is on both exert a force on the cart.

▶ Draw an arrow that shows the direction of the force applied to the cart by the horse.

Changes in motion all have one thing in common. They require a **force**, which is a push or a pull. Forces can cause an object at rest to move. They can cause a moving object to speed up, slow down, change direction, or stop. Forces can also change an object's shape.

Forces are measured with a spring scale in units called newtons (N). The larger the force, the greater the change it can cause to the motion of an object. Smaller forces cause smaller changes. Sometimes more than one force can act together in a way that does not cause a change in motion.

When the rowers pull back on the oars, the oars push against the water.

▶ Weight is a measure of the force that gravity exerts on an object. You can measure weight with a spring scale. Record the weight shown on each spring scale in the spaces below.

_____

_____

The water pushes back against the oars. This force causes the boat to move.

When the ball hits the floor, the force of the floor makes the ball stop and change its direction of movement. When the ball hits the player's hand, the same thing happens.

TWO COMMON
Forces

What do the skydivers and some of the flower petals have in common? They are both falling! What causes this?

Active Reading As you read these pages, circle the sentence that describes a force that causes things to slow down.

▶ Draw an arrow showing the direction of the gravitational force between Earth and the falling flower petals.

→ Gravity

Gravity is a force of attraction between two objects. The size of this force increases as the mass of the objects increases. It decreases as the distance between the objects increases. Gravity acts on objects even if they are not touching.

Large objects such as Earth cause smaller objects, such as the skydivers, to accelerate quickly. We expect to see things fall toward Earth. However, the force of attraction is the same on both objects. If you place two objects with the same mass in outer space, they will move toward one another. If one object is "above" the other, the bottom object will appear to "fall up" as the other "falls down"!

Friction changes the energy of motion into thermal energy. When you use sandpaper to smooth wood, you can feel the temperature rise.

→ Friction

Is it easier to ride your bike on a smooth road or on a muddy trail? Why?

Friction is a force that opposes motion. Friction acts between two objects that are touching, such as the bike tires and the road. Friction can also exist between air and a moving object. This is called air resistance.

It is easy to slide across smooth ice because it doesn't have much friction. Pulling something across rough sandpaper is a lot harder because there is lots of friction.

An air hockey table blows air upward. This layer of air reduces the surface friction, so the pieces move quickly.

▶ In the pictures on this page, circle the places where there is friction between two objects. In the small boxes, write *Inc* if the object is designed to increase friction and *Dec* if the object is designed to decrease friction.

The tires on this bike are designed to keep the rider from slipping. You have to pedal harder on a rough surface to overcome the force of friction.

BALANCED
or Unbalanced?

The tug-of-war teams are both applying
forces. So why isn't anyone moving?

Active Reading Draw a circle around a sentence that explains
why objects don't always move when a force is applied.

When you sit on a chair, the force of gravity pulls you down. The
chair pushes you up. You stay in one place because the forces
on you are balanced. **Balanced forces** are forces on an object that are
equal in size and opposite in direction. They cancel each other out.

The tug-of-war teams in the picture don't move because the forces
are balanced. Friction keeps them from sliding. They
won't move until one side exerts a larger force.
Then, the forces are no longer balanced.
Unbalanced forces are forces that cause a
change in motion. A force must also overcome
the force of friction before an object will move.

The push on the first domino was a(n) _____ force that caused it to fall into the next domino. As each domino fell, it transferred the force to the next domino.

When a plane flies at a constant velocity, all the forces on the plane are balanced. If they weren't, the plane would speed up, slow down, or gain or lose altitude.

The force exerted on this domino by the falling dominoes is balanced by the force of the box. Because the forces are _____, the domino doesn't fall.

▶ Are there any forces acting on the dominoes that have fallen? If so, are they balanced or unbalanced? How do you know?

_____

_____

_____

_____

The forces on the dominoes are _____ when they are standing upright. When a falling domino hits them, the forces become _____ and they fall.

PULL (or Push) Harder!

Would you expect a bunt in baseball to go out of the park? Why or why not?

Active Reading As you read, circle the sentences that explain the relationship between the size of a force and motion.

▶ Use forces to explain why the boy can't ring the bell.

_____

_____

_____

When the man swings the hammer, he exerts a force on a plate. The plate transfers the force to a piece of metal that rises up the column and rings the bell.

The boy swings the same kind of hammer at the same kind of machine. Why doesn't the metal hit the bell?

TEST YOUR STRENGTH

TEST YOUR STRENGTH

If you want to make the cue ball knock another ball into a pocket, you hit the cue ball with a lot of force. This large force makes the cue ball change its velocity, or accelerate, quickly. It has lots of energy to transfer to the other ball. The energy causes the other ball to accelerate.

The greater the force applied to the cue ball, the more force it can transfer to the other ball. A large force will cause a large change in the motion of the other ball. A small force will cause little change. Changes in velocity can also include changes in direction.

Do the Math!
Display Data in a Graph

Use the data in the table to make a graph that shows the relationship between the force applied to an object and its acceleration.

Force (N)	Acceleration (m/sec^2)
1	0.5
2	1
5	2.5
8	4
10	5

I'M NOT Moving!

It's easy to lift your empty backpack off the ground. Could you use the same force to lift it when it's full of books?

Active Reading As you read these pages, circle cause-and-effect signal words, such as *because*, *so*, or *therefore*.

The springs in the pictures all exert the same force on the balls, causing them to roll across the page. The ball with the least mass accelerates the fastest. Therefore, it travels the farthest. The same force causes a greater effect on an object with a small mass than an object with a larger mass.

▶ Rank the balls by writing *greatest*, *middle*, or *least* in the six blanks.

Foam Ball

mass: _____

acceleration: _____

Baseball

mass: _____

acceleration: _____

► Both drivers began to brake at the same time. The brakes applied the same force to the truck. Why did one truck take longer to stop?

_____

_____

_____

An object's acceleration depends on the object's mass and the force applied to it. The larger the force, the greater the acceleration is. Suppose you push a wagon gently. The wagon speeds up slowly. If you use more strength to push, then the wagon's speed changes quickly.

The less an object's mass is, the less force is needed to change its motion. It's easier to push an empty shopping cart than a full one. Light cars are used in drag races because a car with less mass speeds up faster than a car with more mass.

If you want to slide a heavy box across the floor faster, you have two options. You could take some items out of the box, which decreases its mass. Or you could have a friend help you, which increases the force you apply.

Steel Ball

mass: _____

acceleration: _____

How did I get to Mars?

LET'S GO to Mars!

How did an understanding of forces help to send a rover to Mars and safely land it there?

1 The first force you need is an unbalanced force to oppose Earth's gravity. A huge booster rocket produces nearly 900,000 N of force that accelerates the rocket upward.

2 After the booster rocket falls away, smaller rockets in the second stage fire. The rockets change the direction of the vehicle's motion and put it in orbit around Earth.

3 The third-stage rocket firing produces enough force to reach "escape velocity." Earth's gravity can no longer pull it back down. We're on our way!

► What forces act on the rocket while it's at rest on Earth's surface? Are they balanced or unbalanced?

_____

_____

_____

_____

Balanced

▶ At what points during the Rover's trip to Mars are the forces on it balanced?

_____

_____

_____

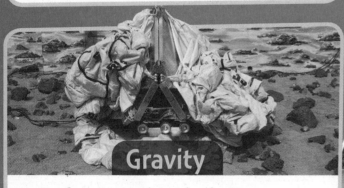

Unbalanced

▶ What unbalanced forces are acting on the Rover as it parachutes toward Mars?

_____

_____

_____

Gravity

▶ Use forces to explain why the Rover required a parachute and "air bags."

_____

_____

_____

uring much of the time it takes the spacecraft to travel to Mars, it travels at a constant velocity. The forces acting on the spacecraft are balanced, so its motion does not change.

Tiny rockets occasionally fire to keep the spacecraft on course. During these times, the forces are unbalanced.

As the spacecraft approaches Mars, gravitational attraction begins to accelerate it toward the surface. Like a person jumping from a plane, the spacecraft releases the Rover. Parachutes open to slow its fall. Then a big ball inflates around the Rover. When the Rover hits the surface of Mars, it bounces around until it comes safely to rest.

Mars Rover air bag testing

When you're done, use the answer key to check and revise your work.

Change the part of the summary in blue to make it correct.

1. Forces are pushes and pulls that increase the speed of objects.

_____

_____

2. Gravity is the force of attraction between a planet and another object.

_____

_____

3. An object moving through the air slows down because it is affected by the force of gravity.

_____

_____

4. When balanced forces act on an object, the object falls.

_____

_____

5. In order for an object to change its speed or direction, someone has to push it.

_____

_____

Answer Key: 1. can change the motion or shape of objects 2. any two objects 3. the force of friction 4. doesn't change its motion 5. an unbalanced force must act on it

© Houghton Mifflin Harcourt Publishing Company

Name _____

Word Play

1 A foreign-language teacher placed words from other languages into the following sentences. For each sentence, write the English word that means the same as the foreign word. Then use the circled letters to complete the riddle.

1. **Italian**
A push is an example of a forza. Another example is a pull.

_ ⬡ _ ⬡ _
   11 3

2. **French**
The force of attraction between Earth and objects on its surface is pesanteur.

_ ⬡ _ _ _ _ _
 8

3. **Russian**
The force between two moving objects that are touching is Трелие.

⬡ _ _ _ _ ⬡ _
4   7

4. **German**
Two forces that are equal in size but opposite in direction are ausgeglichene Kräfte.

_ _ _ _ _ ⬡ _ _ _ _ ⬡ _ _ ⬡
         10   5   9

5. **Portuguese**
Two forces that are not equal in size are Forças desequilibradas.

⬡ _ _ _ _ _ _ _ _ _ _ _ ⬡ _
2   6

6. **Chinese**
A 彈簧秤 is a tool that can be used to measure the size of a force.

⬡ _ _ _ _ _ ⬡ _ _ ⬡
1   12   13

Riddle: What conclusion did the student draw?

The _ _ o _ r _ e of the _ _ o _ c _ is the h _ _ _ _ _ e, of _ _ _ u r _ _ _.
    1 2 3   4 5 6   7 8 9   10 11   12 13

Try saying that five times fast!

Apply Concepts

2 Draw pictures of two activities that you might do. In the first, draw a pushing force. In the second, draw a pulling force.

> pushing force

> pulling force

3 The golfer applied a force when he hit the ball. Describe at least two forces acting on the ball as it rolls. Draw arrows to show the forces.

_____

_____

_____

4 Two students are using a catapult to try and hit a target. The catapult has only one setting. The first time they tried, they used Rock B. Which of the remaining rocks is likely to come closer to the target? Why?

_____

_____

_____

5 Use the words *balanced* and *unbalanced* as you name and describe the forces acting in each of these pictures.

a.
accelerating

b.

c.

_____   _____   _____

_____   _____   _____

_____   _____   _____

_____   _____   _____

6 Draw what will happen to a ball that you throw straight up into the air. Explain why this happens.

_____

_____

_____

_____

_____

7 Explain why it is easy to slip on a floor that is wet.

_____

_____

_____

_____

8 Look at the drawings to the right. Mary measured the distance each ball traveled. Draw lines to match the ball with the distance it traveled.

Explain why each ball traveled a different distance.

25 cm

15 cm

20 cm

_____

_____

_____

9 Give an example of each of the following.

a. A force is applied but nothing happens.

_____

b. A force causes an object to change shape.

_____

c. A force causes an object to change position.

_____

d. A force causes an object to stop moving.

_____

10 Circle the object(s) whose velocities are not changing. Draw an up arrow next to the object(s) whose speeds are increasing. Draw a down arrow next to the object(s) whose speeds are decreasing.

A car travels 35 miles per hour around a bend in the road.

A car comes to a stop when a traffic light turns red.

A race car accelerates when a race begins.

A car is driving 45 miles per hour down a straight road.

Take It Home! Discuss with your family what you've learned about forces. Together, identify five forces that you use to change the motion of objects in your everyday life. Consider forces that weren't discussed in the lesson.

Name _____

SC.5.N.1.1 … plan and carry out scientific investigations…. SC.5.N.1.3 Recognize and explain the need for repeated experimental trials. SC.5.P.13.1 Identify familiar forces that cause objects to move…. SC.5.P.13.2 Investigate and describe that the greater the force applied to it, the greater the change in motion of a given object. SC.5.P.13.3 Investigate and describe that the more mass an object has, the less effect a given force will have on the object's motion.

Essential Question

How Do Forces Affect Motion?

Set a Purpose
What will you learn from this experiment?

_____

_____

_____

State Your Hypothesis
Write your hypothesis, or testable statement.

_____

_____

_____

_____

_____

Think About the Procedure
Why do you use a rubber band to start the cars rather than your hand?

_____

_____

_____

_____

Why do you add bolts to the car?

_____

_____

_____

_____

Record Your Data
In the table below, record the data you gathered.

How Forces Affect Motion						
Part I:	Distance rubber band was stretched					
	1 cm		3 cm		5 cm	
Distance traveled (cm)						
Part II: Rubber band stretched to 3 cm						
	Empty car		Car with 4 bolts		Car with 8 bolts	
Distance traveled (cm) Trial 1						
Distance traveled (cm) Trial 2						
Distance traveled (cm) Trial 3						

Draw Conclusions

Each time you changed a variable and launched the car, you ran three trials. Calculate the average distance traveled by the car in each experimental setting.

Experimental Settings	Average distance traveled (cm)
Rubber band at 1 cm	
Rubber band at 3 cm	
Rubber band at 5 cm	
Car with 0 bolts	
Car with 4 bolts	
Car with 8 bolts	

Draw two bar graphs to display your data.

Analyze and Extend

1. Interpret your data. How is an object's mass related to its change in motion when acted on by a force?

_____

_____

_____

2. How does the size of the force applied to an object affect its motion?

_____

_____

_____

3. Why is it important to repeat an experiment several times or to have several people perform the same experiment?

_____

_____

_____

_____

4. Write another question you could ask about using forces and motion. What experiment could you do to answer your question?

_____

_____

_____

_____

_____

_____

Name _____

SC.5.N.1.1 ... plan and carry out scientific investigations of various types....
SC.5.N.2.2 ... evidence produced by ... investigations should be replicable by others.
SC.5.P.13.1 Identify familiar forces that cause objects to move, such as pushes or pulls, including gravity acting on falling objects.
SC.5.P.13.4 Investigate and explain that when a force is applied to an object but it does not move, it is because another opposing force is being applied by something in the environment so that the forces are balanced.

Essential Question

What Are Balanced and Unbalanced Forces?

Set a Purpose
What will you learn from this investigation?

_____

_____

_____

_____

Think About the Procedure
What forces are acting on the blocks when they are sitting on the table?

_____

_____

_____

_____

Why will you pull the block across several different surfaces?

_____

_____

_____

Record Your Data
Record your measurements in this table.

Forces Investigation	
Action	**Force (N)**
Lift one block	
Lift two blocks	
Lift three blocks	
Pull block on sandpaper	
Pull block on waxed paper	
Pull block on oiled paper	

Draw Conclusions
What is required to start an object moving?

_____

_____

_____

Analyze and Extend

1. The block below is being pulled to the right. Draw arrows to show the forces acting on the object. Label each arrow.

2. At what point during this activity were the forces on the block balanced? Draw the block, and show the forces as arrows.

3. How is an object's mass related to the upward force needed to overcome the pull of gravity?

_____

_____

_____

_____

4. What forces acted on the block as you tried to pull it horizontally? Were the forces balanced or unbalanced?

_____

_____

_____

_____

_____

_____

5. Why did the blocks require a different force to begin moving on the three different surfaces?

_____

_____

_____

_____

6. What other questions would you like to ask about balanced and unbalanced forces? What investigations could you do to answer the questions?

_____

_____

_____

_____

_____

_____

_____

_____

1 A safety engineer helps design and test devices to make them safer.

2 Safety engineers make changes to designs to avoid possible dangers.

3 I'm a crash test dummy. Some safety engineers use me as a model.

10 THINGS TO KNOW ABOUT Safety Engineers

4 Safety engineers can make machines, such as cars, safer to use.

5 Safety engineers make cars safer with inventions such as seat belts and air bags.

6 Some safety engineers focus on stopping specific dangers, such as fires.

7 Safety engineers help society have fewer injuries and illnesses.

8 Some keep germs from spreading into our food and making us sick.

9 They may focus on protecting workers from getting hurt on the job.

10 To do their jobs, safety engineers need to study physics, chemistry, math, and human behavior.

Now You Be the Engineer!

1 What do you think is the best thing about being a safety engineer?

2 How do safety engineers help society?

3 What safety features in cars have safety engineers helped to develop?

4 What question would you like to ask a safety engineer?

1 _____

2 _____

3 _____

4 _____

Multiple Choice

Identify the choice that best answers the question.

SC.5.P.13.3, SC.5.N.2.1

1 Suri places magnets on three identical toy cars, as shown below. Then, Suri measures how far each car rolls when she launches it from the same starting point using the same stretched rubber band.

Car 1   Car 2   Car 3

How will the force of the rubber band affect the cars?

Ⓐ Car 3 will travel the longest distance.

Ⓑ Car 1 will travel the shortest distance.

Ⓒ Car 1 will be the least affected by the force acting upon it.

Ⓓ Car 3 will be the least affected by the force acting upon it.

SC.5.P.13.1

2 When you coast down a hill on a bicycle, you move faster and faster. Then when you keep coasting on a level surface, you eventually stop moving. What causes you to stop?

Ⓕ No force is acting on your bike on the level surface, so it stops moving.

Ⓖ After you reach the bottom of the hill, you run out of energy, so you stop moving.

Ⓗ Friction between the tires and the ground is an unbalanced force that changes your motion.

Ⓘ Gravity affects you when you move downhill, but there is not gravity when you move on a level surface.

SC.5.P.13.3

3 Katie uses all her force to push a bowling ball away from her body. Then, Katie repeats the same procedure with a soccer ball. How does the movement of the two balls contrast?

Ⓐ The soccer ball moves a greater distance because more force is acting on it.

Ⓑ The soccer ball moves a greater distance because it has less mass.

Ⓒ The bowling ball moves a greater distance because it has more mass.

Ⓓ The bowling ball moves a shorter distance because less force is acting on it.

SC.5.P.13.1

4 A spring scale measures force.

What is the force that causes the reading on the spring scale shown in the illustration?

Ⓕ friction   Ⓗ gravity

Ⓖ mass   Ⓘ weight

SC.5.P.13.4

5 Four forces are acting on the block shown in the following illustration:

- *F* is the applied force.
- F_f is friction.
- F_g is the gravitational force.
- F_n is the normal force—the upward push of the table on the block.

If a force *F* is applied to the block and it does not move, which statement is true?

(A) *F* and F_f are equal.
(B) *F* and F_g are equal.
(C) F_f is greater than *F*.
(D) F_g is greater than *F*.

SC.5.P.13.1, SC.5.N.1.1

6 A group of students measured the amount of force needed to move a weight across a dry plastic tabletop. Then they poured some water on the table and repeated the experiment on the wet surface. The students found that less force was needed to make the weight start moving on the wet surface than the dry surface. What caused the difference in the results of the two experiments?

(F) change in the amount of gravitational force on the weight
(G) change in the mass of the weight used in the experiment
(H) change in the friction between the weight and the surface
(I) change in the friction between the weight and the scale used to measure force

SC.5.P.13.4

7 Jean held a spring scale with a weight hanging on its hook. She observed that the force on the scale was 3 N. Why was the force greater than 0 N even though the weight was not moving?

(A) The 3-N force was balancing the force of gravity.
(B) The weight was not moving, but the forces on it were constantly changing.
(C) The spring scale was broken, so it showed 3 N even though the real force was zero.
(D) The 3-N force was the amount of unbalanced force on the weight.

SC.5.P.13.1

8 A crane raises and lowers objects and also moves them back and forth. The following illustration shows a crane lifting a heavy box.

What must the crane work against in order to lift the box upward?

(F) wind
(G) friction
(H) gravity
(I) cable tension

SC.5.P.13.3

9 The following table shows the masses of several different objects. You want to toss each object a distance of 2 meters.

Object	Metal washer	Plastic disk	Rock	Wooden block
Mass (g)	1.5	34	16	22

Which object will require the most force to toss it 2 meters?

(A) metal washer (C) plastic disk
(B) rock (D) wooden block

SC.5.P.13.4

10 The worker shown in the following illustration is pushing a box with a force, which is shown by the arrow. The box does not move.

What keeps the box from moving even though the worker is pushing on it?

(F) The worker is pushing the box in the wrong direction.

(G) There is too much air resistance for the box to move.

(H) The force of gravity opposes the force exerted by the worker.

(I) The force of friction opposes the force exerted by the worker.

SC.5.P.13.3, SC.5.N.1.5

11 The following table shows the masses of four blocks and the forces that are being applied to them.

Block color	Mass (g)	Pushing force (N)	Friction (N)
red	50	24	6
green	100	24	6
blue	40	24	6
yellow	75	24	6

Which block will have the **greatest** change in motion?

(A) red   (C) green

(B) blue   (D) yellow

SC.5.P.13.1

12 The following illustration shows the forces that are acting on a box.

What type of motion will the forces cause?

(F) The box will remain in its current position.

(G) The box will move downward in a straight line.

(H) The box will move to the right in a straight line.

(I) The box will move back and forth from the left to the right.

SC.5.P.13.2

13 Michael is watching the blades of a windmill spin. He decides to measure the speed of the spinning blades. Which of the following would cause the windmill's blades to spin at a slower speed?

(A) a decrease in the speed of the wind

(B) a decrease in the mass of the windmill's blades

(C) a decrease in friction by greasing the windmill's gears

(D) a decrease in the size and number of blades on the windmill

SC.5.P.13.1

14 For which of these surfaces will friction be **greatest** when a block of wood slides across it?

(F) wet ice   (H) glass mirror

(G) thick carpet   (I) waxed wood

SC.5.P.13.2

15 Two race cars with the same mass started moving on a race track at the same time. One car reached the finish line of the track in 15 sec, and the other reached the finish line in 20 sec. Why did the cars take different amounts of time to reach the finish line?

(A) The force of gravity slowed one car, but not the other car.

(B) The slower car did not experience any force, so it moved more slowly.

(C) The forces on one car were balanced and on the other car unbalanced.

(D) The engine of the faster car exerted more force than the engine of the other car.

SC.5.P.13.1

16 Which of these is an example of a force being applied?

(F) watching TV

(G) pulling a wagon

(H) reading a book

(I) standing at the top of a hill

SC.5.P.13.1

17 The spring scale shown in the following figure has a weight attached to it. When the weight was attached, the pointer on the scale moved downward.

What will happen if a second weight is added to the spring scale?

(A) The pointer will move upward because force is increased.

(B) The pointer will move upward because force is decreased.

(C) The pointer will move downward because force is increased.

(D) The pointer will move downward because force is decreased.

SC.5.P.13.4

18 A book is on top of a table. Earth's gravity exerts a constant force of 15 N on the book. Why does the book not move as a result of this force?

(F) The force of gravity is balanced by the force of friction.

(G) The force of gravity is balanced by an upward push of the table.

(H) The force of gravity is exerted on an object only when it is falling toward Earth.

(I) The force of gravity is a balanced force by itself, so it does not cause motion.

SC.5.P.13.2

19 An object is traveling in a straight line in space. No forces are affecting it. What will happen to the object's motion?

(A) It will move faster and faster because there is no force to stop it.

(B) It gradually will stop because there is no force to keep it moving.

(C) It will stop immediately when the force that started its motion goes away.

(D) It will not change. It will continue in the same direction at the same speed.

SC.5.P.13.1

20 A car was stuck in the mud. Two people pushed the car, but it did not move. Why did the car not move even though a force was exerted on it?

(F) Cars are too large to be affected by forces.

(G) A force in the opposite direction balanced the push.

(H) The people were not strong enough to exert a force on the car.

(I) The force of gravity is so strong that people cannot push hard enough to move a car.

The Structure of Living Things

Big Idea 14

Organization and Development of Living Organisms

Tampa Bay, FL

I Wonder Why

These football players are working hard and sweating. Why do athletes use sports drinks instead of just water? *Turn the page to find out.*

Here's Why When the body gets hot, sweat helps cool it down. Sweat is made up of water and salts. Salts are important to keep the body working. Sports drinks replace water and salts that are lost by sweating.

Track Your Progress

Essential Questions and Florida Benchmarks

Big Idea 14   *Organization and Development of Living Organisms*

Now I Get the Big Idea!

© Houghton Mifflin Harcourt Publishing Company (bkgd) ©Al Messerschmidt Archive/Getty Images; (cow) ©John Foxx

SC.5.L.14.1 Identify the organs in the human body and describe their functions, including the skin, brain and sensory organs.
SC.5.L.14.2 Compare and contrast the function of organs and other physical structures of plants and animals, including humans....

Lesson 1

What Are Organs and Body Systems?

Engage Your Brain!

Find the answer to the following question in this lesson and record it here.

What part of your body serves the same function as the part of the octopus shown here?

_____

_____

_____

_____

Active Reading

Lesson Vocabulary

List the terms. As you learn about each one, make notes in the Interactive Glossary.

_____   _____

_____   _____

_____

Main Ideas and Details

Detail sentences give information about a main idea. The information may include examples, features, characteristics, or facts. Active readers look for details that support the main idea.

Building a BODY

Your body has hundreds of different parts! These parts work together to keep you healthy.

Active Reading As you read these two pages, circle each lesson vocabulary term and underline its definition.

Every living thing needs certain things to survive. An **organism** is a living thing. It is made of parts that work together to meet its needs. Some parts are extremely small. Others are large.

An **organ** is a body part that is made up of smaller parts that work together to do a certain job. For example, your eye is an organ. It is made of a clear lens, a colored iris, and other parts that work together to enable you to see.

Groups of organs work together. An **organ system** is a group of organs that work together to do one type of job. Your mouth and stomach are part of one organ system. They work together to supply your body with energy from food. You have many organ systems in your body.

Eyes

Eyes are organs that help you _____. They send information about the world around you to another organ, your brain.

Teeth

Your teeth are bones, and bones are organs. What do teeth do?

_____

Muscles

Muscles are organs that help you _____. Messages from your brain tell your muscles what to do.

Animals are organisms. Plants are organisms, too. Did you know that plants have organs? Roots absorb nutrients and water for the plant. Leaves use sunlight to make food for the plant. Stems support the leaves. Stems also transport water from the roots and food from the leaves. A protective layer covers the plant and keeps the plant from drying out.

Like plants, humans have organs that work together to help us stand. We have an organ that protects us from drying out. We have organs that supply us with food. Plant and animal organs are different, but they are all alike in one way: They all help an organism meet its needs so it can live.

Match It!

▶ Draw a line to connect the plant part to an animal part that does a similar job.

Bones

Bones support your body. They enable you to stand. Each bone in your body is an organ.

Mouth

Your mouth brings food into your body. Your lips, teeth, and tongue work together to help you chew and swallow food.

Skin

What's the largest organ in your body? Your skin is. It protects your body from germs and keeps your body from drying out.

Bark

Stems

Leaves

The Information HIGHWAY

Keep your eye on the ball! In just seconds you can see a ball, run toward it, and swing a racket! How does the body relay all of the information needed to do this? Read on to find out.

Sensing your surroundings and communicating information within the body are the main jobs of your *nervous system*. Your nervous system is made of tiny structures called *nerve cells.* Chains of long nerve cells make up nerves. Nerves carry information to and from the **brain**. The brain is the organ that processes information. It's like a computer made of millions of nerve cells working together.

A rope-like bundle of nerves, called the *spinal cord,* runs along your backbone. Your spinal cord is the main pathway for information traveling to and from the brain. Nerves connect to your spinal cord from all over your body. Some of these nerves send information to the brain. Others receive signals from the brain.

Imagine that you're playing tennis. Nerves in your eyes sense light. These nerves, like other nerves in your head, send information directly to your brain without routing the signal through your spinal cord. You see the ball coming toward you. Your brain decides on an action. It sends instructions through your spinal cord to nerves in your body. The messages from your brain "tell" your legs to run across the court and your arms to swing the racket and hit the ball. All of this communication takes place in seconds!

Information Relay

Fill in the blanks to describe the path that a nerve signal might take in this tennis player.

1. The boy's _____ sense the ball coming toward him.

2. His _____ processes this information.

3. Messages from the _____ travel down the _____ _____.

4. _____ in his arms deliver the message from his brain to swing the racket.

SENSING Surroundings

A carnival is a feast of sights, sounds, tastes, and smells! How do you sense all of that information?

As you read this page, draw a box around phrases that describe sensory structures.

Senses are your body's way of gathering information about the world around you. Special structures in certain parts of your body can detect light, sound, and chemicals in the air and in the food you eat.

A **Sight:** The part of the eye that gives us our eye color is a muscle called the *iris.* Light enters the eye through a hole in the iris called the *pupil,* passes through the lens, and hits the back of the eye, called the *retina.* Inside the retina are special nerve cells that detect light. They send signals that travel along nerve pathways to the brain. The brain interprets this information and we see.

B **Hearing:** The part of your ear that you see is called your outer ear. The outer ear funnels sound into the middle ear. In the middle ear, sound causes the eardrum to vibrate. The vibrations are passed to tiny bones called the hammer, anvil, and stirrup. These bones pass vibrations to the inner ear. There, a fluid-filled structure called the cochlea [KOH•klee•uh] passes vibrations to tiny hairs attached to nerves. The nerves send messages about the vibrations to the brain, and you sense sound.

C **Smell:** When you breathe, air travels through your nose. Inside your nose are structures that sense chemicals in the air. They are attached to nerve cells in the olfactory bulb that send messages to the brain about the chemicals they sensed. This makes up your sense of smell.

D **Taste:** Have you ever noticed small bumps all over your tongue? These bumps are called *taste buds.* They sense the chemicals in food. Taste buds are attached to nerves that send messages to the brain about the chemicals they sense. The brain interprets this information as the sense of taste.

A Eyes

Light enters the eye through the _____, passes through the _____, and hits the _____, where special structures detect _____.

pupil

lens →
← retina

iris

B Ears

Sound enters the ear. Vibrations pass from the _____ to tiny bones, through the _____, to tiny hairs attached to nerves.

eardrum

hammer
anvil

outer ear
stirrup
cochlea

C Nose

When you breathe, structures in the nose detect _____ that are carried in the air.

olfactory bulb
↓

nasal passages

D Tongue

When food enters the mouth, special structures on the tongue sense _____ in food. These structures are called _____ _____.

taste buds

Sensory
OVERLOAD

All organisms have sensory structures that help them survive. Flies have compound eyes. Instead of 1 lens, they have over 5,000!

Active Reading As you read these two pages, find and underline four facts about plant and animal senses.

Animal Senses

Draw an animal that you are familiar with. Label its sensory organs, and describe how it uses them.

Sight

Snails have their eyes on the ends of stalks. The eyespots can sense light and dark. You can see eyespots on the tip of each eyestalk shown here.

Sound

Bats "see" with their ears! They make squeaking noises and listen for the sounds to echo back to them. The way the sound bounces and the amount of time it takes for the sound to return let the bat know what is in its path. Dolphins use a very similar system under water.

Smell

Moths have "noses" on the tops of their heads. The moth's antennae [an•TEN•ee] have structures that sense chemicals in the air.

Touch

The Venus' flytrap has special leaves that are sensitive to touch. When a fly lands on them, the fly touches trigger hairs. The hairs send a message to the leaves of the plant, and the leaves snap shut. The fly is trapped!

The SKIN You're In

Some people don't think of skin as an organ, but it is. Our bodies couldn't survive without it.

Covering your body is a protective layer called **skin**. Skin is part of the *integumentary* [in•teg•yoo•MEN•ter•ee] *system*. Fingernails, toenails, and hair are, too. This system helps to protect the inside of your body.

Skin keeps germs out. If you've ever had a cut that got infected, you know how important it is to keep germs from entering your body. At the same time, skin keeps water in. Your waterproof skin keeps you from becoming dehydrated.

What happens when you get too hot? Sweat helps cool your body. Also, tiny blood vessels near the surface of the skin help to cool your blood.

But what if you get cold? Hair helps to keep your head warm in cold weather. Hair also helps to protect your scalp from injury and shades your scalp from the sun's harmful rays.

Fingerprinting

Draw your own friction ridges in the circles at the tips of these fingers.

Epidermis

This is the outer layer of the skin. It is thin in some places, like your eyelids, and thick in others.

Dermis

This is the inner layer of the skin. It contains hair follicles, sweat glands, blood vessels, and nerve endings.

Nerve endings

These are special structures that sense touch, heat, cold, pain, pressure, and vibration.

hair

oil gland

blood vessels

sweat gland

fat

Look at your fingers. Do you see swirls, loops and waves? These are friction ridges, which form your fingerprints. They allow your fingers to be more sensitive to touch.

Plant and Animal COVERINGS

Would you want to pet a cactus? There are many different kinds of plant and animal coverings. They all protect the plant or animal.

Active Reading Circle the different types of plant and animal coverings that are listed below.

Take a look at the examples of animal coverings on these pages. Can you identify them? Animals such as monkeys, horses, and rabbits are covered in soft fur. Birds are covered with feathers. Fish and snakes are covered in scales. Some animals, such as lobsters and turtles, have hard shells.

Plants do not have skin, but they do have special coverings. Many trees are covered with a thick, hard bark to protect the inner plant. Plant leaves have a waxy coating that keeps the plant from drying out.

Even though plant and animal coverings may look different, they still protect the organisms from predators, disease, injury, and drying out.

These colorful feathers cover the bird's skin. They keep the bird warm and keep water out. Feathers on the wing help the bird fly.

tree bark

Plant leaves have a waxy coating that helps keep the plant from drying out when the weather is hot and dry.

Ouch! This cactus has sharp spines that keep predators away.

Do the Math!
Use a Scale

scale = 1 centimeter

Look at these magnified belly scales from a green tree snake. The black line on the picture is also called a scale. It shows how many belly scales are in 1 centimeter. If the snake is 1 meter long, how many belly scales would the snake have?

_____

_____

_____

This monkey has thick fur. Fur helps to keep the monkey warm in cold weather.

When you're done, use the answer key to check and revise your work.

Fill in the blanks in the following sentences.

1

All living things are called (a)_____ .

An (b)_____ is a body part that does a certain job in the body.

Several of these parts work together to make up an (c)_____ _____ .

Read the summary statements. Match each statement with the correct image.

A.

B.

C.

D.

E.

2 The brain, spinal cord, and nerves form the nervous system. The nervous system senses the environment, sends information to the brain, processes information, and sends instructions to the body.

3 The eyes, ears, nose, and tongue are sense organs. They have special parts that sense the environment.

4 Skin, hair, and nails are part of the human integumentary system. It protects internal organs, helps maintain body temperature, and provides waterproofing.

5 Plants and animals have specialized organs for sensing the environment, like compound eyes, antennae, and trigger hairs.

6 Plants and animals have special body coverings such as bark, fur, feathers, quills, scales, and shells.

Brain Check

Lesson **1**

Name _____

Word Play

1 Unscramble the words on the right to fill in the blanks in each sentence.

1. The __ __ __ __ __ __ __ system sends messages throughout your body.	s r n u o e v
2. The __ __ __ __ __ __ __ __ __ __ __ __ __ __ system protects the body's organs.	n e n i g e m t t a y r u
3. An __ __ __ __ __ __ __ __ is a living thing. It is made up of parts that work together.	s n g m a r o i
4. The __ __ __ __ is the largest organ in the body. It covers and protects the other organs.	i n k s
5. The __ __ __ __ __ receives messages from the body, processes the information, and sends instructions to the body.	r b i n a
6. An __ __ __ __ __ system is a group of organs that work together to do a job.	o g n r a
7. __ __ __ __ __ __ __ __ are used by moths to "smell" the world around them.	e t n n n e a a
8. The __ __ __ __ __ __ include sight, taste, smell, hearing, and touch.	s s s e e n

Bonus: How many body parts can you think of that have only three letters?

_____   _____

_____   _____

_____   _____

_____   _____

_____

Apply Concepts

2 Some areas of the body have more sensory structures than others. Which do you think would have more? For each pair of body parts, circle the one you think would have more sensory structures. Then state your reason.

Why? _____

_____

Why? _____

_____

_____

_____

_____

_____

3 Draw a line to connect the animal to the description of its senses.

Have "noses" on their antennae to "smell" the air

Has compound eyes on moveable eyestalks

Uses a sonar system to find objects in water

4 How are the senses of taste and smell alike?

_____

_____

_____

_____

5 Which of the following structures is used to sense touch?

a. eyestalk

b. antenna

c. trigger hair

d. compound eye

Take It Home!

Make a model of the nervous system using items around the house, such as string and cardboard tubes. Explain to your family members what each part represents and how messages travel.

SC.5.N.1.4 Identify a control group and explain its importance in an experiment. SC.5.N.1.6 Recognize and explain the difference between personal opinion/ interpretation and verified observation. SC.5.L.14.1 Identify the organs in the human body and describe their functions, including the skin....

Name _____

Essential Question

How Does the Body Stay Cool?

Set a Purpose
What will you learn from this experiment?

_____

_____

_____

State Your Hypothesis
Write your hypothesis, or testable statement.

_____

_____

_____

Think About the Procedure
Which sample is the control? What is its purpose?

_____

_____

_____

Record Your Data
Record your observations in a data table.

Draw Conclusions
How did your results compare with your hypothesis?

_____

_____

_____

_____

Analyze and Extend

1. What was the difference between the starting temperature and the ending temperature for each of your experimental groups? Show your work in the space below.

_____

_____

_____

_____

2. Make a bar graph in the space below to display your data.

_____

3. How does this activity relate to the role of sweating?

_____

_____

_____

4. A swamp cooler is a type of air conditioner that blows air over a wet surface. Use your data to explain whether you think this would be an effective way to cool a building.

_____

_____

_____

_____

5. Why is it important that your body be able to cool itself?

_____

_____

_____

_____

_____

6. Think of other questions you would like to ask about evaporation and cooling.

_____

_____

_____

_____

_____

SC.5.L.14.1 Identify the organs in the human body and describe their functions, including the … brain, heart, lungs … muscles and skeleton…. **SC.5.L.14.2** Compare and contrast the function of organs and other … structures of plants and animals, including humans, for example: some animals have skeletons for support—some with internal skeletons others with exoskeletons—while some plants have stems for support.

Lesson **3**

Essential Question

What Body Parts Enable Movement, Support, Respiration, and Circulation?

Engage Your Brain!

Find the answer to the following question in this lesson and record it here.

What is the difference between you and an animal that can breathe underwater?

_____

_____

_____

Active Reading

Lesson Vocabulary
List the terms. As you learn about each one, make notes in the Interactive Glossary.

_____   _____

_____   _____

_____

Main Ideas
The main idea of a paragraph is the most important idea. The main idea may be stated in the first sentence, or it may be stated elsewhere. Active readers look for main ideas by asking themselves, What is this section mostly about?

Strong Bones and Mighty Muscles

What would your body be like without bones and muscles? Your body would be a shapeless blob!

Active Reading As you read these two pages, draw two lines under each main idea.

Organs that support and protect the body and store minerals are called **bones**. The ribs and skull are bones that protect internal organs. Bones attached to muscles help move the body. Bones have a hard outer layer that contains calcium. Inside bones is a spongy layer where blood cells are made.

The place where two or more bones meet is called a joint. Some joints, like the joints in your skull, don't allow the bones to move. Others joints, like the joint in your shoulder or knee, allow different types of movement. *Ligaments* [LIG•uh•muhntz] connect the bones of a joint.

Feel the tip of your nose. This is cartilage. Cartilage cushions the ends of bones and forms flexible parts like your ears and nose. Bones, ligaments, and cartilage form the *skeletal system*.

What Do Bones Do?

- support the body
- anchor muscles
- protect internal organs
- store minerals like calcium
- make blood cells

354

Muscles often work in pairs. When one muscle contracts, the other muscle in the pair relaxes. Cooperation allows the contracting muscle to move the bone that it's attached to. When the opposite muscle contracts, the first muscle relaxes. What happens if both muscles contract at the same time?

Let's Get Moving

Circle the muscle that bends your arm.

Muscles are organs that contract to produce movement in the body. There are three different types of muscles. The heart is made of one type of muscle. Another type makes up the walls of blood vessels and organs. Still another type of muscle pulls our bones to help us move.

The major function of the *muscular system* is to produce movement in the body. You control some movements, like running. These movements are *voluntary*. Other movements, like the beating of your heart, happen without your having to think about them. These are *involuntary* movements.

Strength and Motion

Like humans, plants and animals have systems that support their bodies and allow them to move.

Sunflower blooms can be over two feet wide! The thick stem helps to support the heavy flower at the top. The flower and leaves slowly turn throughout the day to follow the movement of the sun across the sky.

Cicadas [si•KAY•duhz] have a hard outer layer, called an **exoskeleton**. It's like having bones outside their bodies. Exoskeletons help protect them from being eaten. Their muscles are attached to their exoskeletons and move their bodies by pulling from the inside. As cicadas grow, they shed the old exoskeleton. Underneath is a new one.

A Hardened Life

How would your life be different if you had an exoskeleton?

_____

_____

_____

The seal's flexible body lets it glide through water. Its flippers help it swim.

Sea stars use water in tiny tubes, called tube feet, to move. Muscles squeeze water into and out of the tubes, causing the tube feet to move. Suction cups on the ends of the feet help the sea star grip surfaces.

This sensitive plant responds to touch by closing its leaves.

357

Breathe In, Breathe Out

Take a deep breath. Do you feel "inspired"? You should. *Inspire* is another word for breathing in. Breathing out is called *expiring*.

Active Reading As you read the text below, draw boxes around the five parts of the respiratory system that are described.

Organs in the *respiratory system* bring in oxygen that the body needs and release carbon dioxide, the body's waste gas. The main organs of the respiratory system are the **lungs**. Lungs are spongy organs that expand to fill with air.

Air enters your body through your nose or mouth. It flows through a tube in your throat called the *trachea* [TRAY•kee•uh]. The trachea branches into two smaller tubes called bronchi [BRAHNG•ky]. Where the bronchi enter the lungs, they branch into many bronchioles [BRAHNG•kee•ohlz]. At the end of each bronchiole are tiny sacs called alveoli [al•VEE•uh•ly]. Alveoli make up most of the lungs. When you inhale (breathe in), air flows into the lungs and the alveoli inflate like tiny balloons. When you exhale (breathe out) air flows back out of the alveoli and out of the lungs.

Do the Math!
Solve Word Problems

On average, a person breathes about 20 times per minute.

There are 60 minutes in an hour. How many times does a person breathe in one hour? _____

_____

There are 24 hours in a day. How many times does a person breathe every day?

_____

If you take in about 1 liter of air with each breath, how much air passes through your lungs every day?

_____

358

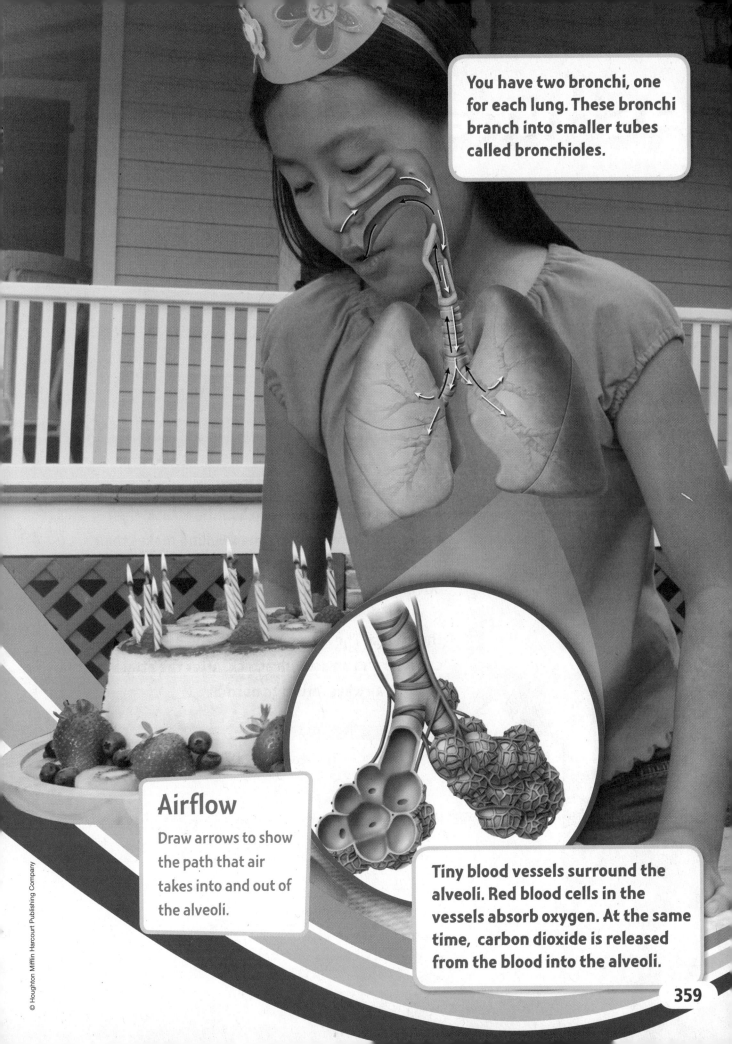

You have two bronchi, one for each lung. These bronchi branch into smaller tubes called bronchioles.

Airflow

Draw arrows to show the path that air takes into and out of the alveoli.

Tiny blood vessels surround the alveoli. Red blood cells in the vessels absorb oxygen. At the same time, carbon dioxide is released from the blood into the alveoli.

Asthma Attack

Asthma is an illness that makes it hard for a person to breathe. During an attack, some kids say it feels like breathing through a straw.

Active Reading As you read these two pages, draw a star next to what you consider to be the most important sentence, and be ready to explain why.

Constricted Airways

When people are having an asthma attack, their bronchi become swollen. The swelling makes their airways smaller. It is much harder to get air in and out of the lungs. People having an asthma attack may cough, wheeze, or feel like a weight is sitting on their chest. They struggle to breathe. Medication can help end an asthma attack. After the attack, a person's airways return to normal.

▶ Fill in the sequence of events that lead to an asthma attack.

| Asthma trigger enters airway | → | Airway becomes irritated | → | Bronchi become _____ |

| Airways become smaller | → | It becomes difficult to _____ |

Pollen from plants can trigger an asthma attack.

Air pollution can trigger attacks.

Normal bronchi are open wide. Air can flow easily.

Constricted bronchi are smaller, making it difficult for air to pass through.

Triggers

The exact causes of asthma aren't known. Many people are born with it, but people sometimes develop asthma as they get older. Doctors do know that there are things that can cause an asthma attack. These things are called asthma triggers. Smoke, air pollution, and allergies are all possible triggers that start the process of an asthma attack.

Management

People who have asthma try to avoid things in the air that trigger attacks. However, a person can't always avoid triggers such as pollen or air pollution. A doctor can give people who suffer from asthma a device called an inhaler. An inhaler releases a mist of medicine that a person breathes in. This medicine can help open up airways during an attack. Other types of medicine help to prevent asthma attacks.

Beat It

Your heart is a powerful muscle. It never rests! The drum-like sound of your heart's contractions is called your heartbeat.

Active Reading As you read these two pages, underline the four parts of blood and their jobs.

Your **heart** is a muscular organ that pumps blood throughout your body. It contracts in two phases. When the top part is relaxed, it fills with blood. Then the top contracts and the bottom relaxes. Blood is squeezed into the lower part of the heart. The lower part contracts and squeezes blood out of the heart, into vessels, and to all parts of the body.

Blood is made up of a clear liquid called plasma and small structures called blood cells. There are three main types of blood cells—red cells, white cells, and platelets.

Arteries are blood vessels that carry blood away from the heart to different parts of the body. Veins are blood vessels that bring blood back to the heart from the lungs and the body. Capillaries [KAP•uh•lair•eez] are tiny vessels with very thin walls. Oxygen and nutrients can pass through capillary walls to the body. Carbon dioxide passes from the body, through capillary walls, and into the blood to be carried back to the lungs.

The heart, vessels, and blood are all part of the *circulatory system*.

Red blood cells carry oxygen throughout your body.

White blood cells help fight disease.

Platelets stop bleeding by sticking together and forming clots.

Plasma carries nutrients and blood cells throughout the body.

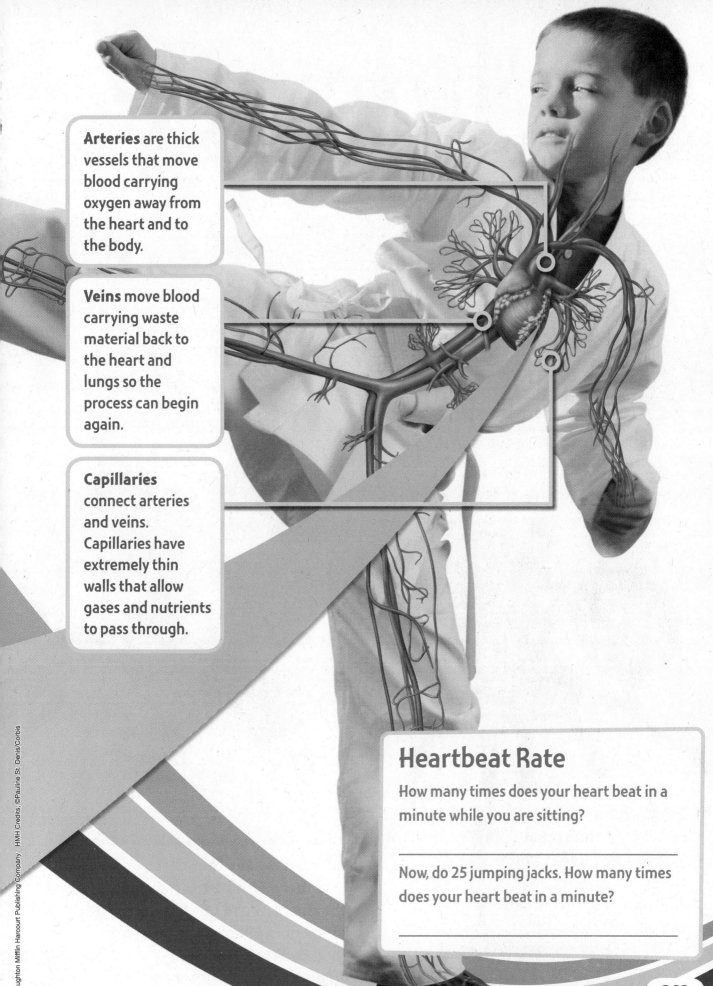

Arteries are thick vessels that move blood carrying oxygen away from the heart and to the body.

Veins move blood carrying waste material back to the heart and lungs so the process can begin again.

Capillaries connect arteries and veins. Capillaries have extremely thin walls that allow gases and nutrients to pass through.

Heartbeat Rate

How many times does your heart beat in a minute while you are sitting?

_____

Now, do 25 jumping jacks. How many times does your heart beat in a minute?

_____

Got Lungs?

Respiration and circulation may look very different in plants and animals, but these systems still have the same purposes.

Circulation or Respiration?

Write a C or an R in the circle next to each picture to tell whether circulation or respiration is being described.

Fish cannot breathe in air. Instead, they have special structures called gills that can take oxygen from water.

Spiders have structures called book lungs that look like tiny books whose pages can fill with air. Book lungs bring oxygen to the spider's blood.

Our hearts have four parts, or chambers. Fish hearts have only two chambers. Blood goes from the heart to the gills, then to the body, and then back to the heart.

lungs

air sacs

Birds use huge amounts of energy to fly. They also use a lot of oxygen. To keep air flowing through their lungs constantly, birds have special sacs that store air. With these sacs, even when a bird is breathing out, air is moving into the lungs.

Plants take in air through special openings in leaves called *stomata*. The word *stoma* means "mouth," which is what these tiny structures look like.

Most plants have a transport system that moves fluid throughout a plant's body. This cross-section of a stem shows bundles of plant vessels.

When you're done, use the answer key to check and revise your work.

1 Read the summary statements below. Each one is incorrect. Change the part of the summary in blue to make it correct.

1. The circulatory system consists of bone, cartilage, and ligaments. Your lungs work in pairs to move your body.

→ _____
_____

2. The respiratory system brings in carbon dioxide for the body to use and releases oxygen as a waste product.

→ _____
_____

3. The muscular system carries blood through your body. It consists of the heart, blood vessels, and blood.

→ _____

4. Plants bring air into their bodies using structures called mouths.

→ _____
_____

5. Fish take in air through hearts, and spiders take in air through exoskeletons.

→ _____
_____
_____

Name _____

Word Play

1 Use the clues to fill in the crossword puzzle.

Across

1. Body parts that work in pairs to help your body move
3. The organ system that moves air into, around, and out of your body
5. The organ system that supports your body
7. Hard body parts that support your body
8. Hard covering on the outside of some animals' bodies
9. Pumps blood throughout the body

Down

2. The organ system that moves blood around your body
4. The organ system that helps your body move
6. Organs that expand to fill with air
10. Type of feet used by sea stars to move
11. Two tubes that connect to the trachea and to bronchioles

Apply Concepts

2 For each action on the left, write the opposite action in the blank to the right.

contract ⟷ _____

inhale ⟷ _____

bleed ⟷ _____

3 What are two structures in animals that serve the same purpose as lungs?

_____   _____

4 Think about how different types of animals move, breathe, and circulate blood. Place the words from the bank below under the picture of the organism that has that structure. You may not use all the words.

tube feet	stem	muscles	gills
book lungs	bones	exoskeleton	lungs

sea star   dog   spider

_____   _____   _____

_____   _____   _____

_____   _____   _____

5 Fill in the process chart below to describe the path that air takes through the respiratory system.

Air enters through the mouth or nose, and travels through the _____ .

Then it flows through the large tubes called _____ and the smaller tubes called _____ until it reaches the _____ .

There, oxygen enters the blood and _____ _____ leaves the blood and enters the _____ .

Then it passes through the _____ and finally leaves the body through the mouth or nose.

The air flows back out through the _____ and then through the larger _____ .

6 _____is a disease that causes the bronchioles to _____which makes _____difficult.

7 How is the function of muscles and bones related?

_____

_____

_____

_____

8 Label each of the following as an example of respiration or circulation.

_____

_____

_____

_____

_____

_____

9 Think about what is happening and identify the part of blood that is being used.

1. You get a cut. The _____ help to close the cut.

2. The _____ _____ _____ help to fight infection and get rid of germs.

3. The _____ helps carry all of these blood cells to the wound area.

10 Which part of the body has thin walls that allow oxygen to pass through?

a. arteries

b. veins

c. capillaries

d. bronchioles

Take It Home! Make a model of a skeleton using different types of pasta. You can model a human skeleton or the skeleton of another animal. Talk with your family about the different bones and what purpose they serve.

SC.5.L.14.1 Identify the organs in the human body and describe their functions, including … lungs, stomach, liver, intestines, pancreas … reproductive organs, kidneys, bladder….
SC.5.L.14.2 Compare and contrast the function of organs and other physical structures of plants and animals, including humans….

Essential Question

What Body Parts Enable Digestion, Excretion, and Reproduction?

Engage Your Brain!

Find the answer to the following question in this lesson and record it here.

If you could see through your body, this might be what you'd see when you look in the mirror. What is the coiled tube inside your belly, and what does it do?

_____

_____

_____

Active Reading

Lesson Vocabulary
List the terms. As you learn about each one, make notes in the Interactive Glossary.

_____   _____

_____   _____

_____

Using Charts
A chart adds information to the text that appears on the page with it. Active readers pause their reading to review the chart and decide how the information in it adds to what they are reading.

Down the Hatch

When you swallow food, it passes through a long tube in your body. As it travels, it is broken down into smaller pieces, and all of the useful parts are absorbed by the body. All that is left over is waste.

Organ	Job
1 esophagus	It's a long tube that begins in your throat. It moves food from the mouth to the stomach.
2 stomach	It's a muscular bag that mashes food into a liquid and mixes the food with digestive juices. These juices break down some nutrients and kill germs. Then the food, which is now liquid, goes through an opening to the small intestine.
3 small intestine	It's a long coiled tube that digests food and absorbs nutrients your body needs from the digested food. Anything not absorbed is sent to the large intestine.
4 large intestine	It's a large tube that soaks up water and minerals and leaves only the waste. Solid waste passes out of your body.

▶ In each box below, write the name and function of the organ that is shown.

The **liver** makes a juice called *bile* that helps break large blobs of fat into tiny droplets so that the fats can be broken down more easily.

The gallbladder stores bile from the liver and sends it to the small intestine only when food passes through.

The **pancreas** makes juices that are released into the small intestine. These juices break down fats and proteins into small pieces that can be absorbed.

Food for Thought

You have two boxes of cereal in your hand. How do you know which is the healthier choice? You can read their food labels to help you decide.

Active Reading As you read these two pages, draw a star next to what you consider to be the most important sentence, and be ready to explain why.

Packaged foods must have a label that gives you information about what is inside the package. This is called nutrition information. Learning how to use nutrition information can help you make healthy food choices.
Each part of a nutrition label has different information. For example, you can learn how many servings are in the box. You can also learn how many Calories [KAL•uh•reez] each serving has. Calories are a way to measure how much energy your body will get from your food. Carbohydrates, proteins and fats are used by the body for energy.

The nutrition label has information about more than just energy. It also lists the amounts of important nutrients that the food contains. Bones need calcium for strength. Sodium is used by the nerves to send signals. Vitamin A helps with your eyesight. Protein is used to build muscle. Fats are used to make important chemical signals and to store energy. As you can see, reading food labels can help you make choices that fulfill all of your body's nutrition needs.

Do the Math!
Solve Word Problems

One serving of this cereal provides you with 160 mg of sodium. This is 7% of your body's daily needs. How many milligrams of sodium equal 100%?

_____

_____

_____

Nutrition Facts

Serving Size ¾ cup (30g)
Servings Per Container About 14

Amount Per Serving	Corn Crunch	with ½ cup skim milk
Calories	120	160
Calories from Fat	15	20

		% Daily Value**
Total Fat 2g*	3%	3%
Saturated Fat 0g	0%	0%
Cholesterol 0mg	0%	1%
Sodium 160mg	7%	9%
Potassium 65mg	2%	8%
Total Carbohydrate 25g	8%	10%
Dietary Fiber 3g		
Sugars 3g		
Other Carbohydrate 11g		
Protein 2g		

*Amount in Cereal. A serving of cereal plus skim milk provides 2g fat, less 5mg cholesterol, 220mg sodium, 270mg potassium, 31g carbohydrate (19g sugars) and 6g protein.

**Percent Daily Values are based on a 2,000 calorie diet. Your daily values may be higher or lower depending on your calorie needs:

	Calories	2,000	2,500
Total Fat	Less than	65g	80g
Sat Fat	Less than	20g	25g
Cholesterol	Less than	300mg	300mg
Sodium	Less than	2,400mg	2,400mg
Potassium		3,500mg	3,500mg
Total Carbohydrate		300g	375g
Dietary Fiber		25g	30g

The serving size will help you make smart decisions about how much of a food you should eat to get the right amount of nutrients in your diet.

The "% Daily Value" tells you what percent of this nutrient a serving of this food will provide compared to how much you should get in a full day.

This section shows how many grams (g) or milligrams (mg) of each type of nutrient you should get each day, depending on how many Calories you need.

▶ How many Calories are in 1 serving, with ½ cup skim milk?

_____

Waste Removal

Digesting food produces one kind of waste. Using the nutrients produces another. The *excretory system* rids the body of this waste and keeps your body's water and salt levels in balance.

Active Reading As you read this page, underline the different types of waste that are described.

Your body "burns" nutrients much like a fire burns wood. Your body doesn't produce ash, but the "burned" nutrients do make waste products. For example, as protein is broken down, ammonia is made. Ammonia is very toxic! The liver converts ammonia to urea [yoo•REE•uh], which is less toxic. But if urea builds up it makes you sick, so your body gets rid of it as urine. A small amount of urea is also released in sweat.

Like a fire, your body uses oxygen and produces a waste gas called carbon dioxide. Carbon dioxide is released by your lungs when you breathe out.

You breathe in oxygen. When you breathe out, your body gets rids of carbon dioxide.

The urinary system filters the blood and rids the body of wastes as urine.

Sweat is mostly water, but some wastes, such as excess salt, are released from the body in sweat.

The Urinary System

kidneys

ureters

bladder

urethra

1 The **kidneys** are organs that remove waste from the blood. They also help to conserve water and to make sure the blood does not have too much or too little salt.

2 After the kidneys filter the blood, the waste, *urine*, collects in tubes called *ureters* [YUR•ih•tuhrz]. These take the urine to the bladder.

3 The **bladder** stores urine and then releases it from the body. The bladder can stretch like a balloon. It can hold up to a pint at a time!

4 The urethra [yu•REE•thruh] is a small tube that takes urine from the bladder to outside of the body.

Organize It—Sequence

Write the organs in order to show the path of urine through the urinary system.

Eating and Excreting

All living things use nutrients and produce waste. Living things have many ways of breaking down nutrients and getting rid of waste.

Active Reading On these two pages, draw circles around descriptions of nutrient use and squares around descriptions of waste removal.

Flies spit out acids onto food. Food is partly digested outside the fly's body! Then the fly sucks up the nutrients through a straw-like mouthpart.

Bird droppings aren't made of urine. Instead, they are made of uric acid and digestive waste. Uric acid is a very powerful acid that damages statues.

No Stomach? No Problem!

Which two organisms below have no digestive system?

_____

Jellyfish bring food into their mouths to digest it. Then they get rid of the waste by sending it back out of their mouths!

Marsh grasses live in salty areas where most plants could not survive. The leaves of marsh grasses get rid of excess salt.

Grass is tough to digest! To get nutrients from grass, cows must chew their food twice and have four sections of stomach! The arrows show the path of food through a cow's digestive system.

Tapeworms have no digestive system. Instead they live inside other animals' digestive systems. As digested food flows past, a tapeworm soaks up nutrients through its skin.

Cycles of Life

What do babies, plantlets, tadpoles, and larvae have in common? They're all organisms that came from other organisms.

Active Reading As you read these two pages, find and underline the different names for young organisms.

Animals and plants all have *reproductive systems*. This system has one very important job: to make new organisms.

Human males and females have reproductive organs that make special cells. The male reproductive cells are made in the testes [TES•teez]. Female reproductive cells are made in the ovaries [OH•vuh•reez]. These reproductive cells join to form an embryo [EM•bree•oh]. The embryo develops in the mother's body for nine months. It grows and changes until it can survive outside the mother's body. At this time, a baby is born.

ovaries

testes

A spider plants grows little "plantlets" at the end of some stems. These plant buds can be broken off to grow new plants.

Insects lay eggs that hatch into larvae [LAR•vee], like the ones shown here. Insects go through several stages before they reach adult form.

Many plants make seeds. Male plant reproductive cells join with female reproductive cells and develop into a seed. Dandelion seeds are carried by wind. If they land in soil, they begin to grow and develop into a new plant.

Frogs lay their eggs in a jelly-like pile. The eggs must stay wet, or they will die. Tadpoles hatch from the eggs. Tadpoles start out looking like fish with large heads. Slowly they grow legs and their tails become smaller and smaller. Little by little they turn into adult frogs.

When you're done, use the answer key to check and revise your work.

Complete the summary paragraph by filling in the blanks. Then place the words in the list below the summary paragraph with the correct system at the bottom of the page.

Summarize

Your body is made up of many 1._____ that work together in systems. The 2._____ system is a long tube that travels through your body. It takes the nutrients out of food for your body to use. The 3._____ system is responsible for removing waste from your body. The 4._____ system makes special cells that produce new organisms. Plants and animals also have ways to get energy, remove waste, and reproduce.

testes	small intestine	esophagus
kidneys	ovaries	ureters
stomach	large intestine	
urethra	bladder	

Digestive System

5._____

6._____

7._____

8._____

Urinary System

9._____

10._____

11._____

12._____

Reproductive System

13._____

14._____

Answer Key: 1. organs **2.** digestive **3.** excretory **4.** reproductive **5.–8.** (in any order) esophagus, stomach, small intestine, large intestine **9.–12.** (in any order) kidneys, ureters, bladder, urethra **13.–14.** (in any order) testes, ovaries

Word Play

1. Read the clues. Write the answers on the lines. Then find these words in the puzzle.

1. These bean-shaped organs filter the blood and remove wastes.

   _____

2. This long tube connects the mouth to the stomach.

   _____

3. These organs produce special reproductive cells in the male body.

   _____

4. This organ expands and fills up with urine until it is ready to be released.

   _____

5. In this organ, water is removed until the waste is solid.

   _____

6. This organ makes juices that break down protein in the small intestine.

   _____

7. This system moves food through your body and absorbs the nutrients.

   _____

8. This organ makes a juice that breaks large blobs of fat into smaller blobs.

   _____

9. This system helps an organism make new organisms.

   _____

10. This term includes all the different stages in an animal's life.

    _____

```
d u r i n a r y l a t o d i
n o e t n a o i i e s r p a
t v p t e l o s v v s k a t
l a r g e i n t e s t i n e
t r o u u f r d r c t d c s
i i d i g e s t i v e n r t
i e u e d c t b i e p e e e
t s c e f y o v h r d y a s
i e t d r c m y e o e s s c
n e i i b l a d d e r r e i
t o v i t e c p n d o n t o
a r e s o p h a g u s e e v
e i a d v s s r k s y i e e
i r u e c c v r m r p r y k
```

11. These organs produce special reproductive cells in the female body.

    _____

12. This organ mashes food and mixes food with digestive juices.

    _____

13. This system filters wastes from the blood.

    _____

Apply Concepts

2 Think about how organs depend on other organs to do their work. Complete each sentence.

1. Food couldn't reach the stomach without the _____ and the _____ .

2. Kidneys couldn't work without the _____ because _____ couldn't leave the body.

3. The small intestine couldn't work without the _____ because fats couldn't be broken down.

3 Describe the life cycle of the tadpole shown here.

_____
_____
_____
_____

4 Explain how each of the items shown below are alike.

stomach and blender   kidney and coffee filter   bladder and water balloon

_____   _____   _____

_____   _____   _____

5 Scientists have discovered a new animal. Is it possible for it to have no digestive system? Why or why not? _____

_____ .

Take It Home!

Write the words *small intestine, pancreas, esophagus, liver, large intestine, gall bladder,* and *stomach* on index cards. Eat a snack. Ask your family to explain how each organ helps to digest your food.

SC.5.L.14.2 Compare and contrast the function of organs and other physical structures of plants and animals, including humans....

People in Science

Meet the Grays of Biology

Henry Gray

Henry Gray was a surgeon in London. He was fascinated by the science of anatomy. Anatomy is the study of the parts of the body. In 1858, when he was only 31 years old, Henry Gray published a book on anatomy. It became one of the most famous scientific books of all time: *Gray's Anatomy*. The book included drawings of all of the organs and systems of the human body. Henry Gray died three years later from smallpox, but his work lives on. In 2009, the 40th edition of *Gray's Anatomy* was published. It is still used today by doctors, students, and other scientists.

Asa Gray

Asa Gray was an American botanist. He studied plants. He lived around the same time as Henry Gray, but the two men were not related. They never even met. Still, their work had some things in common. Asa Gray wrote a book known as *Gray's Manual*. Working with a scientific illustrator named Isaac Sprague, Asa Gray published a book that had information about almost every plant in the Northern United States. It was written more than a century ago. But *Gray's Manual* is still used by botanists today. Asa Gray is considered to be one of history's most important botanists.

Be a Scientific Illustrator

Try your hand at scientific illustrations! See how well you can produce an anatomical drawing of the bones of the human hand. Then try making a botanical illustration of the raspberry branch.

Bones of the Human Hand

Raspberry Branch

Multiple Choice

Identify the choice that best answers the question.

SC.5.L.14.1, SC.5.N.1.1

1 David has five thermometers. He wraps each one in a strip of cloth. He dips four of them into different liquids. He leaves the fifth one dry. He sets all of them outside in the shade for five minutes. The table below shows the temperature that he records for each thermometer:

Alcohol	Mineral oil	Salt water	Water	Dry
72 °F	82 °F	78 °F	78 °F	83 °F

Which liquid evaporates fastest?

(A) water

(B) alcohol

(C) salt water

(D) mineral oil

SC.5.L.14.1

2 During recess, Renee scraped her knee, so the nurse put a bandage on it. Which of the functions below that are normally provided by skin is now being provided by the bandage?

(F) preventing dehydration

(G) regulating body temperature

(H) keeping bacteria out of the body

(I) sensing when it is being touched

SC.5.L.14.1

3 A group of students are exploring a cave. Their flashlight's battery runs out of power. They must wait for another group of explorers to catch up with them. In the meantime, which of their senses has become nearly useless?

(A) hearing

(B) smell

(C) sight

(D) touch

SC.5.L.14.2

4 Manatees have whiskers. Manatees use their whiskers to sense their environment. When the whiskers touch an object, a message is sent to the manatee's brain. Which statement best describes what is happening?

(F) Only the nervous system is involved.

(G) Only the integumentary system is involved.

(H) Neither the integumentary nor the nervous system is involved.

(I) Both the integumentary and nervous systems are working together.

SC.5.L.14.1, SC.5.N.1.4

5 Latoya knows that skin produces oil, water, and salt. She wants to find out which of these elements causes cooling. She designs an experiment and creates the following table to record her data.

	Towel soaked in oil	Towel covered in salt	Towel soaked in water	Towel that is clean and dry
Starting temperature				
Temperature after 1 min				
Temperature after 10 min				

Which towel is the control?

(A) towel soaked in oil

(B) towel covered in salt

(C) towel soaked in water

(D) towel that is clean and dry

SC.5.L.14.1

6 In the early days of telephone use, there were no computers. To make a phone call, a person had to call an operator. The operator would connect two callers. The operator performed a function that is most similar to which human body part?

- (F) brain
- (G) nose
- (H) eyes
- (I) skin

SC.5.L.14.2

7 An ant's antennae sense temperature and pressure. Which human structure serves the same function?

- (A) skin
- (B) olfactory bulb
- (C) taste bud
- (D) rods and cones

SC.5.L.14.2

8 Great white sharks can sense electrical impulses from great distances with a sense called electroreception. Which statement best describes the sense of electroreception?

- (F) the ability to smell blood in very small amounts
- (G) the ability to sense nerve impulses produced by another creature's movement
- (H) the ability to hunt underwater for long periods of time
- (I) the ability to cause pain to prey by producing electric impulses

SC.5.L.14.2

9 Animals have body coverings, such as skin, that protect them. This protective layer can be used to protect the animal from extreme temperatures and to help it blend in with its environment to avoid predators. Look at the body coverings of these animals. Which animal has a body covering that will best protect it from bites and scratches during an attack by a predator?

SC.5.L.14.1

10 The following picture shows some muscles and bones of the arm.

Triceps   Biceps   Radius   Ulna

As this arm bends, which word describes what the biceps muscle is doing?

- (F) relaxing
- (G) retracting
- (H) contracting
- (I) constricting

SC.5.L.14.2

11 Fish get oxygen from water through their gills. They also use their gills to release carbon dioxide. Which organ in humans is similar to fish gills?

(A) heart

(B) lungs

(C) intestine

(D) mouth

SC.5.L.14.1

12 How do nutrients in digested food reach the bloodstream?

(F) They are absorbed by the large intestine.

(G) They pass from the esophagus into the blood.

(H) They are absorbed into the bloodstream by the small intestine.

(I) They are absorbed into the bloodstream through the pancreas wall.

SC.5.L.14.1

13 Digestion takes place in the digestive tract, shown here.

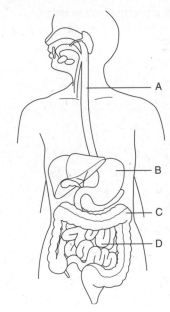

In what order does food move through the organs of the digestive tract?

(A) A, B, C, D

(B) A, C, B, D

(C) A, B, D, C

(D) A, D, B, C

SC.5.L.14.2

14 The following picture shows how plant tissues carry water and nutrients throughout a plant.

Sugars flow from leaves to roots.

Water flows from roots to leaves.

Which human body system is similar to this plant vascular system?

(F) circulatory system

(G) respiratory system

(H) muscular system

(I) skeletal system

SC.5.L.14.2

15 The diagram below shows how a butterfly develops.

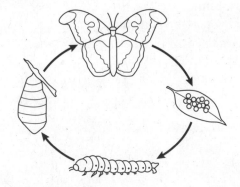

What process is illustrated in the diagram?

(A) digestion

(B) a life cycle

(C) a food chain

(D) photosynthesis

SC.5.L.14.1

16 There are similarities and differences between the male and female reproductive systems. What is one difference between the male and female reproductive systems?

F) The bladder is the main organ of the male reproductive system, but not the female reproductive system.

G) Only the female reproductive system has specialized structures, but not the male reproductive system.

H) Babies develop inside part of the female reproductive system, but not the male reproductive system.

I) Babies begin development inside the male reproductive system and finish development inside the female reproductive system.

SC.5.L.14.1

17 The following picture shows the flow of blood through the human circulatory and respiratory systems.

Which statement is true of the large blood vessel called the aorta?

A) It carries blood to the heart.

B) It carries blood to the lungs.

C) It carries blood that is high in oxygen.

D) It carries blood that is high in carbon dioxide.

SC.5.L.14.1

18 Cells in the body use nutrients and oxygen for energy. Which body system transports oxygen and nutrients throughout the body?

SC.5.L.14.1

19 Urine is a product of the urinary system. What makes up normal human urine?

A) oxygen

B) nutrients

C) water and waste products

D) all the fluids a person drinks

SC.5.L.14.2

20 Insects have a hard outer covering called an exoskeleton. Which process below is the function of an insect's exoskeleton and a human's skeletal system?

F) gas exchange

G) structural support

H) removal of waste

I) temperature control

390 Unit 8

Changes in Environments

Big Idea 15

Diversity and Evolution of Living Organisms

Clearwater, Florida

I Wonder Why

Sea turtles hatch in the sand and make their way to the ocean. Why do sea turtles need to be protected? *Turn the page to find out.*

SAVE OUR SEA TURTLES

PROTECTED ENDANGERED SPECIES

NESTING SEASON MAY–OCTOBER
REPORT NESTING TURTLES

CLEARWATER
MARINE SCIENCE CENTER

Here's Why Human activities, such as walking on nests, can accidentally harm turtle eggs. Turtle nests are protected so that the young turtles can safely hatch and reach the ocean.

Essential Questions and Florida Benchmarks

Big Idea 15 *Diversity and Evolution of Living Organisms*

Now I Get the Big Idea!

SC.5.L.15.1 Describe how, when the environment changes, differences between individuals allow some plants and animals to survive and reproduce while others die or move to new locations.

Essential Question

How Do Environmental Changes Affect Organisms?

Engage Your Brain!

Find the answer to the following question in this lesson and record it here.

A forest fire can change a landscape in a matter of minutes! Trees are burned, and animals run for shelter. How could a forest fire be a good thing?

_____

_____

_____

Active Reading

Lesson Vocabulary
List the terms. As you learn about each one, make notes in the Interactive Glossary.

_____ _____

_____ _____

_____

Compare and Contrast
Many ideas in this lesson are connected because they explain comparisons and contrasts—how things are alike and different. Active readers stay focused on comparisons and contrasts when they ask themselves, How are these things alike? How are they different?

It's All Around You

As far as we know, Earth is the only planet that we can live on. Water and air are two important reasons why life is possible on Earth.

Active Reading As you read this page, circle things that make up environments on Earth.

What do oceans, clouds, fish, and birds all have in common? These things are all part of the environment. The **environment** is all of the living and nonliving things in nature. We depend on the environment for our food, air, and water and for a safe place to live. We share the environment with all other life on Earth. Every other living thing also depends on the environment to meet its needs for food, air, water, and a place to live. In this way, every living thing on Earth is connected.

You and the other living things around you interact with each other and with the nonliving parts of the environment. For example, think about the ways that honeybees interact with the living and nonliving things around them. Bees get nectar from a field of flowers, drink water from puddles, and sting animals if they get too close to the hive. Living things that interact with each other form a community. A community of living things and the nonliving things around them are called an **ecosystem**. Bees, birds, flowers, soil, water, and sunlight are all part of an ecosystem.

water

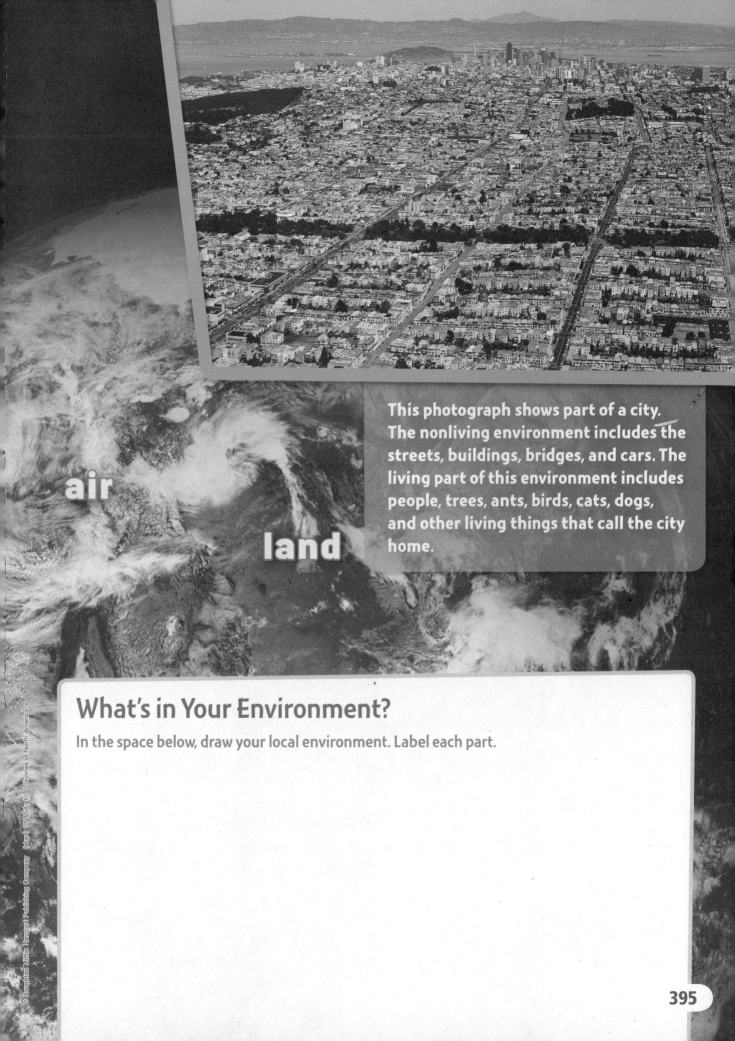

air

land

This photograph shows part of a city. The nonliving environment includes the streets, buildings, bridges, and cars. The living part of this environment includes people, trees, ants, birds, cats, dogs, and other living things that call the city home.

What's in Your Environment?

In the space below, draw your local environment. Label each part.

Change Comes Naturally

The environment can change in response to natural events. Some of these events occur quickly. Others take place more slowly.

Active Reading As you read this page, draw a box around events that change the environment rapidly. Draw a circle around events that change the environment slowly.

Storms can bring heavy rains and flood the land, which changes the environment. Natural events, such as floods, earthquakes, volcanic eruptions, and droughts, can change the environment very quickly.

In contrast, events such as an ice age happen more slowly. An ice age happens when Earth has colder-than-normal temperatures for a very long time. Large areas of land might be covered with ice for thousands of years.

Volcanic eruptions can also change the environment over a long period of time. How? A violent eruption sends gases and dust high into the air. The materials block sunlight from reaching Earth's surface. This can cause temperatures to drop for months or years.

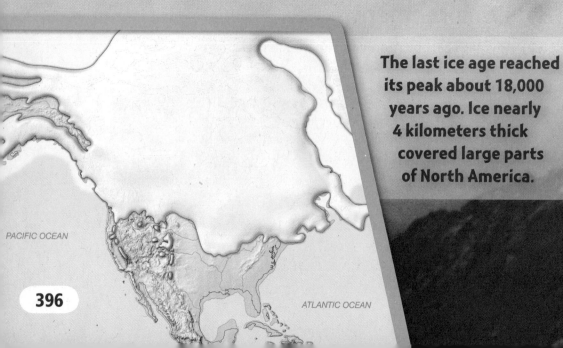

PACIFIC OCEAN

ATLANTIC OCEAN

The last ice age reached its peak about 18,000 years ago. Ice nearly 4 kilometers thick covered large parts of North America.

Volcanoes can cause rapid change as hot flowing lava scorches the surrounding ecosystem. Volcanoes can also cause long-term change as dust and gases block out the sun's rays.

Is It Cold Enough For You?

Think about the environment during an ice age. How do you think the ice age affected living things?

_____

_____

_____

_____

_____

_____

A forest fire is a natural cause of environmental change. Forest fires destroy vegetation. But many ecosystems need fire to stay healthy. Some trees even make seeds that cannot grow unless they have been burned!

Animal Architects

Living things are affected by their environment. Living things, in turn, can cause changes to their environment. These changes can be both helpful and harmful, depending on the point of view.

Active Reading As you read this page, draw boxes around clue words that signal examples.

Beavers are only about 1 meter long, but they have a very large effect on their environment. For example, beavers use their teeth to cut trees. They use the trees to build dams across streams. Beaver dams cause ponds and wetlands to form.

The trees that beavers cut down to build their dam are harmed. In addition, organisms that lived in the flowing water of the stream and on the dry land around the stream must move.

But beaver dams provide a home for organisms that rely on ponds and wetlands. Ponds made by beaver dams increase the number of different kinds of organisms that can live in the area.

© Houghton Mifflin Harcourt Publishing Company (fire ant) ©James H. Robinson/Photo Researchers, Inc.; (tr) ©Francesco Tomasinelli/Photo Researchers, Inc.; (b) ©David Hosking/Photo Researchers, Inc.; (br) ©Paul Souders/Digital Vision/Getty Images

Fire ants are tiny red ants with very painful bites! They tend to attack in swarms and can even kill small animals. They live in dirt mounds that can be home to more than 100,000 ants! Fire ants were accidentally brought to the United States on a cargo ship. Since then, they have spread over all of the southeastern United States.

Harverster ants are large ants that eat seeds. As fire ants spread, they wipe out colonies of native harvester ants. Fire ants are an invasive animal. This means that they are invading an ecosystem that was not their original home. In their new home, they affect the native plants and animals.

Harvester ants are a favorite food of the horned lizard. Because there are fewer harvester ants, horned lizards have less food to eat. Now very few horned lizards remain. If they are not protected, in time there may be no horned lizards left!

Cause and Effect

Fill in the graphic organizer below to show a cause-and-effect relationship between fire ants and their ecosystem.

Cause ⟶ **Effect**

_____   _____

_____   _____

Humans Change the Environment

Humans are part of the environment and we have a large impact on our ecosystem. The effects of humans on the environment are both harmful and beneficial.

Many human activities are harmful to an ecosystem. For example, people mine coal to get energy to power homes and businesses. Open-pit mining, like the mine shown here, kills all the plants living in that area. Other organisms must move to find food.

People cut down forests to use the wood or to clear space for homes. When the trees in an area are cut down, as they were in the bottom photograph, organisms that usually live in the forest must move or die. This effect is called habitat destruction. A *habitat* is a place where an organism usually lives.

Humans produce a large amount of waste that is disposed of as trash. Most trash ends up in landfills. If landfills are not built properly, wastes can pollute soil and water. **Pollution** is any harmful substance that gets into the environment. Pollution can kill organisms or cause diseases.

Not all changes caused by humans are harmful. People work to protect their environment and to protect organisms from harm as a result of ecosystem change. Protecting ecosystems and the organisms living in them is called **conservation.**

People try to restore habitats and repair damaged ecosystems by replanting trees and cleaning up pollution. People also remove invasive plants and animals so native organisms can survive.

In addition, people try to help organisms affected by natural disasters. People care for animals injured or orphaned by these disasters.

What Can You Do To Help?

In the space below, list things that you can do to help the environment. Include things you already do and things you would like to do in the future.

_____

_____

Living Things Change

Look at the snakes slithering down this page. Each snake looks different, but they are all the same kind of snake. Why don't they look the same?

Active Reading As you read these two pages, circle the clue words or phrases that signal a detail such as an example or an added fact.

You don't look exactly like your parents. You have many similarities, but there are also small differences that make you unique. Every organism is slightly different from every other organism. Sometimes these differences can be very important.

Corn snakes, like the ones shown here, come in many colors and patterns. Some are very light colored, some are golden brown, and some are bright orange. Suppose a hawk is flying over a wheat field, looking for a snack. Which of these snakes is least likely to become lunch? If you guessed the golden brown snake, you are correct. Why? Its color would blend in with the wheat. The hawk would not see it, and the snake would survive. The snake would reproduce and pass on its coloring to its offspring. Its golden brown offspring would have a better chance of surviving in the wheat field and would also produce more offspring. Eventually, most of the snakes living in the wheat field would be golden brown.

Do the Math!
Find Median and Mean

Length of Corn Snakes	
Snake 1	3.5 m
Snake 2	5.5 m
Snake 3	4.6 m
Snake 4	5.1 m
Snake 5	4.8 m
Snake 6	3.9 m
Snake 7	5.3 m

Adult corn snakes vary not only in color, but also in length. The table shows the lengths of several adult corn snakes. Study the data, and then answer the questions.

1. The median is the middle number of a data set when the numbers are placed in numerical order. Find the median of the data set. _____

2. The mean is the average of a data set. Find the mean of the data set. _____

Sometimes living things change because their environment changes. For example, bacteria have changed as a result of their changing environment. Since the discovery of antibiotics, people have learned how to kill bacteria. The first antibiotic, penicillin, saved many lives by killing bacteria that cause disease.

But in a very large population of bacteria, a few are not affected by penicillin. These bacteria survive and multiply. Over time, they produce large populations of bacteria that are not affected by penicillin.

Researchers have had to find new antibiotics to kill these bacteria. But, again, some bacteria are not killed. These bacteria continue to multiply.

Many types of antibiotics have been developed. And bacteria have become resistant to many of them. Now there are bacteria that are resistant to almost all known types of antibiotics. These bacteria are extremely difficult to kill.

Antibiotics in soaps and cleaners kill many bacteria. However, when not all of the bacteria are killed, the ones that survive multiply. Little by little, bacteria are becoming resistant to antibacterial soap and cleaners.

Gone!

Some living things change when their environment changes. Some living things move to new places. Others simply do not survive.

Active Reading As you read these two pages, underline the definition of *extinction*. Circle pictures of organisms that became extinct because of natural environmental change.

Millions of years ago, Earth was covered with giant reptiles! Now, most of those reptiles are extinct. **Extinction** happens when all the members of a certain kind of living thing die. Giant reptiles, such as the *Tyrannosaurus rex* shown here, lived in a time in which Earth was warm. Over time, the environment cooled, and many of the reptiles could not survive.

These dinosaurs, *Diplodocus* and *Triceratops* (from left to right), were large plant-eaters. They became extinct about 65 million years ago.

The Tasmanian wolf lived in Australia and New Guinea. Ranchers believed the wolves killed sheep and cattle, but this was never proven. The Tasmanian wolf was hunted to extinction by the 1930s.

The dodo bird lived on an island in the Indian Ocean. Around 1600, people came to the island. People hunted the birds for food. They cut down the island's forests to make room for houses. Nonnative animals, such as cats and pigs brought by people, destroyed the dodo birds' nests. Within 80 years after they were discovered, the dodo birds were extinct.

Time Traveler

If you could go back to the island of the dodo birds in 1600, what advice would you give to people to help conserve the dodo birds?

_____

_____

_____

_____

Today, people work to conserve habitats and protect organisms from extinction. Even so, many organisms are in danger of becoming extinct. As these organisms' environments continue to change, some will adapt, some will move, and some will not survive.

When you're done, use the answer key to check and revise your work.

Read the summary statements below. Each one is incorrect. Change the part of the summary in blue to make it correct.

1

1. Pollution is all the living and nonliving things that affect an organism's life.

_____

2. Some natural events that cause the environment to change slowly include earthquakes and floods. _____

3. People can help conserve habitats by mining, building landfills, and cutting down forests.

_____

_____

4. Protecting ecosystems is an example of extinction. _____

2 **The idea web below summarizes the lesson. Complete the web.**

If the environment changes, living things change, 6. _____, or do not survive.

A community of living things and their environment are an 7. _____ .

Living things rely on their environment for 5. _____, air, _____, and a place to live.

In a city, the buildings, streets, air, and water are all 8. _____ parts of the environment.

Fast environmental change can be caused by 9. _____ and _____ .

Name _____

Word Play

1 Use the clues to unscramble the words below.

1. iavinvse __ __ __ __ __ __ __ __ : A nonnative animal that moves into a new place

2. ecnntavosroi __ __ __ __ __ __ __ __ __ __ __ __ : Protecting ecosystems and the organisms living in them

3. nlpituloo __ __ __ __ __ __ __ __ __ : Litter on the ground or harmful chemicals in the water

4. tsymeeocs __ __ __ __ __ __ __ __ __ : A group of organisms and their environment

5. radonsiu __ __ __ __ __ __ __ __ : A type of giant extinct animal

6. eeautrtpmer __ __ __ __ __ __ __ __ __ __ __ : How hot or cold something is

7. vebera __ __ __ __ __ __ : Can be helpful or harmful, depending on point of veiw

8. aaicbter __ __ __ __ __ __ __ __ : Have adapted to antibiotics

9. vmetneonrin __ __ __ __ __ __ __ __ __ __ __ : Everything around a living thing, including air, water, land, and sunlight

10. txoniecnit __ __ __ __ __ __ __ __ __ __ : Happened to dodo birds and Tasmanian wolves

11. navoolc __ __ __ __ __ __ __ : Can cause long-term environmental change by blowing dust and gases into the sky.

Bonus: What kind of dinosaur accidentally smashes everything in its path?

_____ _____

Apply Concepts

2 Label each of the following pictures as a change caused by people, by animals, or by a natural event.

_____

_____

_____

_____

_____

_____

3 List some nonliving things found in Earth's environment. Give an example of how you use each thing.

_____

_____

_____

_____

_____

_____

_____

4 Draw one circle around animals that became extinct because of natural events. Draw two circles around animals that became extinct because of human activities.

5 In the first box below, draw a landscape that includes a river. In the second box, draw how the same landscape might look after a flood. Include captions explaining how the environment changed.

6 Fill in the graphic organizer below to describe how beavers change the environment. The first box is already completed.

Beavers build a dam in a stream.

↓

_____
_____

↓

_____
_____

Describe a way that people might be able to solve each environmental problem listed below.

7 Coal mining can harm habitats and cause pollution.

_____

_____

_____

8 Cutting a forest destroys habitats and can lead to soil erosion.

_____

_____

_____

9 Waste from garbage in landfills can enter the ground and pollute soil and water.

_____

_____

10 Imagine that an orange tree frog eats only a certain type of small blue fly. A giant red fly starts moving into the tree frog's ecosystem. The red fly eats all the blue fly's food. In the space below, draw and illustrate a flow chart that shows what might happen to the frog.

Bonus: How might orange frogs change because of the red fly? _____

_____

Take It Home! Share what you have learned about conservation with your family.
Come up with at least four ways to help conserve resources at home.
Carry out your family's plan, and report the results to the class.

Quest for the Serpent Eagle

Jane Juniper is a wildlife surveyor. She is deep in the forest of Madagascar, an island off the coast of Africa, observing birds.

What's that sound? Jane hears a loud, screeching bird call that she never expected to hear. It sounds like... But could it be?

Jane tiptoes quietly through the forest, searching the trees for movement. There!

Jane stands perfectly still. The bird has a dark back and a striped chest. It has yellow eyes, and sharp talons. But it's not supposed to exist!

Jane Juniper has studied all about African birds. It takes her just a moment to be sure. But she is still amazed! With her camera she collects evidence of her find.

Jane Juniper, wildlife surveyor, found a bird that was thought to be extinct—a Madagascar Serpent Eagle!

Now You Be the Surveyor

Imagine you're a wildlife surveyor. Survey the forest below. Write the kinds of animals you find and the number of each kind.

_____   _____

_____   _____

_____   _____

_____   _____

_____   _____

Name _____

SC.5.N.1.1 ... plan and carry out scientific investigations.... **SC.5.N.1.4** Identify a control group and explain its importance in an experiment. **SC.5.L.15.1** Describe how, when the environment changes, differences between individuals allow some plants and animals to survive and reproduce while others die or move to new locations.

Essential Question

How Does Drought Affect Plants?

Set a Purpose
What will you better understand about plants after doing this experiment?

_____

_____

_____

_____

State Your Hypothesis
Write your hypothesis, or testable statement.

_____

_____

_____

Think About the Procedure
What parts of your experiment stay the same for each test group?

_____

_____

_____

What part of the experiment did you change?

_____

_____

_____

Record Your Data
Record your observations in the table below.

Plant Observations	
Cup A	
Cup B	
Cup C	
Cup D	
Cup E	

Draw Conclusions

Was your hypothesis supported? Why or why not?

_____

_____

_____

_____

What conclusions can you draw from this investigation?

_____

_____

_____

_____

_____

Analyze and Extend

1. What natural conditions did Cup A and Cup E represent?

_____

_____

_____

2. Did the plants in the cups that got the most water do the best? What can you infer based on your results?

_____

_____

_____

_____

3. Suppose you are studying pea plants. You find that half of the individual pea plants are able to survive in mild drought conditions. Why might this data be imporant?

_____

_____

_____

_____

_____

4. How would you set up an experiment to test the following hypothesis: The amount of fertilizer does not affect how quickly plants grow. Draw and label a picture that shows your setup.

5. Think of other questions you would like to ask about how environmental conditions affect plants.

_____

_____

_____

_____

Multiple Choice

Identify the choice that best answers the question.

SC.5.L.15.1

1. Twenty years ago, Mr. Jackson planted four trees in his front yard. The thickness of the bark on each tree is given in the table below.

Tree	Bark thickness (cm)
A	3.5
B	5.2
C	4.1
D	4.5

In Mr. Jackson's back yard, woodpeckers are nesting. Woodpeckers can damage a tree if they drill all the way through the bark. Based on these data, which tree is most likely to not be damaged by the woodpeckers?

(A) Tree A

(B) Tree B

(C) Tree C

(D) Tree D

SC.5.L.15.1

2. The state bird of Florida is the mockingbird. Mockingbirds eat many types of food, including insects, berries, and seeds. Insects and seeds have hard coverings, but berries are soft.

If the plants that make berries don't grow well one year, which individual mockingbirds are most likely to survive?

(F) those who sing the loudest

(G) those with the strongest beaks

(H) those with the longest tail feathers

(I) those that lay eggs with the most spots

SC.5.L.15.1

3 When the environment changes, differences between individuals allow some plants and animals to survive while others die or move to new locations. Which of these statements best describes how this happens?

(A) Environmental changes cause variations in animals that lead to adaptations.

(B) All animals are able to survive when the environment changes, which leads to their variations and adaptations.

(C) Animals have variations, and when the environment changes, these variations allow populations to adapt and survive.

(D) Animals have different adaptations that allow them to survive when the environment changes, which leads to variation.

SC.5.L.15.1

4 Some zebras are taller, and some can run faster. Some have longer hair, and some have longer tails. What is the most important reason for a population to have individual variation.

(F) Variation helps individuals recognize each other.

(G) Variation ensures that every individual will survive.

(H) Variation determines how large a population can be.

(I) Variation ensures that at least some individuals may be able to survive if the environment changes.

SC.5.L.15.1

5 Environmental changes happen all the time. Some of these changes are easy to spot. For example, the figure below shows a sign that you might see while riding along a road in Florida.

What can you conclude about environmental changes after seeing this sign?

(A) Changes in the environment happen in cycles.

(B) All changes to the environment happen naturally.

(C) This environment will soon be changed by human activity.

(D) Any change made to the environment will lead to extinction.

416   Unit 9

SC.5.L.15.1

6 Beach mice live on the Gulf coast of Florida's barrier islands. Despite their name, these beach mice are found in inland areas as well as along the beach. However, the beach mice that live inland are usually darker in color than those that live on the sandy beaches along the coast. Which of these statements explains this color difference?

(F) The mice are not related to each other.

(G) The mice that live inland are colored by the mud.

(H) The mice have adapted to living in their specific environment.

(I) The mice on the sandy beaches have become lighter in the sun.

SC.5.L.15.1, SC.5.N.1.1

7 In a science experiment, soil was placed in four different beakers. The following diagram shows the conditions of the soil for each beaker.

Which of the following beakers models drought conditions?

(A) Beaker A

(B) Beaker B

(C) Beaker C

(D) Beaker D

SC.5.L.15.1

8 A farmer plants corn every year. One year, the farm experiences a drought and receives less rainfall than is normal during the growing season. Which of the following is the most likely result?

(F) The corn plants will not grow at all.

(G) The corn plants will be taller than they usually are.

(H) The corn plants will be shorter than they usually are.

(I) The corn plants will grow the same as they usually do.

SC.5.L.15.1

9 The following picture shows a wetland in Florida and the plants that grow there.

Which of the following conditions do the plants shown have to cope with?

(A) wet soil

(B) low rainfall

(C) drought conditions

(D) very cold temperatures

SC.5.L.15.1, SC.5.N.1.1

10 Ricardo planted 50 grass seeds in three identical pots of soil. He watered one pot every day, watered one pot every third day, and gave one pot no water. He observed each pot and recorded the number of seeds that had sprouted after 30 days. The following table shows his results.

Pot	Watered	Number of seeds sprouted
A	every day	36
B	every third day	25
C	not watered	0

Which of the following conclusions is best supported by the experiment?

(F) Grass seeds need water to sprout.

(G) Grass seeds do not need water to sprout.

(H) The more often seeds are watered, the less likely they will sprout.

(I) How often seeds are watered has no effect on whether the seeds sprout.

Plant and Animal Adaptations

Big Idea 17

Interdependence

Pensacola, FL

I Wonder Why

Look at the shape of the pelican's beak.
Why is a pelican's beak shaped like that?
Turn the page to find out.

Here's Why Living things, including pelicans, have characteristics that help them survive in their environment. The pelican's beak helps it scoop up and eat fish.

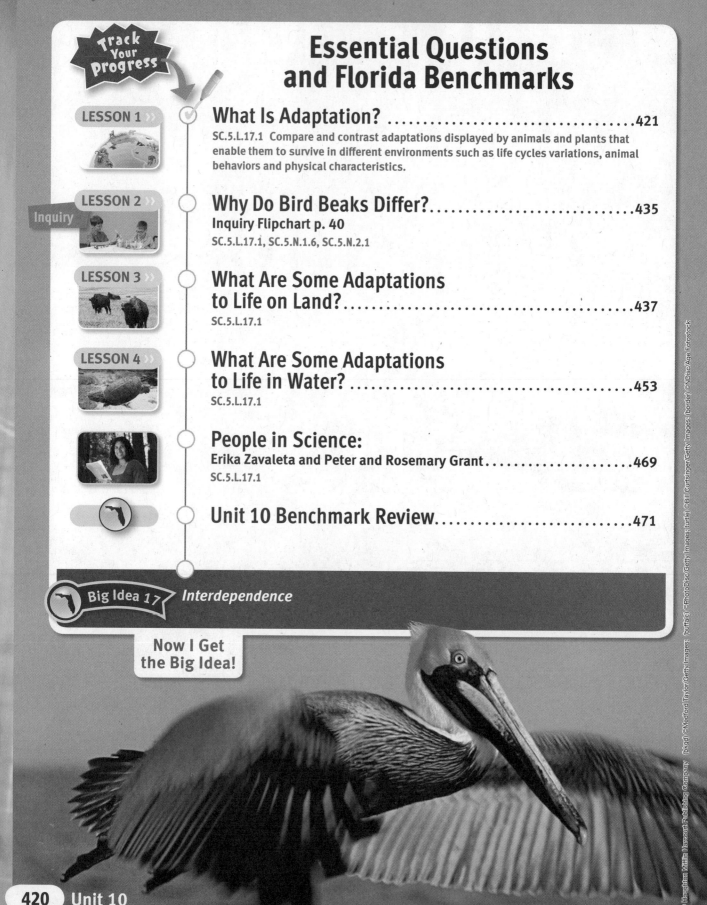

Track Your Progress

Essential Questions and Florida Benchmarks

Big Idea 17 *Interdependence*

Now I Get the Big Idea!

SC.5.L.17.1 Compare and contrast adaptations displayed by animals and plants that enable them to survive in different environments such as life cycles variations, animal behaviors and physical characteristics.

Essential Question

What Is Adaptation?

🧠 Engage Your Brain!

Find the answer to the following question in this lesson and record it here.

Watch out! Don't get bit by that... caterpillar? What type of adaptation does this caterpillar have?

_____

_____

_____

Active Reading

Lesson Vocabulary

List the terms. As you learn about each one, make notes in the Interactive Glossary.

_____

_____

_____

Signal Words: Details

This lesson gives details about how living things are suited to where they live. Signal words link main topics to added details. *For example* and *for instance* are often used as signal words. Active readers look for signal words that link a topic to its details.

A Place to Call Home

Where are living things found on Earth?
They can be found deep underground, high
up in the air, and everywhere in between!

Active Reading As you read this page, put a star next to the main idea of each paragraph.

Think about all the different kinds of living things on Earth. They each live in a different location. The place where a living thing lives is called its **habitat**. There are many different kinds of habitats. Some habitats are hot and dry. Other habitats are frozen. Still other habitats are found deep under the ocean.

All of a living thing's needs must be met within its habitat. Because of this, only certain kinds of living things can live in certain habitats. For example, an animal that has gills for breathing under water cannot live in a dry habitat. A plant that needs very little water cannot live in a wet habitat. As you look at the different types of habitats shown on this page and the next, ask yourself why each plant or animal is found in a certain kind of habitat.

mountain

jungle

Where Do I Live? Write the type of habitat in which these animals are found.

_____   _____   _____   _____

Habitats on Earth

Each type of habitat is home to different plants and animals. Which type of habitat shown here is most similar to a habitat found where you live?

polar

ocean

desert

grassland

Adaptations

Living things have many similarities. They also have many interesting differences.

As you read this page, underline the definition of *adaptation*.

Deserts are home to many kinds of snakes. This is because snakes have characteristics that help them survive in a desert. For example, snakes have tough, scaly skin that keeps them from drying out.

A characteristic that helps a living thing survive is called an **adaptation**. Suppose an animal is born with a new characteristic. If this characteristic helps the animal survive, the animal is likely to reproduce and pass on the characteristic to its young. As long as the animal's habitat doesn't change, young that have this characteristic are also likely to survive and reproduce. Over time, the adaptation becomes more common in the population. In this way, populations of plants and animals become adapted to their habitats.

These rabbits live in very different habitats. Because of this, they have different adaptations.

An arctic hare lives in a cold habitat. It has thick fur to keep it warm and small ears that keep heat from being lost.

A jackrabbit lives in a hot habitat. Jackrabbits have large ears that help keep their blood cool.

Ostriches, rheas, and emus all live on different continents. Even though they live very far from each other, they look almost the same! Their habitats are very similar, and so they share similar adaptations. These birds are all adapted for running fast. Ostriches are the fastest flightless birds on Earth. They can reach speeds of 72 km/hr (45 mi/hr)!

ostrich

emu

rhea

▶ Vines and trees are both plants, but they are very different from each other. What adaptations can you see in these plants, and how do you think these adaptations help them survive?

_____

_____

_____

_____

_____

_____

Physical Fitness

Whether blending in or standing out, physical adaptations help organisms survive.

As you read the next two pages, circle signal words that alert you to details about the main idea.

Can you see the owl in this picture? The owl is camouflaged to look like bark.

The bright color of this rose attracts pollinators, but the thorns keep plant-eating animals away.

Some adaptations are differences in the bodies of plants and animals. These are called physical adaptations. For example, sharp teeth, webbed feet, and large eyes are physical adaptations.

Some physical adaptations protect living things from being eaten. For example, roses have sharp thorns that help keep their stems from being eaten. Other physical adaptations help to keep an animal hidden. This type of adaptation is called *camouflage* [KAM•uh•flazh]. Green lizards hiding in green grass are camouflaged.

Catching Flies

Bright coloring on an animal is often a warning that an animal is dangerous. Many animals know that paper wasps, like the one shown below, have a painful sting. The black and yellow hoverfly doesn't have a stinger. It is completely harmless. But because it looks like a wasp, animals will think twice before trying to eat it. This adaptation is called *mimicry*.

▶ Draw a line from the chameleon's tongue to the insect it would most likely eat.

paper wasp

hoverfly

house fly

Chameleons have many adaptations that help them catch insects. They have long, sticky tongues that capture an insect in the blink of an eye. They have eyes that move in all directions, helping them see not only food but also possible danger. They also have feet and a tail that wrap around branches, making them excellent climbers. With all of these adaptations, a tasty fly must look like a wasp to avoid being eaten by a chameleon!

Animals that hunt, such as eagles, have adaptations that help them catch food. Eagles have very good eyesight. They also have sharp claws on their feet, which they use to capture their food.

Many plants have adaptations that help spread their seeds. Some seeds can be carried by the wind. Other seeds are inside berries. When the berries are eaten, the seeds are carried to a new location.

On Your Best Behavior

The way living things act is called behavior. Some behaviors are adaptations that help animals survive.

Active Reading As you read the paragraph below, circle examples of instinctive behavior and underline examples of learned behavior.

Some things that animals do seem to come naturally. Babies do not have to be taught how to cry. Spiders are not taught how to spin webs. Behaviors that animals know how to do without being taught are called **instincts**. Animals have to learn other types of behaviors. For example, a lion cub is not born knowing how to hunt. It learns to hunt by watching its mother. Raccoons learn to wash food by watching other raccoons.

Many animals have behaviors that help protect them from predators. When an octopus is frightened, it releases ink into the water. If the octopus is being attacked, the animal attacking it will not be able to see, and the octopus can escape.

Some bats are *nocturnal*. This means they are active at night and sleep during the day. This allows bats to hunt insects that are active only at night.

Do the Math!
Interpret Data in a Bar Graph

Ground squirrels hibernate. They must eat a lot during the spring, summer, and fall to store up enough energy to survive hibernation. Study the graph below.

Ground Squirrel Body Mass

About how much mass does a ground squirrel have in March?

_____

During which month do ground squirrels start to hibernate? How do you know?

_____

_____

Some animals move to different locations at certain times of the year to find food, reproduce, or escape very cold weather. This instinctive behavior is called *migration*. Many birds, butterflies, and some bats migrate long distances.

Other animals hibernate. *Hibernation* is a long period of inactivity that is like sleeping. But hibernation is not the same as sleeping. When an animal hibernates, its body processes slow down and it stays inactive for months. Can you imagine taking a three-month nap?

The way that animals act toward other animals of the same type is called *social behavior*. Honeybees have very complex social behavior. They communicate using movements called the "waggle dance." A bee that finds food will return to the hive and do a waggle dance. The pattern of the dance gives other bees a lot of information! The dance communicates which direction to go, how far away the food is, how much food there is, and even what kind of food it is!

The Circle of Life

All living things grow and develop. The way that living things develop can be an adaptation.

Active Reading Circle two different examples of organisms whose life cycles keep adults and young from competing for food.

Living things go through stages of growth and development called a *life cycle*. A living thing's life cycle is related to its habitat. Because of this, differences in life cycles are a type of adaptation.

Most frogs are adapted to live near water. A frog's life cycle starts when its eggs are laid in water. When the eggs hatch, tadpoles emerge. Tadpoles live in water until they grow legs and lungs. At this point, they are ready to live on land. In places where water tends to dry up quickly, tadpoles develop more quickly. This difference, or variation, in frog life cycles helps tadpoles survive.

Tadpoles and adult frogs live in different places, and they eat different foods. This is another kind of adaptation. Adult frogs and tadpoles don't compete with each other for food. This helps more frogs survive. Many other living things have similar adaptations. For example, caterpillars eat plant leaves and adult butterflies sip nectar from flowers.

salmon eggs

Adult salmon live in the ocean, which is a dangerous place for young salmon. Adults migrate from the ocean to shallow rivers to lay eggs. More young salmon are able to survive in rivers.

A female impala has one or two calves and then spends months feeding and protecting them. A female salmon lays thousands of eggs and then returns to the ocean. What are some advantages of each type of life cycle?

_____
_____
_____
_____
_____
_____
_____

Some animals can adjust their life cycle to changes in their habitat. In a very dry year, a pregnant impala can wait up to a month, until rain falls, to give birth. This life cycle variation helps make sure there is enough food and water for the young impalas to survive.

luna moth caterpillar

adult luna moth

It does not rain very often in the desert. When it does rain, the seeds of desert wildflowers, such as those shown below, immediately begin to grow. The plants bloom, make new seeds, and complete their whole life cycle within a few weeks! Explain how the life cycle of desert wildflowers helps them survive in the desert.

_____
_____
_____
_____

Sum It Up!

When you're done, use the answer key to check and revise your work.

The outline below is a summary of the lesson. Complete the outline.

Summarize

I. Habitats: The place where a living thing lives is called its habitat. Earth has many different types of habitats.

    A. Example: _____

    B. Example: _____

    C. Example: _____

    D. Example: _____

II. Adaptations: A characteristic that helps a living thing survive is called an adaptation. Kinds of adaptations include:

    A. Physical Adaptations

        1. Example: _____

        _____

        2. Example: _____

        _____

    B. Behavioral Adaptations

        1. Example: _____

        _____

        2. Example: _____

        _____

    C. Life Cycle Adaptations

        1. Example: _____

        _____

        2. Example: _____

        _____

Answer Key: Your answers may vary. Sample answers: I.A. Desert I.B. Ocean I.C. Forest I.D. Polar II.A.1. camouflage II.A.2. thorns that keep plant-eating animals away II.B.1. migration II.B.2. hibernation II.C.1. controlling when offspring are born II.C.2. having young that don't eat the same food as adults

Name _____

Word Play

1 Use words from the lesson to complete the puzzle.

Across

1. What type of adaptation helps a living thing hide in its environment?
5. The place where an animal lives is its _____.
7. An animal that is active at night is described as being _____.
8. All of the stages a living thing goes through as it develops are called its life _____.

Down

2. An example of _____ is birds flying south in winter.
3. What is any characteristic that helps an animal survive?
4. What behavior causes an animal to be inactive for a long period of time?
6. A behavior that an animal doesn't need to learn is a(n) _____.

Apply Concepts

2 Draw a picture of three habitats described in this lesson. Underneath each drawing, label the habitat.

_____   _____   _____

3 Circle the camouflaged animal.

4 In winter, ground squirrels retreat into burrows and do not come out until spring. Circle the term that bests describes this behavior.

Communication   Hibernation

Migration   Nocturnal hunting

5 A narrow-mouthed frog's eggs do not hatch into tadpoles. Instead, they hatch directly into tiny frogs. What type of habitat would you expect the narrow-mouthed frog to live in? Explain your answer.

_____

_____

_____

Take It Home! Go on a walk through your neighborhood or a local park with your family. Look at different plants and animals, and point out different adaptations that the plants or animals have.

SC.5.N.1.6 Recognize and explain the difference between personal opinion/ interpretation and verified observation. **SC.5.N.2.1** ... explanation must always be linked with evidence. **SC.5.L.17.1** Compare and contrast adaptations displayed by animals and plants that enable them to survive in different environments such as life cycles variations, animal behaviors and physical characteristics.

Name _____

Essential Question

Why Do Bird Beaks Differ?

Set a Purpose

Why do you think different birds have beaks with different shapes?

_____

_____

_____

_____

Write a statement summarizing what you plan to investigate.

_____

_____

_____

What will you be modeling in this investigation?

_____

_____

_____

_____

Record Your Data

In the space below, make a table in which you record your observations.

435

Draw Conclusions

Did some beaks work for more than one kind of food? What might this suggest about the bird's ability to survive?

_____

_____

_____

_____

Did one kind of beak work for eating all of the different foods?

_____

_____

_____

Analyze and Extend

1. Which bird's beak would be best for eating flower nectar? Which beaks would be best for picking insects out of wood and worms out of sand?

_____

_____

_____

_____

2. A toucan is a bird that eats very large, tough tropical fruit. What would you expect a toucan's beak to look like?

_____

_____

3. Look at the bird beaks below. Tell which tool in the investigation was most similar to each of the beaks.

hummingbird

_____

finch

_____

macaw

_____

shorebird

_____

woodpecker

_____

duck

_____

4. Think of other questions you would like to ask about how adaptations relate to the food an animal eats.

_____

_____

_____

_____

Essential Question

What Are Some Adaptations to Life on Land?

Engage Your Brain!

Find the answer to the following question in this lesson and record it here.

Is that a pine cone with eyes? No, it's a pangolin! Pangolins have strong claws for climbing and digging, and their strong tail wraps around objects. Where might you find a pangolin?

_____

_____

_____

Active Reading

Lesson Vocabulary

List the terms. As you learn about each one, make notes in the Interactive Glossary.

_____

_____

_____

_____

Visual Aids

This lesson has many photographs of animals and plants that live on land. Active readers pause their reading to review the photographs and captions and decide how the information in them adds to what is provided in the running text.

Take a Walk in the Woods

Forests are habitats filled with trees. Many living things call forest habitats their home.

Active Reading As you read this page, circle the types of organisms found in a forest.

Some of the largest forests in the United States are temperate forests. Temperate forests have warm summers and cold winters. Trees that grow in a temperate forest have wide leaves that absorb a lot of sunlight. Many kinds of plants grow beneath the trees. These plants are adapted to live with less light than plants that are not shaded. Vines, such as ivy, climb the trees to reach light.

Many animals live in a forest. Some of them have adaptations that help them climb or live in trees. Birds are common in forests. Many forest birds have feet that help them perch on branches. Insects are also common in forests. Many of them have special mouth parts that let them bore into wood. These insects can live under a tree's bark. Woodpeckers are adapted to eat insects that burrow into wood.

Describe the Temperate Forest	Describe Adaptations for Living Here

Woodpeckers eat insects that live in trees. They use their hard, pointy beak to drill holes in the tree.

Young deer, called fawns, have spots on their fur. When a fawn is curled up on the forest floor, the spots help camouflage it.

Most trees in temperate forests are *deciduous*. Their leaves change color as nights become longer in the fall. They lose their leaves before winter begins to help prevent water loss in the cold, dry air. Before the leaves fall, deciduous trees pull important nutrients from the leaves into the trunk and stems. When the weather becomes warmer in spring, the trees sprout new leaves.

Rain, Rain Every Day

Deep in the jungles live amazing plants and animals that can't be found anywhere else on Earth.

Active Reading As you read this page and the next, underline plant adaptations and circle animal adaptations.

Tropical rain forests, often called jungles, are warm and rainy all year. As a result, many different kinds of plants live there. The tallest trees reach out over the top of the forest to get sunlight. Another layer of trees spreads below those giants. With so many trees, not much light reaches the forest floor. A third layer of plants live close to the ground. These are adapted to low light. Some plants, called *epiphytes* [EP•ih•fyts], have adapted to reach light by living in the trees.

Daily rain washes dirt into rivers. As a result, the soil is very thin in a tropical forest. Because their roots cannot grow very deep, large trees in tropical forests have special adaptations that help keep them from falling over. Some trees have roots that grow down from the branches to prop the tree up. Other trees have roots that make walls that spread out around the tree.

Buttress roots form walls at the base of trees. This helps keep the tree from falling over in shallow soil.

Describe the Tropical Forest	Describe Adaptations for Living Here

A howler monkey's calls are very loud. They can be heard up to four kilometers away! This helps howler monkeys communicate in a dense tropical forest.

This plant is an epiphyte. It gets the water it needs from the air and rain. Living in the trees allows it to get enough sunlight.

Many different types of animals live in a tropical forest. Larger animals such as jaguars, monkeys, and sloths live in and around the trees. Jaguars have sharp claws to climb trees and to hunt. Sloths and pangolins have long arms and strong claws that they use to hang from branches. Monkeys are able to grip branches with their hands, feet, and sometimes even their tails!

Many animals in a tropical forest are brightly colored. Some bright colors warn predators that the colorful animal is poisonous. For other animals, bright colors help them find their family in the dimly lit forest environment.

Epi- means "on top of" and *-phyte* means "plant." Using this information, write your own definition for *epiphyte*.

_____

_____

Fields of Gold

In some habitats, there is not enough rain for many trees to grow. What grows in place of trees?

Active Reading As you read this page and the next, underline the types of animals that eat plants. Circle the types of animals that eat meat.

African hyenas are dog-like hunters and scavengers. They have powerful, bone-crushing jaws and live in packs with complex social behavior.

Grasses are the main plant life in a **grassland**. Grasslands receive less rain than forests, which is why few trees grow in grasslands. Grassland fires are common.

The long, narrow leaves of grasses keep them from losing very much water. Grasses have large root systems in which energy is stored. This helps them grow back quickly after a fire or after they've been eaten. Plant eaters in African grasslands, shown here, include elephants, zebras, giraffes, and gazelles. They have flat teeth that help them chew grass.

Many grassland animals are very fast runners. Gazelles and cheetahs are two of the fastest animals on earth. Grassland hunters have long legs, sharp teeth and claws, and powerful jaws. This helps them chase down and capture their prey. Lions' golden color helps them blend with the grass. Smaller insect-eating animals, such as meerkats, live in burrows in African grasslands. Eagles and vultures are meat eaters that search for food from far overhead. Their keen eyesight helps them spot food from high above the ground.

Describe the Grasslands	Describe Adaptations for Living Here

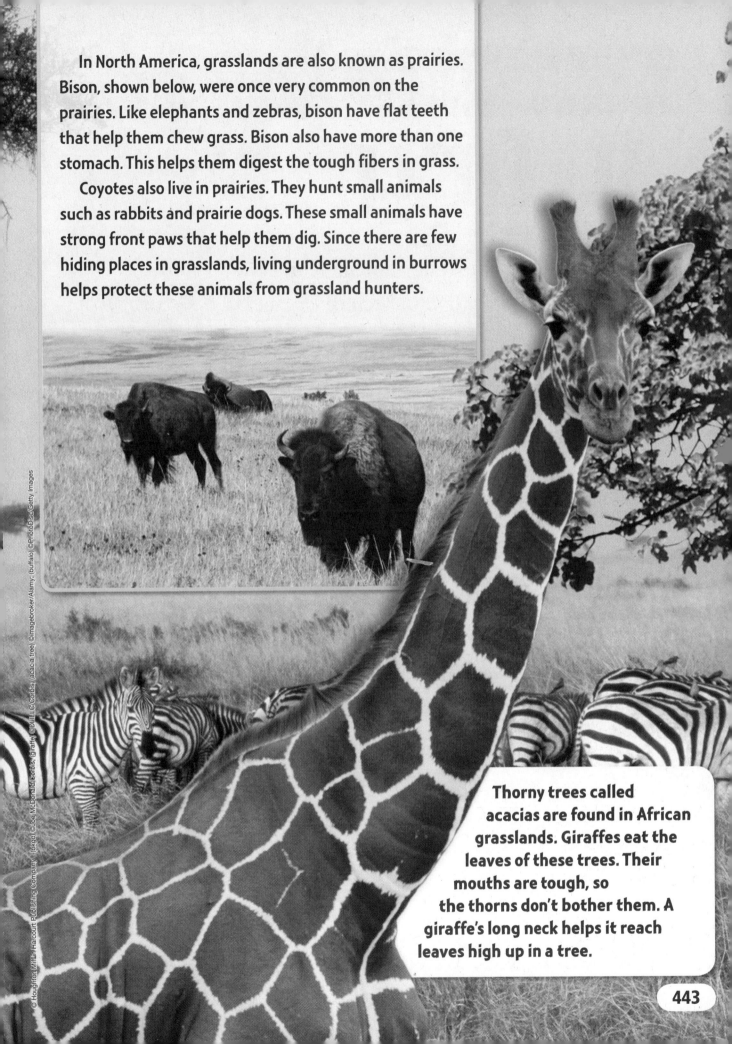

In North America, grasslands are also known as prairies. Bison, shown below, were once very common on the prairies. Like elephants and zebras, bison have flat teeth that help them chew grass. Bison also have more than one stomach. This helps them digest the tough fibers in grass.

Coyotes also live in prairies. They hunt small animals such as rabbits and prairie dogs. These small animals have strong front paws that help them dig. Since there are few hiding places in grasslands, living underground in burrows helps protect these animals from grassland hunters.

Thorny trees called acacias are found in African grasslands. Giraffes eat the leaves of these trees. Their mouths are tough, so the thorns don't bother them. A giraffe's long neck helps it reach leaves high up in a tree.

Some Like It Dry

Some habitats get almost no rain all year. Few plants and animals can live in such dry places.

Active Reading As you read this page, circle signals words that alert you to details about the main idea.

Sandy. Rocky. Dusty. DRY! These words describe a **desert**, which is a place that receives very little rain. Lack of water makes a desert a hard place to survive. Some deserts are very cold. Other deserts are the hottest places on Earth. Plants and animals must have special adaptations to live in deserts.

Many desert plants, such as these Arizona cactuses, have thick bodies that store a lot of water. Their stems and leaves have a tough, waxy coating. They often have very small leaves. This helps keep water from escaping into the dry air.

Desert animals also have adaptations that help them conserve water. For example, many animals in hot deserts are nocturnal. They sleep during the heat of the day and only come out at night, when the desert is much cooler.

Describe the Desert	Describe Adaptations for Living Here

In the North African and Middle Eastern deserts, camels are common animals. Camels have wide feet for walking on sand. They are able to drink large amounts of water and go a long time without drinking. Camels store all of their fat in their humps. This helps their bodies cool more easily. A camel's long lashes protect its eyes from blowing sand. A camel can also close its nostrils during a sandstorm to keep sand out of its lungs.

This American sidewinder rattlesnake is adapted to move over the smooth desert sand. It takes sideways "steps" with its body, so that it doesn't slip in the sand.

Do the Math!
Make a Bar Graph

Deserts that are very hot during the day often cool down quickly after sunset. This happens because there is no cloud cover to trap the heat. In the Sahara, in Africa, daytime temperatures may reach as high as 55 °C (131 °F). The temperature may drop to 10 °C (50 °F) at night. Plot this information on a bar graph below.

Some Like It Cold

A tropical forest isn't the only place where trees are green all year round. Some trees are tough enough to stay green even when they're covered with ice!

Active Reading As you read this page, find and underline the meanings of *conifer* and *taiga*.

Pines, firs, and spruces are evergreen trees—they stay green all year long. They live in the **taiga** [TY•guh], a far northern habitat with very cold winters and short, warm summers. Trees called conifers are common in the taiga. *Conifers* are evergreen trees that grow seeds inside of cones.

Conifers are well adapted to the taiga. They have pointed tops and flexible branches. This helps them shed snow and allows them to bend without breaking when they're weighed down with ice. They are also dark green in color. This helps them absorb more light from the sun. In addition, the cones that contain seeds are hard. This helps protect the seeds inside from harsh weather and hungry animals.

lynx

Describe the Taiga	Describe Adaptations for Living Here

Most conifers have needle-like leaves.

Animals that live in the taiga have many cold-weather adaptations. Animals such as wolverines and lynxes have thick fur coats. The color of their fur helps camouflage them among the trees.

During the summer, many birds live in the taiga. These birds feed on berries and insects that are abundant during the summer months. Most of these birds migrate south in autumn. This helps the birds avoid the harsh winter months when few berries and insects can be found. The birds that stay in the taiga during the winter have thick layers of feathers. These feathers insulate the birds from the cold.

A moose grows a thicker coat of fur for the long winter.

This crossbill's beak is adapted to open pine cones. The bird can then eat the seeds hidden inside the cones.

Life on Ice

Some habitats are winter wonderlands all year long!

Active Reading Look at the photos and read the captions on this page and the next page. Place a star next to the animal that changes color.

Habitats that are near the North Pole and South Pole are called **polar** habitats. In some areas, called the *tundra,* snow on the surface of the ground melts during the summer. The ground below stays frozen, but the thin layer of soil on top is just enough to allow plants to grow. These plants must grow and reproduce before the ground freezes again in late summer. The arctic willow, shown above, is one example of this kind of plant. It is a small, woody plant that is dormant all winter. When summer arrives it sprouts furry leaves , grows flowers, and makes seeds all in a few short months.

In places closest to the poles, the ground is always fozen. No plants can survive here. Plantlike organisms called *lichens* [LY•kuhns] live on the rocks. Many animals, including reindeer, eat lichens in polar habitats.

This arctic willow plant has very fuzzy leaves. The fuzz stops snow from collecting on the leaves.

Describe Polar Habitats	Describe Adaptations for Living Here

Polar habitats that are covered with ice year-round are home to many animals. Penguins, like the emperor penguins shown here, live near the South Pole. They are excellent swimmers and dive for fish in the icy ocean. These amazing hunters have thick layers of fat and a layer of water-proof feathers.

Polar bears live near the North Pole. They hunt seals and are excellent swimmers. Both polar bears and seals can close their nostrils. This keeps water from entering their noses when they swim.

A willow ptarmigan has white feathers in winter. This camouflages the bird in the snow. The feathers on its legs and feet help to keep it warm.

In the summer, ptarmigans shed their white feathers and grow brown feathers. This camouflages them against the brown soil and tundra plants.

When you're done, use the answer key to check and revise your work.

Read the summary statements below. Each one is incorrect.
Change the part of the summary in blue to make it correct.

(1) Most of the trees in a temperate forest stay green in winter.

(2) Many animals in a tropical forest are very loud so that they can hide from predators.

(3) A habitat dominated by grass is called a taiga.

(4) Desert plants have waxy stems and tiny leaves so that they can use more water.

(5) Many birds in the taiga become nocturnal before the winter comes.

(6) Animals that live in polar habitats often have black fur for camouflage.

Answer Key: 1. lose their leaves in winter. 2. communicate in the dense forest. 3. grassland. 4. reduce water loss. 5. migrate 6. white

Name _____

Word Play

1 Draw lines to match the words in the column on the left to the correct picture on the right.

1. polar

2. conifer

3. deciduous

4. desert

5. epiphyte

6. grassland

7. taiga

A

B

C

D

E

F

G

Apply Concepts

2 Beside the picture of each living thing, write the name of the habitat where it would be found and two adaptations it has that help it survive in that habitat.

Habitat: _____

Adaptations: _____

_____

Habitat: _____

Adaptations: _____

_____

Habitat: _____

Adaptations: _____

_____

Habitat: _____

Adaptations: _____

_____

3 How is a camel adapted for life in the desert?

_____

_____

_____

4 Write the adaptation from the list next to the animal that it belongs with.

_____   _____   _____

_____   _____   _____

> furry leaves
> fast runner
> strong beak
> loud call
> camouflage
> waxy leaves
> buttress roots

Take It Home!

Research an animal that lives in a habitat you learned about in this lesson. Draw the animal in its habitat. Label your drawing with at least three adaptations the animal has for surviving in its habitat.

SC.5.L.17.1 Compare and contrast adaptations displayed by animals and plants that enable them to survive in different environments such as life cycles variations, animal behaviors and physical characteristics.

Lesson 4

Essential Question

What Are Some Adaptations to Life in Water?

Find the answer to the following question in this lesson and record it here.

Can you spot the sea horse? Pygmy sea horses are adapted to blend with their brightly colored habitat. Where would you find a pygmy sea horse like this one?

_____

_____

_____

Active Reading

Lesson Vocabulary

List the terms. As you learn about each one, make notes in the Interactive Glossary.

_____

_____

Problem-Solution

You can think of differences in habitats as problems, or challenges. You can think of adaptations as solutions to these problems. Active readers keep track of problems and solutions as they read. This helps them stay focused on the way information is organized.

Life in Lakes and Ponds

There are many kinds of water habitats. Some are salty and some are not. Water found on Earth that is not salty is called *fresh water*, but ocean water is just as "fresh."

Active Reading As you read the text below, circle the descriptions of the three zones of a lake.

Ponds and lakes are examples of freshwater habitats. Lakes and ponds are wide bodies of water that do not flow very much. These habitats are divided into zones. The zone close to the shore has many living things in it. Many kinds of water plants grow near the shore. Their roots grow in the soil at the bottom, but the water is shallow enough that their leaves get plenty of sunlight. Other plants, such as water lilies and water hyacinth, float near the shore. Many animals, including ducks, snails, and fish, eat water plants.

▶ What are two meanings for the word "fresh"?

_____

_____

Further away from the shore is the open-water zone. Floating plants and plantlike organisms called algae can grow here. But the water is usually too deep for non-floating plants to reach light. The deep part of a lake or pond, where light does not reach, is called the deep-water zone. No plants can grow here. Catfish, worms, and bacteria are found in the deep-water zone. They feed on dead plants and animals that fall down from above.

A snapping turtle has webbed feet that help it swim through the water.

Water lilies have air-filled pockets in their leaves. This helps them float on the surface of the water.

Catfish spend much of their time in the dark near the bottom of a pond or lake. Their whiskers are adapted to sense chemicals, which helps catfish find food in the dark.

▶ Which living thing shown on this page has an adaptation that helps it find food in the dark?

_____

Go with the Flow

Unlike lakes and ponds, the water in rivers and streams is always on the move. How do living things keep from being washed away?

The kind of living things found in a river or stream depends on how fast the water is moving. The faster the water moves, the harder it is for living things to make a home. Because of this, fast-moving streams are often clear. Very few plants and animals live there.

In places where the water slows down, more living things will be found. Many plants can grow near the banks of rivers and streams. Tiny plants called mosses make a fuzzy green carpet on rocks in and around rivers and streams. Mosses have hair-like structures that cling to rocks. This keeps them in place. Insects also live in flowing water. They can often be found floating on the surface, clinging to plants, or living under rocks in shallow water.

Of course, many fish are also found in rivers and streams. Fish must constantly swim upstream so that they are not carried away by the current.

▶ If a filter in a fish tank creates a stream of flowing water near the edge of the tank, what might happen?

_____

_____

_____

Why aren't any plants growing in this stream?

_____

_____

_____

© Houghton Mifflin Harcourt Publishing Company

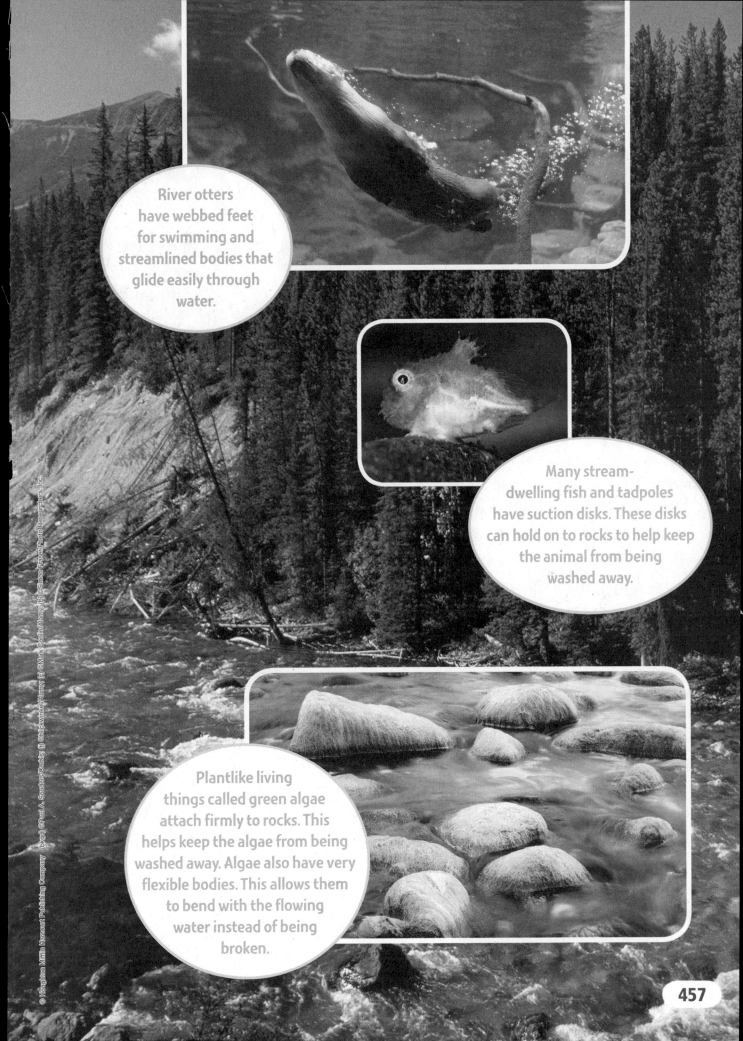

River otters have webbed feet for swimming and streamlined bodies that glide easily through water.

Many stream-dwelling fish and tadpoles have suction disks. These disks can hold on to rocks to help keep the animal from being washed away.

Plantlike living things called green algae attach firmly to rocks. This helps keep the algae from being washed away. Algae also have very flexible bodies. This allows them to bend with the flowing water instead of being broken.

Soggy Bogs

What do a bog beast and a swamp creature have in common? These imaginary creatures are adapted to live in muddy, wet habitats.

Active Reading Underline the phrases that explain why wetlands are important habitats.

A **wetland** is an area of land covered by a shallow layer of water for most of the year. Bogs, swamps, and marshes are three types of wetlands. Bogs tend to be covered in a layer of thick mud. Swamps, like the one shown here, are forested wetlands. The trees often have roots both above and below the water. *Marshes* are wetlands without trees. Grasses and reeds are common marsh plants. Wetland plants have special tissues that carry air from the plant's leaves to its roots. Marshes on ocean coasts are covered with salt water. Plants here also have adaptations to get rid of excess salt.

Wetlands are very important habitats. Many kinds of birds make their nests in wetlands. Migrating water birds use shore wetlands as rest areas on their journeys to spend winter in warmer habitats. Wetlands are also home to many different kinds of plants and animals, such as carnivorous plants, insects, fish, snakes, alligators, frogs, and even giant water rodents!

▶ Circle the two birds' feet that are best adapted for living in a wetland.

Herons have very long legs. These legs blend in with wetland reeds, so fish don't notice herons hunting from above.

Pitcher plants grow in many bogs. Bogs tend to lack certain nutrients in the soil. Pitcher plants get these nutrients by trapping and digesting insects.

Alligators live in American wetlands. Their eyes and nostrils are raised to enable them to hide in shallow water while hunting.

Between a Rock and a Hard Wave

One of the harshest habitats on Earth is found on the edge of the ocean along coastlines.

The place where the ocean meets the coast is called the **intertidal zone**. Every day the tide comes in and covers the intertidal zone in salt water. Then the tide goes out and the intertidal zone is exposed to air and bright sunlight. Between high tide and low tide, the intertidal zone is constantly bashed by waves. Living things in the intertidal zone have adaptations that protect their bodies from being crushed, washed away, or dried out. Seaweed, sea stars and sea urchins, barnacles, clams and oysters, tube worms, and anemones [uh•NEM•uh•neez] call the intertidal zone home.

▶ Put an *H* next to what the sea anemone and clam look like during high tide. Put an *L* next to what they look like during low tide.

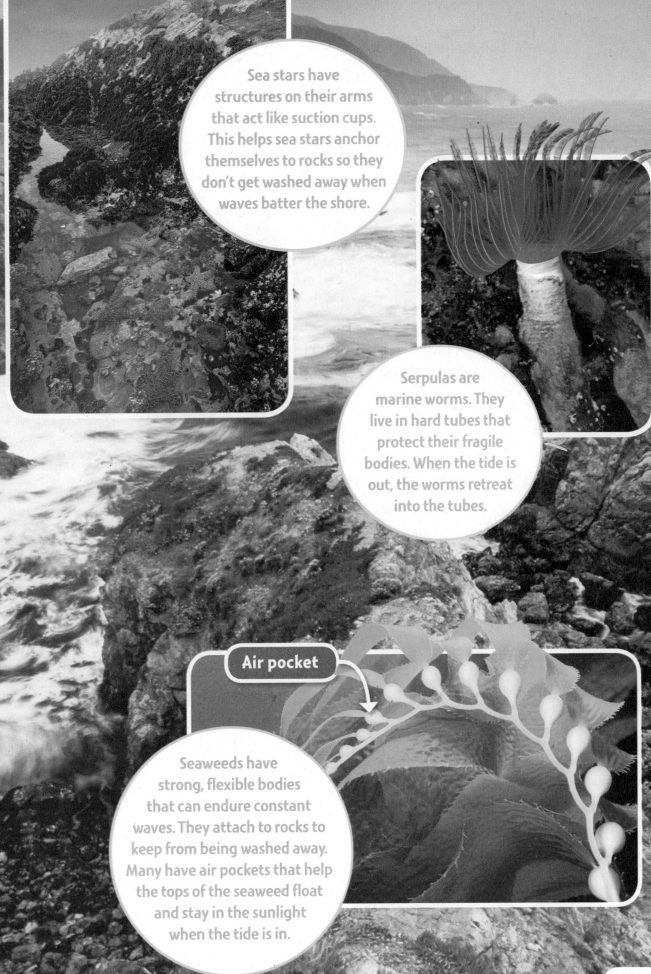

Sea stars have structures on their arms that act like suction cups. This helps sea stars anchor themselves to rocks so they don't get washed away when waves batter the shore.

Serpulas are marine worms. They live in hard tubes that protect their fragile bodies. When the tide is out, the worms retreat into the tubes.

Air pocket

Seaweeds have strong, flexible bodies that can endure constant waves. They attach to rocks to keep from being washed away. Many have air pockets that help the tops of the seaweed float and stay in the sunlight when the tide is in.

Out to Sea

The ocean is the largest habitat on Earth! Life can be found all the way from its edges down to its deepest depths.

Active Reading Read the text below and circle the names of the two major zones of the ocean.

Like lakes, the ocean can be divided into zones. Light reaches the top zone, known as the photic [FOH•tik] zone. Close to shore, corals and seaweeds live. Colorful fish and pygmy sea horses blend with brightly colored coral reefs. In the open ocean, floating seaweed and tiny plantlike organisms use the sun to make food. The photic zone is also full of animal life, including jellyfish, squid, fish and sharks, dolphins, and whales.

Underneath the sunlit zone is the part of the ocean where light does not reach. This part is called the aphotic [ay•FOH•tik] zone. It is very dark and very cold. Some animals move back and forth between the photic and aphotic zones.

The ocean floor is covered with mountains, valleys, and canyons, much like on land. There are undersea volcanoes and hot springs called vents. Hot water full of minerals shoots out of these deep-sea vents. Many living things depend on the heat and use the minerals to make food. Animals living here are very different from other ocean animals. Their bodies are adapted to living under extreme water pressure. Most cannot survive closer to the surface.

Coral reefs are found near many coasts. They are filled with a great diversity of sea life.

▶ Match each zone with its description.

APHOTIC ZONE	Seaweeds and corals live here.
DEEP OCEAN FLOOR	Mid-ocean level where no light reaches.
PHOTIC ZONE	Animals that glow are found here.

dolphins

Large floating mats of a seaweed called sargassum provide a safe habitat for many animals, including young sea turtles.

Jellyfish float in the open ocean, catching fish that accidentally wander into their tentacles.

shark

Deep-sea fish live in total darkness. Some have adaptations that allow them to produce light. They use this light to lure food or find mates.

Some marine tube worms live near the hot vents at the bottom of the ocean. They filter tiny organisms out of the water for food.

Oceans in Peril

Most living things are very well adapted to their habitats. When their habitats change, living things can be put in danger.

Active Reading As you read this page, find and underline three problems faced by sea life.

Today, many changes are taking place in ocean habitats. Large areas of coral reef are losing their color, a process called *coral bleaching*. Many bleached patches are dying. Possible reasons for coral bleaching include rising water temperatures and ocean pollution.

People take too many fish out of the sea. Animals that depend on these fish for food do not have enough to eat. The fish that are left cannot reproduce fast enough to rebuild their population. It is possible that the fish we and many other animals depend on for food could become extinct.

Some countries dump their garbage in the ocean. This harms sea life. Chemicals from the trash are harmful. Living things in the ocean easily get caught in trash, such as the plastic rings used to package drink cans. Recently, a giant patch of garbage has been discovered floating in the middle of the ocean. Ocean currents have brought garbage from many countries to one area, and now the Great Pacific Garbage Patch is about twice the size of the state of Texas!

▶ Draw an X where coral bleaching has occurred in the picture.

Do the Math!
Understand Fractions

About 75 percent of Earth's surface is covered by oceans. Change this percentage into a fraction. Then complete the circle graph and label the amount of Earth's surface covered by land and the amount covered by water.

Sum It Up!

Read the summary statements. Then match each statement with the correct image.

1 Many animals in wetlands have adaptations that allow them to blend with grasses while they hunt for food. _____

Ⓐ

2 Seaweed such as sargassum lives near the surface of the ocean. _____

Ⓑ

3 Because rivers and streams flow, plants that live in them must have adaptations that keep them from floating away. _____

Ⓒ

4 Many animals living in lakes and ponds have webbed feet to help them swim. _____

Ⓓ

5 In intertidal areas, many animals have protective shells or casings that they retreat into during low tide. _____

Ⓔ

Name _____

Word Play

1 Use words from the lesson to complete each sentence.

1. The ocean has salt water, but rivers and streams have __ __ __ __ __ water.

2. Animals that live at the edge of the ocean are adapted to life in the __ __ __ __ ˎ __ __ __ __ __ zone.

3. A swamp and a bog are both examples of a __ __ __ __ __ __ __.

4. An area of land with many grasses and reeds that is covered by water is known as a __ __ __ __ __.

5. About 75% of Earth's surface is covered by __ __ __ __ __ __.

6. A reef may lose its color due to __ __ __ __ __ bleaching.

7. The many rows of sharp, jagged teeth on some sharks is an example of an __ __ __ __ __ __ __ __ __ __ __ for catching food.

Figure out how to place the answers in the boxes below so that the letters in the red boxes answer the riddle.

Riddle: Who am I? You may have seen my latest blockbuster movie. It's playing now in underwater theaters. I am a __ __ __   __ __ __ __ __.

Apply Concepts

2 What adaptations would a plant living in a river need that a plant living in a pond would not need?

_____

_____

_____

3 Circle the animal that is best adapted to live in an intertidal zone.

4 What type of habitat does this bird most likely live in? Explain your answer.

_____

_____

_____

_____

5 How are these two fish similar?

_____

_____

Take It Home!

Walk with your family at a local body of water. Observe living things in the water and list the living things that you see. Talk with your family about how these living things are adapted to their habitat.

People in Science

Meet the Environment Detectives

Erika Zavaleta

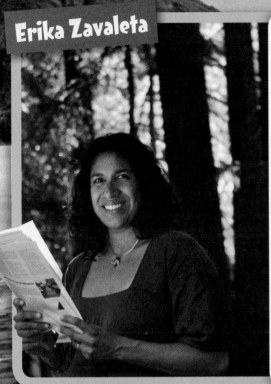

Erika Zavaleta is an ecologist in California. She studies the links between the environment and people. Cities grow and climates change. These changes make it hard for some plants and animals to survive. Part of Erika Zavaleta's job is figuring out good ways for people, plants, and animals to live in harmony.

Recently, Erika Zavaleta has studied oak trees. Fires and other disasters can kill a whole forest of these trees. She is studying the best ways to help new trees grow after such a disaster.

Peter & Rosemary Grant

Peter and Rosemary Grant study animal adaptation. On the Galápagos Islands off the coast of South America, they study how birds called finches change over time. They are most interested in changes in the birds' beaks. The Grants have found that beak shape and size change when the environment changes.

During severe droughts many birds die of starvation. When the only seeds remaining on the ground are large, hard seeds, only the birds with the biggest beaks can crack them. They survive and the small-beaked birds die. The next year, the big-beaked birds produce big-beaked young like themselves.

Now You Look For Clues

Answer the questions below about the scientists you just read about.

What kind of problems in the environment does Erika Zavaleta study?

_____

_____

_____

_____

What measurements do you think the Grants made as part of their studies?

_____

_____

_____

_____

What have these scientists learned about plant and animal adaptation?

_____

_____

_____

_____

_____

Multiple Choice

Identify the choice that best answers the question.

SC.5.L.17.1

1 A cardinal is a type of bird that lives in North America and South America. There are many kinds of cardinals. Most have bright, colorful feathers that are red, orange, or blue. Look at the drawing of the cardinal.

What does a cardinal **most likely** eat?

Ⓐ insects   Ⓒ nectar
Ⓑ seeds   Ⓓ worms

SC.5.L.17.1

2 The picture on the right shows flowers with an unusual shape.

Which beak shape would **best** allow a bird to reach the nectar inside the flower?

Ⓕ long and thin   Ⓗ long and thick
Ⓖ short and thin   Ⓘ short and thick

SC.5.L.17.1

3 A stilt is a bird found in the Florida wetlands. It wades in shallow water and has a long, thin, sharp beak. What do stilts **most likely** eat?

Ⓐ seeds and nuts
Ⓑ nectar and sap
Ⓒ frogs and large fish
Ⓓ burrowing animals

SC.5.L.17.1

4 In warm weather, the egg of a house fly takes about seven days to mature. In cooler weather this takes much longer. What type of adaptation does this illustrate?

Ⓕ change in habitat
Ⓖ change in behavior
Ⓗ change in life cycle
Ⓘ change in environmental conditions

SC.5.L.17.1

5 Catfish can live in rivers and lakes where the water is not very clear. The following picture shows a catfish.

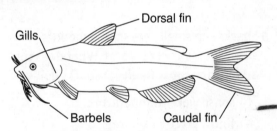

What do the barbels most likely help the catfish do in muddy water?

Ⓐ grab objects   Ⓒ dig holes
Ⓑ sense objects   Ⓓ breathe better

SC.5.L.17.1

6 Rivers and streams are sometimes fast moving. What characteristics would help plants live in swiftly moving water?

Ⓕ stiff stems and broad leaves
Ⓖ shallow roots and long stems
Ⓗ thin leaves and large flowers
Ⓘ flexible stems and ability to cling to rocks

SC.5.L.17.1

7 The picture shows an alligator that lives in the Florida Everglades.

What advantage does this swimming position give the alligator?

Ⓐ It keeps its skin from drying out.

Ⓑ It keeps it away from muddy water.

Ⓒ It keeps it mostly hidden under water, but the alligator can still see prey.

Ⓓ It keeps its body temperature from getting too high.

SC.5.L.17.1

8 Sharks can smell very small amounts of substances in ocean water. What does this adaptation **most likely** let sharks do?

Ⓕ sense water temperature

Ⓖ find a place to lay eggs

Ⓗ find a safe place to hide

Ⓘ find food that is far away

SC.5.L.17.1

9 Compared to other marine habitats, very few kinds of fish live on the ocean floor. To live in the deep ocean, what condition do fish need to be adapted for?

Ⓐ lack of food   Ⓒ high pressure

Ⓑ low salt levels   Ⓓ lots of light

SC.5.L.17.1

10 The following picture shows a mother deer and her baby, called a fawn.

The markings on the fawn's fur are different from the markings on the mother. How does the pattern in the fawn's fur help it survive?

Ⓕ It helps the fawn stay warm in cool weather.

Ⓖ It helps the fawn stay cool in warm weather.

Ⓗ It helps the fawn blend in with the forest background.

Ⓘ It helps the fawn stand out against a forest background.

SC.5.L.17.1

11 Bryce drew the picture on the right. It is a tree commonly found in a tropical forest.

How do buttress roots help this tree survive in the ecosystem in which it lives

Ⓐ They keep the tree from freezing during a very cold winter.

Ⓑ They help support the tree in shallow soil so it does not fall over.

Ⓒ They help the tree make sugars from carbon dioxide and sunlight.

Ⓓ They help the tree reach deep into sandy soil for nutrients and groundwater.

12 A pitcher plant is a carnivorous plant—a plant that traps and digests insects. The American pitcher plant lives in bogs.

Insects that fall into the slippery opening of the pitcher plant get trapped inside. The plant digests the insect and absorbs the nutrients. Which of the following is a characteristic of bogs that pitcher plants are adapted to?

(F) Bogs get little sunlight so plants compete with insects for sunlight.

(G) Bog soil is low in nutrients so some plants are adapted to digest insects.

(H) Bogs are filled with plant-eating insects that plants need to defend against.

(I) Bogs get little rain, so plants need to store water to live through dry periods.

13 Camouflage is coloring or texture that helps a living thing blend in with its environment. Which describes an animal with camouflage that is best suited for a grassland ecosystem?

(A) solid, dark black

(B) solid, bright white

(C) light brown, vertical stripes

(D) bright, colorful patterns

14 Many desert plants, such as the welwitschia, have long central roots called taproots. Taproots grow deep underground to reach groundwater. How is a taproot a useful adaptation for a desert ecosystem?

(F) It helps protect the plant from animals that might eat it to get water.

(G) It helps the plant get water in an ecosystem that gets very little rain.

(H) It helps the plant produce seeds that can sprout when there is water.

(I) It helps the plant move to an ecosystem that gets more rain than a desert.

15 A ptarmigan is a bird that walks on the ground. Ptarmigan feet are completely covered with tiny white feathers.

How are the ptarmigan's feet adapted for living in its environment?

(A) The feathers help keep its feet warm in the cold.

(B) The feathers keep fish from noticing the ptarmigan's feet in marshes.

(C) The feathers help the ptarmigan walk quietly so it can sneak up on prey.

(D) The feathers help protect the ptarmigan's feet from sharp cactus spines.

SC.5.L.17.1

16 It is estimated that fewer than 100 Florida panthers are still living. Florida now has a protected habitat for the panther. How will the protected habitat affect the panthers?

(F) The panthers will probably become extinct.

(G) Panthers will no longer be adapted to living in Florida.

(H) The Florida panther population will decrease in the near future.

(I) The panther population may increase now that they are being conserved in a protected habitat.

SC.5.L.17.1

17 Florida has a wide variety of habitats where plants grow. Some of these habitats are shown in the illustration below.

What statement is supported by this illustration?

(A) Land habitats support the same types of plants as water habitats do.

(B) Water habitats do not provide a suitable environment for plant life.

(C) Land habitats and water habitats do not contain the same types of plants.

(D) The variety of plants in a land habitat is much greater than in a water habitat.

SC.5.L.17.1

18 The coloring of the rough green snake allows it to blend in with its background. What type of adaptation is the rough green snake's color?

(F) life-cycle adaptation

(G) physical adaptation

(H) behavioral adaptation

(I) reproductive adaptation

SC.5.L.17.1

19 Which behavioral adaptation below allows the alligator to control its body temperature?

(A) Alligators mate in April and May.

(B) The alligator basks in the sunlight.

(C) Alligators lay between 20 and 50 eggs at one time.

(D) The alligator eats turtles, small mammals, and birds.

SC.5.L.17.1

20 The diagram below shows how an ant lion catches its food.

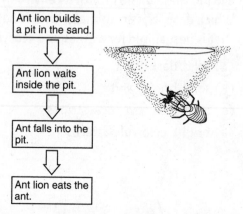

What does the diagram suggest about the ant lion?

(F) The ant lion is not adapted to its habitat.

(G) The ant lion has a diet of both plants and animals.

(H) The ant lion survives by hunting and chasing food.

(I) The ant lion has behavioral adaptations for its environment.

Don't Wait

Tick...tick...tick. Time is wasting. Don't wait until the last minute. Start your research and planning now!

What kind of project is it?

What is the goal of the project? Is it an experiment, an engineering challenge, or something entirely different? Find out about the rules and expectations.

Projects in
Science

by Michael DiSpezio

Since you're reading this section, there's probably a science project in your future. Right?

Don't worry, we're here to guide you along. Whether you were given specific steps to follow or want to create your own totally awesome project, you've come to the right place. We'll show you how to put it together.

What topic should I pick?

You'll be spending quite a bit of time on this undertaking, so select a topic that you're interested in.

What's the plan?

When you know your goals, formulate a plan. Make a calendar that shows completion dates for various steps. Try to stick to that schedule, but update it as needed.

What materials do I need?

Make sure you use materials that are safe, available, and affordable.

Gathering Information

The first step in any project is to learn as much as you can about the subject.

You'll need to fine-tune your research skills to help you complete your project. As you learn more about your topic, you'll be able to design a better project. You may even change your topic based on what you uncover.

Home   A Search Engine for Kids
                                    Search   GO

These days, it's easy to access a global library of information. All it takes is an Internet connection and the ability to use a search engine. A search engine is a tool that scours the Internet and locates web pages containing documents, images, and videos. All you have to do is enter keywords or phrases that relate to your subject. The search engine does the rest and generates a list of relevant links. Click on a link, and a new web page opens that contains information related to your search.

▶ Suppose the subject of your project is hurricane damage. Write down five keywords or phrases that you would enter into a search engine to learn more about this subject.

_____

_____

_____

_____

_____

Print References

A library has books, magazines, pamphlets, and other kinds of print references. If you still need a topic for your project, you might try flipping through some of the references. You can ask a librarian for assistance.

Computerized Catalog

Many libraries have computerized their catalog of books. Enter keywords or phrases into the catalog search engine. In response, the computer screen displays an assortment of books and references that are part of the library's holdings.

Interview Questions

You might want to interview a local expert. Find out which individuals are likely to have knowledge of your topic. Politely ask to set up an interview. Before you speak with an expert, make sure that you have your questions thought out and written down.

Tell It or Type It...
Transmit Information!

The world is at your fingertips! Communication is important at every step of a science project, from working with members of a team to sharing your results with others. Technology makes sending and receiving information easier than ever before.

Sandy's Science Site

Home   About   Search | GO

Report Your Findings
Report Your Data

Recent posts
Bug of the week
Books on Nature

Archives
June
July

Can you help us find this butterfly?

Friends might use cell phones to communicate, but text messages aren't always clear. Are there better ways to communicate scientific information? ▶

Here's a ? 4 U. What's the 411 with our project? Are we meeting L8R? Give me a shout. TTFN :o)

▲ Scientists used to communicate by writing books and journal articles. This process could take several months or even years. Today, you can communicate instantly using the Internet.

Say What?

What message was sent on the cell phone?

_____

_____

_____

_____

478

SCIENCE BLOG SITES

Search

Home   **About**   **Video**

Blogs and Websites

The Internet is a great tool for communicating with others. You can send e-mails about a project to team members. You can make a website to post your results and share them with others. You can read blogs to find out what projects others are doing. Computers keep records, so it's easy to track the progress of your project.

Internet Safety Tips

▶ Your parents or teacher should know when you are using the Internet.

▶ Never enter personal information on websites.

▶ If something makes you uncomfortable, tell your parents or teacher immediately.

▶ Just like you shouldn't talk to strangers on the street, you shouldn't communicate with strangers on the Internet.

Share Your Results

Tell Your Story

Field Reports

Internet a global system of computers that are connected together

Website a collection of online pages that a person, an organization, or a company puts on the Internet for others to view

Blog an online diary where people post information about hobbies or experiences

Science Fair
Projects

Is your school going to stage a science fair? You'll have several weeks to prepare an award-winning project. But where should you start? The answer is easy—right here!

Experimental Design

Design an investigation to answer your question. Keep it simple and to the point. Most questions will lead to an investigation that explores how one factor affects a subject. For example, "How does temperature affect seed germination?"

Begin with a Question

Most science fair projects answer a question. A good question can be solved by an investigation. To come up with a good question, you may need to do some research about your topic.

Scientific Methods

Write a hypothesis about how you think things will turn out. During your investigation, make sure you are using scientific methods.

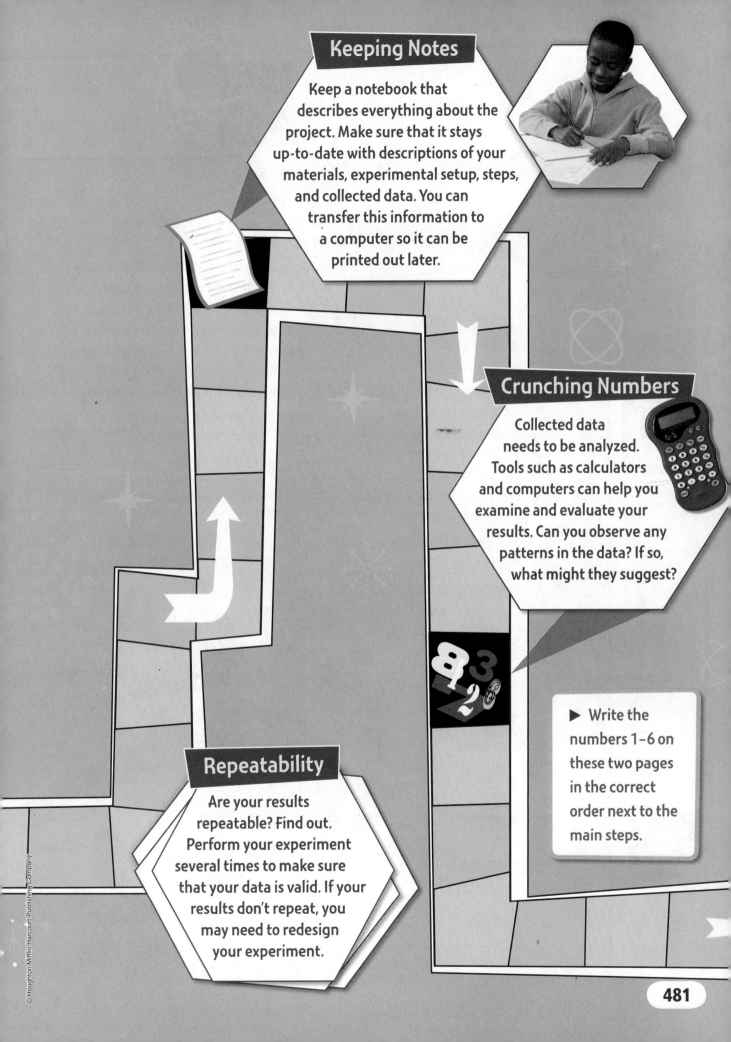

Keeping Notes

Keep a notebook that describes everything about the project. Make sure that it stays up-to-date with descriptions of your materials, experimental setup, steps, and collected data. You can transfer this information to a computer so it can be printed out later.

Crunching Numbers

Collected data needs to be analyzed. Tools such as calculators and computers can help you examine and evaluate your results. Can you observe any patterns in the data? If so, what might they suggest?

▶ Write the numbers 1–6 on these two pages in the correct order next to the main steps.

Repeatability

Are your results repeatable? Find out. Perform your experiment several times to make sure that your data is valid. If your results don't repeat, you may need to redesign your experiment.

Communicate What You've Learned

When you're finished with your project, it's time to communicate your findings at a science fair. Chances are the event will be held in a cafeteria, gym or other large space. Here, you'll have the opportunity to present your project to other students, teachers, parents, and judges.

Drawing Conclusions

Once you've analyzed your data, it's time to evaluate your hypothesis. Do the collected measurements agree with your educated guess? If so, describe this relationship and how it is supported by your data. If not, describe how your hypothesis is disproved by your findings.

Show It Off

You may want to take pictures to document your project.

FINISH

Before you talk about your project, know what to say. Have your key points written down or memorized. Practice in front of a mirror or before friends and family.

▶ Write a title for the science fair project shown below.

_____

Intro

People use lots of paper products every day. Although trees are a renewable resource, strong old trees are usually chopped down so pulpwood trees can be planted. Recycling paper saves trees and energy. It also makes less pollution.

I did a project to show how paper can be recycled. I made my own recycled paper out of used papers common to everyone's home. I also wanted to find out which kinds of paper were easier to recycle so I recorded data to help me decide.

Materials

- newspaper or newsprint
- water
- white printer paper
- laundry starch
- brown paper bags
- eggbeater
- metric ruler
- window screen
- basin
- thick towel
- measuring cup
- 4 pages of newspaper

Methods

1. Tear the paper into strips and put the strips in the basin.
2. Add water.
3. For each 240mL ad 5mL of starch.
4. Beat the mixture with the egg beater until it forms a slightly lumpy pulp.
5. Dip the screen into the mixture, coating one side with a thin layer of pulp. Put screen between 2 sheets of newspaper.
6. Roll the thick towel over the newspaper to remove as much water as possible lower the pulp. Let the pulp air dry and carefully peel the new sheet of paper off the screen.

Data

Energy Used to Recycle Paper

Results

- The newspaper took the 4 minutes to blend to the right consistency.
- The printer paper took 8 minutes to blend to the right consistency.
- The brown paper bags took 5 minutes to blend to the right consistency.

Conclusions

The newspaper took the least amount of energy to recycle, but the recycled sheets were weak and not easy to write on. The printer paper took the most amount of energy to recycle, but the recycled sheets didn't hold together well and were difficult to recycle due to mixture. The brown paper bags took a moderate amount of energy to recycle, and the sheets were strong and easy to write on.

For display and judging, you'll probably set up an exhibit on a tabletop. Most often, science fair projects are communicated using a self-standing display made of cardboard. You can buy a tri-fold display or make your own. If a single sheet is too small, try taping three large pieces together. Each section of the display shows a different part of the project. In addition to a poster, you might want to exhibit materials, parts of the setup, or models of what you investigated.

Citizen Science:
Get Involved

In a citizen science project, you can collect data that can be used by scientists.

Hey, Robin. I've been having this strange feeling that someone's been watching us. It started a few days ago when those students first appeared with binoculars. Be honest. Am I just being paranoid, or do they keep staring at us?

Listen, bird brain, of course they're looking at us. They're doing a bird count. It's part of a citizen science project. That's when ordinary folks collect data and share it with scientists. Using all the collected data, scientists can perform more extensive research.

When people participate in citizen science, scientists can quickly gather a lot of data.

Did you know that there are other citizen science projects? One involves analyzing local water samples to help monitor pollution. Another project has volunteers making local weather observations. To find out more, do a web search.

I see six crows and one robin. We'll e-mail the data to the local bird preserve. They'll post it online and share it with scientists and other bird watchers.

Field Guide to Humans

▶ Make a list of materials you'd need to participate in a local bird count.

_____

_____

_____

_____

_____

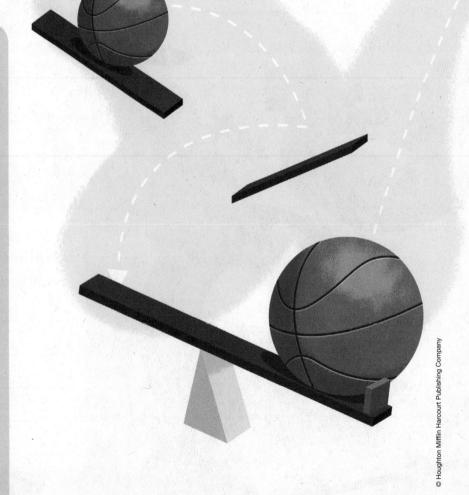

Engineering a
Challenge

Classroom engineering challenges are
like real-world construction projects.
Are you up for the challenge?

Engineering challenges offer the opportunity
to plan, test, and improve original designs.
To start, learn as much as you can about the
challenge and its associated science.
Be familiar with the rules before you
begin to brainstorm ideas.

Creativity

Be creative! Have fun! At this
point, don't worry if your ideas
are perfect. Brainstorm and
generate a list of all design
options. Later on, you'll select
and test your best ideas.

Materials

Consider what sort of
materials would be best to
use. Make sure that you are
aware of the guidelines for
the challenge. There may be
limits to kinds of materials
or to the cost of supplies
used to assemble your entry.

Blueprints

As you start to think up a design, draw simple diagrams or blueprints on paper. It's much easier to change a drawing than an assembled project, so this is the perfect time to update your plans.

Teamwork

If you're working with others, make sure that each person has a specific responsibility. Share what you know. Work together to engineer a design based on the entire team's understanding and experience.

Test and Redesign

Once you have a model assembled, test it. Does it perform as you imagined? Test it again. From what you observe, can you improve your design? Continue making improvements until it's time to show off your completed project.

A Better Design?

How would you change one element in this wacky design?

_____

_____

Try These
Challenges

Would you like to challenge your classmates
to a friendly design competition?
Here are some suggestions.

Bridge Building

When it comes to engineering, bridges
offer an "inside" view of design. Unlike
buildings, whose beams are concealed
by outer walls, the structural framework
of bridges is often exposed. How would
you build a bridge using craft sticks and
white glue? How much weight could
you add to the bridge before the
structure collapsed?

Solar-Powered Racers

Fill 'er up—with sunshine, that is!
Here's your chance to build a solar-
powered vehicle. The energy to run
the car's motor comes from a solar
cell. Beyond the motor and cell, the
design is up to you! Should it have
four wheels or three? Where
should you place the motor and
cells? What style of car body will
you design?

Parachute Drop

3...2...1... Release! Can you design a soft lander that will prevent a dropped egg from cracking? To meet this challenge, you might use a parachute or bumpers that cushion impact.

Towering Towers

How high can you build a tower using only 20 straws and modeling clay? Draw a blueprint to show how you would design your tower.

Robotic Challenges

Robot competitions offer a more difficult challenge. To assemble a robotic device, you'll need construction materials that include motors and other electronic parts. Your entry's design will be guided by the contest's specific task. Perhaps, it will compete in some sort of robotic basketball game? Score!

My Project **Plan**

Title of project:_____

Type of project:_____

Teammates (if any):_____

Describe the project.

_____

_____

List the goals of the project.

_____

_____

What materials are needed for the project?

_____

_____

_____

The safety issues (if any) are:

_____

What are some sources of background research?

_____

_____

_____

How will you communicate or display your project?

_____

_____

How will you evaluate the project?

_____

_____

_____

Interactive Glossary

As you learn about each term, add notes, drawings, or sentences in the extra space. This will help you remember what the terms mean. Here are some examples.

fungi [FUHN•jee] A group of organisms that get nutrients by decomposing other organisms

Mushrooms are an example of fungi.

physical change [FIHZ•ih•kuhl CHAYNJ] A change in the size, shape, or state of matter with no new substance being formed

When I cut paper in half, that's a physical change.

Glossary Pronunciation Key

With every glossary term, there is also a phonetic respelling. A phonetic respelling writes the word the way it sounds, which can help you pronounce new or unfamiliar words. Use this key to help you understand the respellings.

Sound	As in	Phonetic Respelling	Sound	As in	Phonetic Respelling
a	bat	(BAT)	oh	over	(OH•ver)
ah	lock	(LAHK)	oo	pool	(POOL)
air	rare	(RAIR)	ow	out	(OWT)
ar	argue	(AR•gyoo)	oy	foil	(FOYL)
aw	law	(LAW)	s	cell	(SEL)
ay	face	(FAYS)		sit	(SIT)
ch	chapel	(CHAP•uhl)	sh	sheep	(SHEEP)
e	test	(TEST)	th	that	(THAT)
	metric	(MEH•trik)		thin	(THIN)
ee	eat	(EET)	u	pull	(PUL)
	feet	(FEET)	uh	medal	(MED•uhl)
	ski	(SKEE)		talent	(TAL•uhnt)
er	paper	(PAY•per)		pencil	(PEN•suhl)
	fern	(FERN)		onion	(UHN•yuhn)
eye	idea	(eye•DEE•uh)		playful	(PLAY•fuhl)
i	bit	(BIT)		dull	(DUHL)
ing	going	(GOH•ing)	y	yes	(YES)
k	card	(KARD)		ripe	(RYP)
	kite	(KYT)	z	bags	(BAGZ)
ngk	bank	(BANGK)	zh	treasure	(TREZH•er)

Interactive Glossary

A

accurate [AK•yuh•ruht] Very close to the actual value (p. 49)

adaptation [ad•uhp•TAY•shuhn] A trait or characteristic that helps an organism survive (p. 424)

air mass [AIR MAS] A large body of air that has similar temperature and humidity throughout (p. 130)

air pressure [AIR PRESH•er] The weight of the atmosphere pressing down on Earth (p. 128)

anemometer [an•uh•MAHM•uht•er] A weather instrument that measures wind speed (p. 118)

asteroid [AS•ter•oyd] A chunk of rock or iron less than 1,000 km (621 mi) in diameter that orbits the sun (p. 72)

astronomy [uh•STRAHN•uh•mee] The study of objects in space and their properties (p. 84)

atmosphere [AT•muhs•feer] The mixture of gases that surround a planet (p. 101)

atom [AT•uhm] The smallest unit of a pure substance that has the properties of that substance (p. 212)

barometer [buh•RAHM•uht•er] A weather instrument used to measure air pressure (p. 119)

atomic theory [uh•TAHM•ik THEE•uh•ree] A scientific explanation of the structure of atoms and how they interact with other atoms (p. 212)

bladder [BLAD•er] Organ in the excretory system that stores and releases urine (p. 377)

B

balance [BAL•uhns] A tool used to measure the amount of matter in an object, which is the object's mass (p. 46)

bone [BOHN] A hard organ that has a spongy layer inside and that may help support the body or protect other organs (p. 354)

brain [BRAYN] The organ in the human body that processes information (p. 338)

balanced forces [BAL•uhnst FAWRS•iz] Forces that cancel each other out because they are equal in size and opposite in direction (p. 310)

C

chemical change [KEM•ih•kuhl CHAYNJ] A change in one or more substances, caused by a reaction, that forms new and different substances (p. 181)

chemical energy [KEM•ih•kuhl EN•er•jee] Energy that is stored in matter and that can be released by a chemical reaction (p. 239)

circuit [SER•kuht] A path along which electric charges can flow (p. 288)

climate [KLY•muht] The pattern of weather an area experiences over a long period of time (p. 144)

climate zone [KLY•muht ZOHN] An area that has similar average temperatures and precipitation throughout (p. 146)

comet [KAHM•it] A chunk of frozen gases, rock, ice, and dust orbiting the sun (p. 73)

compound [KAHM•pownd] A substance made of two or more different atoms that have combined chemically (p. 216)

condensation [kahn•duhn•SAY•shuhn] The process by which a gas changes into a liquid (p. 102)

conductor [kuhn•DUK•ter] A material that readily allows electric charges to pass through it and therefore carries electricity well (p. 286)

dwarf planet [DWORF PLAN•it] A nearly round body, slightly smaller than a planet, whose orbit crosses the orbit of another body (p. 72)

conservation [kahn•ser•VAY•shuhn] The preserving and protecting of an ecosystem or a resource (p. 401)

E

ecosystem [EE•koh•sis•tuhm] A community of organisms and the environment in which they live (p. 394)

control [kuhn•TROHL] The experimental setup to which you will compare all the other setups (p. 29)

electric current [ee•LEK•trik KER•uhnt] The flow of electric charges along a path (p. 254)

D

desert [DEZ•ert] An area of land that is very dry (p. 444)

electric motor [ee•LEK•trik MOHT•er] A device that changes electrical energy into mechanical energy (p. 266)

Interactive Glossary

electrical energy [ee•LEK•trih•kuhl EN•er•jee] Energy caused by the movement of electric charges (p. 237)

environment [en•VY•ruhn•muhnt] All the living and nonliving things that surround and affect an organism (p. 394)

electromagnet [ee•lek•troh•MAG•nit] A device in which electric current is used to produce magnetism (p. 269)

equator [ee•KWAYT•er] An imaginary line around Earth, equally distant from the North and South Poles (p. 146)

element [EL•uh•muhnt] Matter that is made of only one kind of atom (p. 214)

evaporation [ee•vap•uh•RAY•shuhn] The process by which a liquid changes into a gas (p. 101)

energy [EN•er•jee] The ability to cause changes in matter (p. 230)

evidence [EV•uh•duhns] Information collected during a scientific investigation (p. 6)

exoskeleton [eks•oh•SKEL•uh•tuhn] A hard outer covering, found in many types of animals, that supports and protects the body (p. 357)

friction [FRIK•shuhn] A force that acts between two touching objects and that opposes motion (p. 309)

experiment [ek•SPAIR•uh•muhnt] A procedure carried out under controlled conditions to test a hypothesis (p. 28)

front [FRUHNT] The border where two air masses meet (p. 130)

extinction [ek•STINGK•shuhn] The death of all the organisms of a certain kind of living thing (p. 404)

G

galaxy [GAL•uhk•see] A group of billions of stars, objects that orbit those stars, gas, and dust (p. 87)

F

force [FAWRS] A push or a pull, which may cause a change in an object's motion (p. 306)

gas [GAS] The state of matter in which a substance does not have a definite shape or volume (p. 170)

Interactive Glossary

generator [JEN•er•ayt•er] A device that makes an electric current by converting kinetic energy to electrical energy (p. 271)

heart [HART] A muscular organ that pumps blood through the rest of the circulatory system (p. 362)

grassland [GRAS•land] An area of land covered mostly with grasses that generally receives less rain than a forest (p. 442)

humidity [hyoo•MID•uh•tee] The amount of water vapor in the air (p. 119)

gravity [GRAV•ih•tee] The force of attraction between two objects, such as the attraction between Earth and objects on it (p. 308)

I

instinct [IN•stinkt] A behavior that an organism inherits and knows how to do without being taught (p. 428)

H

habitat [HAB•ih•tat] The place where an organism lives and can find everything it needs to survive (p. 422)

insulator [IN•suh•layt•er] A material that resists the flow of electric charge and therefore does not conduct electricity well (p. 286)

© Houghton Mifflin Harcourt Publishing Company

intertidal zone [in•ter•TYD•uhl ZOHN] The area between the land and the ocean that is covered by water at high tide and uncovered at low tide (p. 460)

investigation [in•ves•tuh•GAY•shuhn] A procedure carried out to carefully observe, study, or test something in order to learn more about it (p. 4)

K

kidneys [KID•neez] Organs in the human excretory system that remove waste materials from the blood (p. 377)

kinetic energy [kih•NET•ik EN•er•jee] The energy an object has because of motion (p. 232)

L

latitude [LAT•ih•tood] A measure of how far north or south a place is from the equator (p. 146)

liquid [LIK•wid] The state of matter in which a substance has a definite volume but no definite shape (p. 170)

liver [LIV•er] A large organ that makes a digestive juice called bile (p. 373)

lungs [LUNGZ] The largest organs in the respiratory system that bring oxygen from the air into the body and release carbon dioxide (p. 358)

Interactive Glossary

M

matter [MAT•er] Anything that has mass and takes up space (p. 166)

muscle [MUHS•uhl] An organ made of bundles of long fibers that can contract to produce movement in living things (p. 355)

mechanical energy [muh•KAN•ih•kuhl EN•er•jee] The total energy of motion and position of an object (p. 238)

O

opinion [uh•PIN•yuhn] A personal belief or judgment that does not need to be backed up with evidence (p. 9)

microscopic [my•kruh•SKAHP•ik] Too small to be seen without using a microscope (p. 43)

organ [AWR•guhn] A body part that is made of smaller parts that work together to do a certain job (p. 336)

mixture [MIKS•cher] A combination of two or more different substances in which the substances keep their identities (p. 197)

© Houghton Mifflin Harcourt Publishing Company

organ system [AWR•guhn SIS•tuhm]
A group of organs that work together to do a job for the body (p. 336)

physical change [FIZ•ih•kuhl CHAYNJ]
A change in which the form or shape of a substance changes but the substance still has the same chemical makeup (p. 180)

organism [AWR•guh•niz•uhm] A living thing (p. 336)

planet [PLAN•it] A large, round body that revolves around a star (p. 64)

P

pancreas [PAN•kree•uhs] An organ that makes a digestive juice and insulin (p. 373)

polar [POHL•er] Near Earth's North Pole or South Pole (p. 448)

parallel circuit [PAIR•uh•lel SER•kit] An electric circuit that has more than one path for the electric charges to follow (p. 291)

Interactive Glossary

pollution [puh•LOO•shuhn] A waste product that harms living things and damages an ecosystem (p. 400)

runoff [RUN•awf] Water that does not soak into the ground and that flows across Earth's surface (p. 105)

potential energy [poh•TEN•shuhl EN•er•jee] Energy that an object has because of its position or its condition (p. 232)

S

science [SY•uhns] The study of the natural world through observation and investigation (p. 5)

precipitation [pree•sip•uh•TAY•shuhn] Water that falls from the air to Earth's surface (p. 103)

scientific methods [sy•uhn•TIF•ik METH•uhds] Different ways that scientists perform investigations and collect reliable data (p. 22)

R

reaction [ree•AK•shuhn] The process in which new substances are formed during a chemical change (p. 181)

R12

series circuit [SIR•eez SER•kit] An electric circuit in which the electric charges have only one path to follow (p. 291)

solution [suh•LOO•shuhn] A mixture that has the same composition throughout because all the parts are mixed evenly (p. 198)

skin [SKIN] The human body's largest organ, which covers the outside of the body (p. 344)

spring scale [SPRING SKAYL] A tool used to measure forces (p. 47)

solar system [SOH•ler SIS•tuhm] A star and all the planets and other objects that revolve around it (p. 64)

star [STAR] A huge ball of very hot, glowing gases in space that produces its own light and heat (p. 84)

solid [SAHL•id] The state of matter in which a substance has a definite shape and a definite volume (p. 171)

Interactive Glossary

static electricity [STAT•ik ee•lek•TRIS•uh•tee] The buildup of electric charges on an object (p. 251)

stomach [STUHM•uhk] A baglike organ in which food is mixed with digestive juices and squeezed by muscles (p. 372)

T

taiga [TY•guh] Land that is very cold in winter and that is covered mostly with conifers (p. 446)

temperature [TEM•per•uh•cher] The measure of the energy of motion in the particles of matter, which we feel as how hot or cold something is (p. 168)

U

unbalanced forces [uhn•BAL•uhnst FAWRS•iz] Forces that cause a change in motion because they act on an object and don't cancel each other out (p. 310)

universe [YOO•nuh•vers] Everything that exists, including galaxies and everything in them (p. 86)

V

variable [VAIR•ee•uh•buhl] Any condition that can be changed in an experiment (p. 29)

volume [VAHL•yoom] The amount of space something takes up (p. 166)

weather map [WETH•er MAP] A map that uses symbols to show weather data (p. 132)

W

water cycle [WAWT•er SY•kuhl] The process in which water continuously moves from Earth's surface into the atmosphere and back again (p. 101)

wetland [WET•land] An area of land covered with shallow water for most of the year (p. 458)

weather [WETH•er] What is happening in the atmosphere at a certain place and time (p. 116)

wind [WIHND] Air that is moving (p. 128)

Index

feathers, 346
heart, 365
heron, 458
ostrich, 425
owl, 426
pelican, 419
penguin, 449
ptarmigan, 449
record data, 435
rhea, 425
serpent eagle, 411
woodpecker, 436, 438–439
Bladder, 377, 382–384
Blizzard, 134, 138. *See also* **Weather**
Blood, 362–363, 366, 370, 377
Boiling, 173, 201
Bone, 337, 340, 354, 366–369
Book lung, 364, 366, 368
Botanist, 13, 385
Brain, 338, 340, 348–349
Breathing, 358–361, 369, 376
Bronchi, 358–361
Bronchial tube, 369
Bronchiole, 358–359, 369
Burning, 181, 189

Calcium chloride in fireworks, 217
Caliper, 44. *See also* **Science tools**
Calories, 374
Camera, 41, 50, 52.
  See also **Science tools**
Camouflage, 426, 432–434, 439,
  449–450
Capillaries, 362–363, 370
Carbon dioxide, 358–359, 362, 366,
  369, 376
Careers in Science
  astronaut, 93
  biologist, 469
  botanist, 13, 385
  ecologist, 469
  electrician, 299
  field scientist, 40
  hydrologist, 157–158

inventor, 11, 275, 282
meteorologist, 116, 130, 132–133,
  135
paleontologist, 4–5
safety engineer, 327–328
surgeon, 385
taxonomist, 13
weather forecaster, 131
wildlife surveyor, 411–412
zoologist, 55–56
Cartilage, 354, 366
Cause and Effect, 148, 252, 269, 305,
  314, 399
Cellulose, 192
Chawla, Kalpana, 93–94
Chemical change, 186, 190–192
  in iron, 181
  in matter, 180–181, 188
Chemical energy, 238–240, 242–244.
  See also **Energy**
Chemical reaction, 181, 191–194
Chlorine, 215
Circuit. *See also* **Electric circuit**
  breaker, 292–293
  overload, 292, 296
Circulatory system
  animals, 364–365, 368, 370
  humans, 362–363, 366–367
  plants, 365, 370
Cirrus clouds, 120–121, 124–125
Classify, 13–15, 66
  clouds, 120–121
Clearwater, Florida, 391
Climate. *See also* **Weather**
  compare and contrast, 147
  in desert, 151
  in different regions, 148–149
  dry, 154
  effect on nonliving things, 150
  effect on organisms, 150
  and environment, 150–151
  factors affecting, 148, 152
  Gulf stream, 148
  in landform, 156
  polar, 146–147, 423, 432, 451
  predict, 149

in swamp, 151
temperate, 146, 152–153, 155
tropical, 146–147, 152–153, 155
tropical rain forest, 151
vs. weather, 144–145, 152
wet, 154
Climate zone, 146, 153–155
Closed circuit, 288–289, 294–295,
  300. *See also* **Electric circuit**
Clouds, 101–102, 108, 120
  altocumulus, 121
  altostratus, 121
  cirrus, 120–121, 124–125
  classify, 120–121
  cumulonimbus, 121
  cumulus, 120–121, 124
  formation of, 110
  heights, 121
Clue words, 132, 398, 402
Cochlea, 340–341
Cold front, thunderstorm, 130
Collect data, 31, 35
Collecting net, 40, 50, 52.
  See also **Science tools**
Color, 167–168, 184.
  See also **Properties of matter**
Comet, 73–74, 77–78, 80
Communicate, 10, 14–15, 32, 42, 429,
  441, 450
Compare, 4–5, 14, 16, 33, 46, 145, 167,
  290, 393
Compare and contrast, 39, 63, 68, 92,
  115, 147, 165, 167, 213, 229, 285
Compound eyes, 342, 348
Compounds, 211, 216–220
  properties of, 216
Compress, 174–175, 177
Computer, 42, 50, 52.
  See also **Science tools**
Condensation, 102, 108–109, 111,
  172, 189. *See also* **Evaporation**
Conductor, 286–287, 294–297.
  See also **Insulator**
Conservation, 401, 406–407
Contract, 189
Contrast, 122, 286

Index

Index

Index

howler monkey, 441
hyena, 442
jackrabbit, 424
jaguar, 441
kangaroo, 56
koala, 56
lynx, 446–447
meerkat, 442
monkey, 347, 441
moose, 447
orangutan, 32
pangolin, 437
river otter, 457
seal, 357
sloth, 441
squirrel, 429, 434
Tasmanian wolf, 405, 408
whale, 25
wolverine, 447
wombat, 55
zebra, 443
Mars, 66–67, 70, 77, 79, 316–317.
See also **Planets**
Mass, 166, 169, 178.
See also **Properties of matter**
measuring, 46–47
Mathematics Skills.
See **Do the Math!**
Matter, 166, 171, 177, 214.
See also **Properties of matter**
chemical change of, 180–181, 188
physical change of, 172, 180–181,
184, 188–189
properties of, 167–169
states of, 170–171, 174–175, 178
and temperature, 172–173,
182–183
Measure, 44–49, 51–52, 122
accurate, 49, 51
distance, 44, 52
force, 47
length, 44, 47
mass, 46–47, 178
radioactivity, 222
rain, 122
temperature, 30, 45, 47, 52, 178

time, 45, 47
units of, 44–45, 47–48
volume, 48–49, 52, 178
weight, 307
Measuring cup, 49, 176, 178.
See also **Science tools**
Mechanical energy, 238–240,
242–244, 264, 266–267, 270, 272,
274. *See also* **Energy**
Melting, 172, 176, 185, 189, 191.
See also **Boiling**
Melting point, 29–30
Meniscus, 49
Mercury, 65–66, 70, 77, 79.
See also **Planets**
Metals
boron, 214
copper, 214–215
gold, 212–213
mercury, 214
silver, 212, 215
tungsten, 184
Meteor Crater, 75
Meteorites, 73, 75, 78
Meteoroids, 73–74, 78
Meteorologist, 116, 130, 132, 135
use tools, 133
Meteors, 73
Meterstick, 44, 50, 52.
See also **Science tools**
Metric units, 44, 48, 51–52
Miami Beach, Florida, 163
Microscope, 42–43, 50.
See also **Science tools**
electron, 43
light, 42–43
Migration, 429, 432–433, 450
Milky Way galaxy, 86–87.
See also **Galaxy**
Mixture, 196–197, 199, 205–206
separation of, 200, 204, 206, 208
Models, 35
computer, 26, 34
of earthquakes, 26–27
physical, 26, 34
two-dimensional, 26

types of, 26, 34
using, 23, 26–27, 34, 36
Moon, 64–65, 68, 70, 72, 74, 76–77,
80, 93
Mountain breeze, 140
Mouth, 337, 358, 384
Muscles
animals, 357, 368
function of, 355, 369
humans, 336, 354–355, 366–369
types of, 355
Muscular System, 355

Nakamura, Shuji, 275–276
Nebula, 83
Neptune, 68–70, 72, 77, 79.
See also **Planets**
Nerves, 338–340, 348
Nervous system, 338, 348–349
brain, 338, 340, 348–349
nerves, 338–340, 348
spinal cord, 338–339
Neutrons, 213, 218–219, 248–249,
256–258
Nitrogen atom, 220
Nocturnal animal, 428, 433
North Atlantic Ocean
water temperature in, 148
Nose
animals, 343
humans, 340–341, 348, 358
olfactory bulb, 341
Nucleus, 213–214, 218–219
Nutrients, 362–363, 372,
374–376, 379
Nutrition information,
374–375

Observe, 4–5, 7, 9, 14–15, 23–24, 50,
81–82
weather patterns, 141–142
Ocean, 199, 432, 467

Index

Index